Citrix XenDesktop Implementation

Citrix XenDesktop Implementation

A Practical Guide for IT Professionals

Gareth R. James

Kenneth Majors
Technical Editor

ELSEVIER

AMSTERDAM • BOSTON • HEIDELBERG • LONDON
NEW YORK • OXFORD • PARIS • SAN DIEGO
SAN FRANCISCO • SINGAPORE • SYDNEY • TOKYO
Syngress is an imprint of Elsevier

SYNGRESS®

Acquiring Editor: Angelina Ward
Development Editor: Heather Scherer
Project Manager: Heather Tighe
Designer: Joanne Blank

Syngress is an imprint of Elsevier
30 Corporate Drive, Suite 400, Burlington, MA 01803, USA

Notices
Knowledge and best practice in this field are constantly changing. As new research and experience broaden our understanding, changes in research methods or professional practices, may become necessary. Practitioners and researchers must always rely on their own experience and knowledge in evaluating and using any information or methods described herein. In using such information or methods they should be mindful of their own safety and the safety of others, including parties for whom they have a professional responsibility.

To the fullest extent of the law, neither the Publisher nor the authors, contributors, or editors, assume any liability for any injury and/or damage to persons or property as a matter of products liability, negligence or otherwise, or from any use or operation of any methods, products, instructions, or ideas contained in the material herein.

Library of Congress Cataloging-in-Publication Data
James, Gareth R.
  Citrix XenDesktop implementation : a practical guide for IT professionals / Gareth R. James.
    p. cm.
  ISBN 978-1-59749-582-0
1. Computer networks–Remote access. 2. Virtual computer systems. 3. Citrix XenDesktop. I. Title.
  TK5105.597J356 2010
  005.4'3–dc22   2010026570

British Library Cataloguing-in-Publication Data
A catalogue record for this book is available from the British Library.

ISBN: 978-1-59749-582-0

For information on all Syngress publications
visit our website at *www.syngress.com*

Printed in the United States of America

10 11 12 13 14   10 9 8 7 6 5 4 3 2 1

Typeset by: diacriTech, Chennai, India

Working together to grow libraries in developing countries

www.elsevier.com | www.bookaid.org | www.sabre.org

ELSEVIER   **BOOK AID International**   **Sabre Foundation**

I want to thank my absolutely gorgeous wife Charlotte, for her advice and direction. Without Charlotte this project would most likely never have been started and almost certainly never have been finished. I also want to thank my children Joel, Rosalie, Daniel and Sarah—children really are God's richest blessing. And lastly to my father who was a family man, musician, writer, journalist, and activist in South Africa's darkest days.

— Gareth James

Contents

Introduction

- Desktop Virtualization
- Components of a Citrix VDI Solution
- The Project-Based Approach

Desktop virtualization is a very broad topic, which can encompass various virtualization technologies. This book is aimed at specifically addressing how to implement a virtual desktop infrastructure (VDI) solution using Citrix XenDesktop.

This book is not meant as a definitive guide to any one of the technologies discussed in this book, but sets out to tie the components together in a simple, easy-to-grasp manner. We certainly hope it enables you, the reader, to accelerate through the discovery stage, straight through to implementing your own proof of concept or pilot of the technology.

DESKTOP VIRTUALIZATION

Desktop virtualization has become a catch all phrase for various mechanisms that simplify the management of the user's desktop environment.

VDI is a concept that has been around for some years. The basic concept is to host the desktops in the datacenter rather than on the user's desk. This concept was pioneered by Hewlett-Packard about 5 years ago. The first iteration of the idea involved taking a rack of blade computers, and installing Windows XP on each blade; users then accessed their assigned blade using a standard Microsoft RDP (Remote Desktop Protocol) client. As a concept, it worked for some high-end requirements. The advent of server virtualization into the mainstream has meant that we can now host 30+ desktops on a single server,[A] such that this technology is now far more affordable. Figure 1.1 is a diagram of a basic VDI.

The Client Hypervisor is another desktop virtualization technology. The Client Hypervisor entails installing a hypervisor on a laptop or PC, which is used to host one or more desktop operating systems. This technology should not be confused with "Type 2" hypervisors like virtual PC or VMware workstation that execute on top of a guest operating system. This differs from a server hypervisor insofar as it allows the guest operating system to be accessible from the device itself.

[A] Citrix has released test results of 130 virtual desktops on one 72GB dual socket, quad-core Intel Xeon x5570. Running Windows XP guests at 512MB RAM per guest.

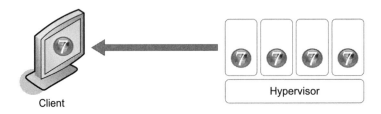

Client   Hypervisor

FIGURE 1.1

A basic VDI layout.

This includes exposing peripherals like USB (Universal Serial Bus), LPT ports, and importantly the graphics processing unit direct to the guest operating system. The user can thus access the guest operating system (Windows 7, for example) as if it were locally installed. There are plans to dovetail this (currently beta) technology into VDI, such that you could access the same guest virtual machine (VM) using the VDI-hosted mechanism, or even "check out" the VM by dragging the whole VM virtual disk down to a laptop to make it available offline.

Depending on your point of view (or who you work for), Microsoft Remote Desktop Services (RDS) – formerly called Terminal Services – Citrix XenApp, Presentation Server, or MetaFrame is also regarded as a form of desktop virtualization. The difference between this method and VDI is that the operating system used is shared by multiple users, and that it is implemented on a Microsoft server rather than a Microsoft desktop operating system. Additionally, because the overhead of running the operating system is shared rather than requiring an individual instance per user, one typically achieves a higher user density using RDS over VDI. Most organizations would benefit from having a blend of both technologies, with RDS catering for minimal environment, task-based users, and VDI providing a richer environment for the users with higher resource requirements. Microsoft has included RDS CAL in its premium VDI suite, such that the user can connect to a hosted desktop operating system, or a server operating system using RDS, or indeed both if required. Citrix, likewise, both as part of desktop virtualization and their new XenDesktop 4 licensing model, allows the user to use a hosted desktop operating system (XenDesktop) and also to connect to a server desktop using their XenApp product, as part of the same licensing suite. For the sake of clarity, I will refer to the Citrix VDI solution as XenDesktop, and to the RDS (Terminal Services) solution as XenApp, although both products are included in the XenDesktop 4 license suite.

Desktop streaming is a further type of desktop virtualization. VDI and RDS are datacenter-based solutions and the Client Hypervisor is client end virtualization, desktop streaming is a combination of both. Desktop streaming involves mounting a virtual disk over the network to a physical device. The device could be a normal PC or a diskless device. Based on the MAC address of the machine, either you could choose a virtual disk to mount or the administrator could assign one to the MAC address. Citrix Provisioning Server is a mature technology that Citrix acquired when they bought Ardence back in 2006. Dell uses this technology as part of its "Flexible Computing Solution" and refers to it as on-demand desktop streaming (ODDS). This technology can be used with physical or even VMs! Citrix integrates the technology into its XenDesktop VDI solution, but it is important to note that it can be used separately and is a valid solution in its own right.

Application virtualization is sometimes included in the definition of desktop virtualization – whether you include it in the definition or not, it should most certainly be included as part of your implementation. Application virtualization products include Citrix XenApp streaming and Microsoft App-V. Both products function in a similar way, instead of installing each application into the operating system, embedding themselves into the file system and registry, the applications are presented with a virtual file system and a virtual registry, unique to that application. Streamed applications work in an isolation environment. This means that applications don't conflict with each other, and they don't need to be installed in order to execute. Decoupling the application from the host operating system means we greatly simplify the application management on our desktop. This modular approach means that we can easily build out complex and unique guest environments from commonly used building blocks.

Virtual Profiles is another component commonly used within the framework of desktop virtualization. Virtual Profiles fits into the category of "complementary technology." Virtual Profiles is an extension of the roaming profile concept. Roaming profiles is essentially the ability to centralize the user settings on a file share, Virtual Profiles extends this capability to include files and registry keys not traditionally included in the users settings. Virtual Profiles also includes sophisticated mechanisms for managing user settings, including the ability to merge settings from multiple user sessions, and to do intelligent conflict handling. Virtual Profiles provides a more robust solution for handling a situation where users may have multiple access mechanisms to access their working environment.

COMPONENTS OF A CITRIX VDI SOLUTION

The Citrix approach to VDI is a layered, modular approach. This approach allows you to leverage different technologies at each layer, when composing the overall solution (see Figure 1.2).

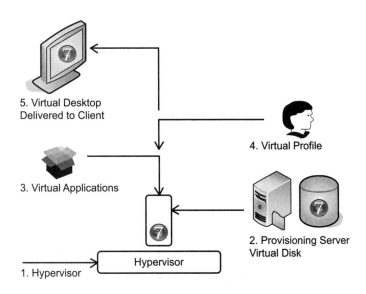

FIGURE 1.2

Conceptual diagram of the complete solution.

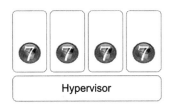

FIGURE 1.3

Multiple guest VMs hosted on server hardware.

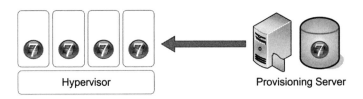

FIGURE 1.4

Provisioning server providing a virtual disk.

Starting at the server hardware level, the Citrix solution is hypervisor agnostic. The hypervisor may be Citrix's XenServer, Microsoft's Hyper-V, or VMware's ESX/vSphere (see Figure 1.3).

Next, you make use of Citrix's provisioning server to mount a virtual disk into the VM – this technology is the one most people are unfamiliar with – it allows you to use one virtual disk to boot multiple VMs simultaneously, thus dramatically reducing storage requirements. The greatest benefit is that you manage one desktop image for multiple users – you have guaranteed consistency across the desktop pool, and updates and patches are applied to one common use instance. The provisioning server acts as a "clever" file server, sharing a VHD format virtual disk, the workstations mount the .vhd file as their hard disk (see Figure 1.4).

Virtual applications are then "delivered" into the user's desktop based on their user credentials. These applications can be installed dynamically, and can integrate user-installed applications. Virtual Profiles then inject the users' application and environment settings. The virtual desktop is then delivered to the end point over a presentation layer protocol. High Definition User Experience (HDX) includes the Citrix ICA protocol and the other technologies built around ICA to connect peripherals and deliver content to the end point.

THE PROJECT-BASED APPROACH

This book has been structured in such a way that you could run a XenDesktop project by simply following the chapters one by one. The "step-by-step" approach to the installation and configuration sections is meant to give you, the implementer, the information and the visual cues of the dialog boxes to successfully perform the implementation. We have tried to arrange the information – as far as possible – in such a way that you can omit sections not relevant to your project. The scope of every project is different, but we hope this gives you a basic framework from which you can extrapolate your own project.

"User profiling" will normally precede a project of this nature. In almost every company, there will be a mix of technologies used to cater to the different needs of different groups of users. This book presumes that either "user profiling" has already been done, or that your proof of concept environment will highlight the groups of users that it would benefit the business to move onto virtual desktops.

Installation of the Broker – Desktop Delivery Controller

HOW THE DESKTOP DELIVERY CONTROLLER WORKS

The Desktop Delivery Controller (DDC) is the core technology used to couple the XenDesktop components together. The DDC is effectively the traffic controller, directing the user to their assigned desktop based on their user credentials (see Figure 2.1).

The XenDesktop technology has drawn from the Citrix XenApp technologies. In the context of XenApp, the users are mapped to assigned applications, whereas in XenDesktop, they are mapped to assigned Desktop Groups. The most notable difference is that the components being assigned are not resident on the machines doing the brokering. The Citrix "Farm" mechanism remains largely the same, but the portion being "presented" to the users – a Windows desktop operating system – had to be rebuilt. The Virtual Desktop Agent components are designated as "PortICA" in some of the registry settings. This is because the ICA (Independent Computing Architecture) protocol[A] was "ported" from Windows server to Windows desktop operating systems. It may be useful – for those familiar with XenApp – to think of it in terms of the XenApp management components remain on the DDC, but the ICA stack has been moved to a Windows XP, Windows Vista, or Windows 7 workstations.

Multiple virtual desktops are installed on a physical server; these virtual desktops have a Virtual Desktop Agent installed on them. The Virtual Desktop Agent registers with the DDC.

Figures 2.2 and 2.3 illustrate how the components interact.

1. The Virtual Desktop Agent queries Active Directory for the DDC address.
2. The Virtual Desktop Agent then registers the virtual desktop as available for use.
3. The user requests a virtual desktop from the DDC.
4. The controller returns the connection information.
5. The virtual desktop launches to the user.

[A]The ICA Protocol is a presentation layer protocol, which allows a Windows desktop to be accessible over a network. ICA transmits screen updates to the end point and receives keyboard and mouse clicks from the end point.

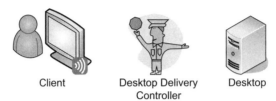

Client   Desktop Delivery Controller   Desktop

FIGURE 2.1

The Desktop Delivery Controller.

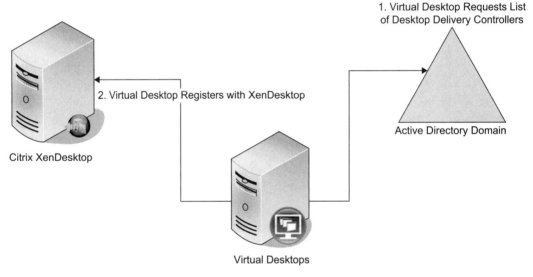

FIGURE 2.2

Virtual desktop registration.

It is important to note that the DDC brokers the connection, but once the connection is established, the communication is directly between the user's device and the virtual desktop. If the DDC is rebooted, it would not affect the connected sessions.

A single DDC can broker literally thousands of virtual desktops. A recent whitepaper cites scalability testing of three DDCs managing a farm of 6000 virtual desktops.[B] (4vCPU 4GB RAM per controller), two of the servers were configured to perform registrations, one to act as only a farm master. Most environments will include at least two DDCs, providing load balancing and failover.

[B]"Delivering 5000 Desktops with Citrix XenDesktop."

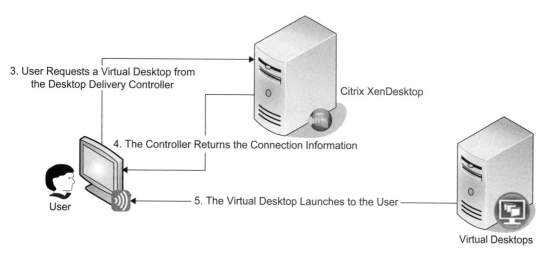

3. User Requests a Virtual Desktop from the Desktop Delivery Controller

Citrix XenDesktop

4. The Controller Returns the Connection Information

5. The Virtual Desktop Launches to the User

User

Virtual Desktops

FIGURE 2.3

Connecting to a virtual desktop.

FAQ

Physical or Virtual?

The DDC is a fairly light load and can be comfortably be run as a virtual machine (VM) on the hypervisor infrastructure.

The very simplest proof of concept can be conducted with two PCs – one configured with a desktop operating system and the other configured with Windows Server 2003 and the DDC software. This can be a quick and effective way of demonstrating the performance when connecting to a remote workstation. The workstation could be a physical machine or a VM.

Prerequisites

Important Considerations

1. The user account performing the installation must be a local administrator on the server. If an enterprise database is being used, it should also be db_owner of the database.
2. Only Windows Server 2003 is supported for the DDC. The version can be SP2 or R2, (System Center Virtual Machine Manager [SCVMM] requires R2 for Hyper-V integration). Both x86 and 64-bit versions are supported. This will change with the next release, but not yet at the time of writing.
3. Terminal Services in application mode must be installed – otherwise, you will be prompted for the Windows 2003 CD during installation to add this component.

The DDC is based on the XenApp software, and this is a legacy link to XenApp.

4. IIS must be installed – otherwise, you will be prompted for the Windows 2003 CD during installation to add this component.
5. Install NET 3.5 SP1 and all the latest Windows Updates.
6. Install JRE 1.5.0_15 – this can be found in the Support folder off the root of the XenDesktop Media.

The Microsoft Updates to the .NET Framework have introduced significant scalability improvements.

For Hyper-V only,

7. Install the SCVMM Administrator Console on the server *before* installing the Citrix DDC software. If the SCVMM Administrator Console isn't installed, only the XenServer and VMware hypervisors are available for integration.[c]

SQL Express or an Access format database is sufficient for a proof of concept. A pilot or production should make use of an Enterprise Database, which can be easily backed up and restored as required.

8. Microsoft SQL 2000 or 2005, or Oracle 11 g Release 1 – Microsoft SQL 2005 is recommended. Microsoft SQL 2008 was not officially supported at the time of writing – it does indeed work with the backward compatibility pack, so I would be comfortable using it for a proof of concept system, but not for a production system.
9. The installer user account must have db_owner rights to the SQL database. We recommend a service account be used for this purpose in production environments.

TIP

Ask the database administrator in your organization to create a database for you. Installing a separate SQL Server will incur extra licensing costs, and probably also annoy the database administrator! It is a small (less than 100 MB), low-impact database that can very easily coexist with other databases on an SQL Server.

Provisioning server requires Microsoft SQL 2005 or Microsoft SQL 2008 if you wish to use the same database server; at the time of writing, we would recommend Microsoft SQL 2005. Check the Citrix Web site for the latest support, the latest XenApp release is geared toward SQL 2008, and XenDesktop support may well be included by the time this goes to press.

DDC INSTALLATION

To obtain the software, log in to www.mycitrix.com and select **Downloads | XenDesktop**.

The XDS_4_0_0_dvd.ISO file is more than 1 GB in size, so this is definitely something you want to start downloading the day before your implementation.

---

[c]If you decided to add Microsoft Integration after installation, **Add/Remove Programs | Citrix Pool Management | Change | Modify | Add Microsoft SCVMM Plug-In**.

If IIS is not installed, you will be prompted for the Windows Server 2003 disk and IIS will be installed. By default, the Setup program will install Web Interface on every DDC.

DDC Installation – Step by Step

1. Mount the XenDesktop 4 DVD on your server.
2. The DVD should autorun, if it doesn't, click **autorun.exe** in the root of the DVD.
3. Click **Install Server Components** (see Figure 2.4).
4. Change the radio button to accept the license agreement, and click **Next** (see Figure 2.5).

You may choose to deselect the Citrix License Server (see Figure 2.6). There is only one license server per farm. For a proof of concept environment, we would recommend that you install all the components on a single server.

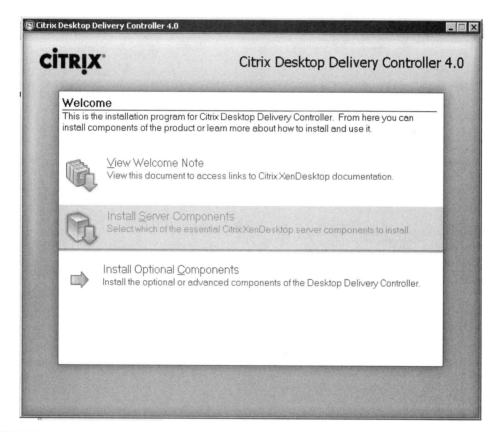

FIGURE 2.4

Installing server components.

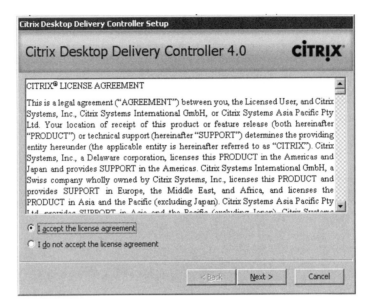

FIGURE 2.5

Accepting the license agreement.

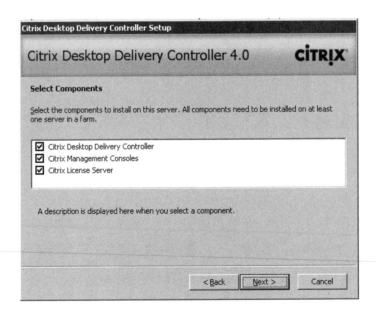

FIGURE 2.6

Selecting components to install on the server.

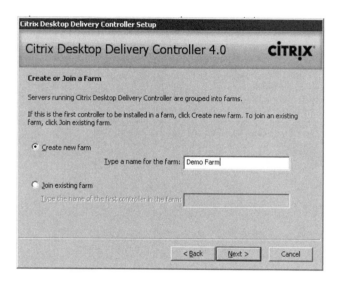

FIGURE 2.7

Creating or joining a farm.

For a live/production environment, it is advisable to install the Citrix License Server on a separate server. The Citrix License Server should preferably reside on a server that is not acting as a DDC. A server that is not subject to down time is ideal; a dedicated VM is commonly used.

5. For the first DDC in your organization, type in the name of the XenDesktop Farm[D] and click **Next** (see Figure 2.7). This section covers creating the first DDC.

If you are adding a second or subsequent DDC, select **Join existing farm** – "Type the name of the first controller in the farm" this will fetch all the configuration settings – including the Active Directory configuration and replay those setting for your additional DDC.

6. Select the correct edition that you have purchased, or plan to purchase. If you are evaluating the software, select **Platinum Edition** – you can choose if you need all the features later (see Figure 2.8).
7. The dialog box shown in Figure 2.9 could be a bit confusing; it doesn't refer to using an existing database, but rather a database server. By this they mean a separate database server, like an SQL Server. For a proof of concept, we recommend that you leave this blank and skip down to Step 15, and for a live/production environment, use an enterprise database server in your environment – such that it is simple to both back up and restore your farm settings.

The SQL Server option is available – Oracle would only appear in the drop-down list if the Oracle client were installed (see Figure 2.10). The following steps are for a Microsoft SQL database.

[D]Farm – Citrix uses the term farm to designate a group of DDCs. The farm will load balance tasks among the servers, the farm also serves as a high availability mechanism – if any of the DDCs were to fail, the XenDesktop virtual workstations would automatically be redirected to another controller in the farm to take over the role of managing the workstations.

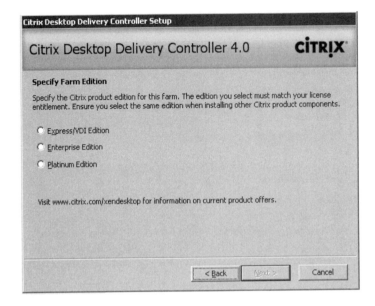

FIGURE 2.8

Selecting the farm edition.

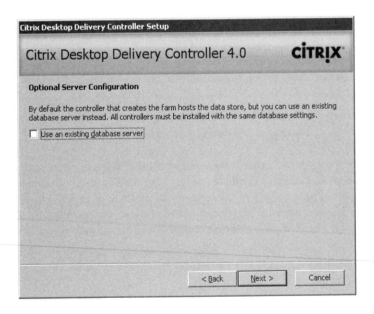

FIGURE 2.9

Choosing SQL express or an enterprise database.

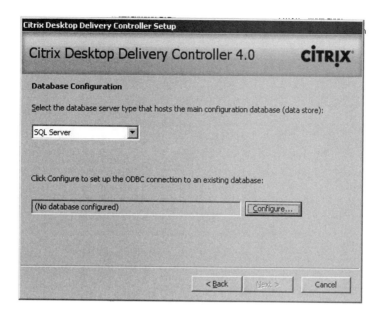

FIGURE 2.10

Enterprise database configuration.

8. Click **Configure**.
9. This brings up a standard Microsoft ODBC (Open Database Connectivity) dialog box (see Figure 2.11). Select the appropriate SQL Server.
10. Select the authentication type, Windows NT authentication is most commonly in use (see Figure 2.12).
11. From the drop-down list, select the database that the SQL administrator has created for you (see Figure 2.13).
12. Click **Finish** (see Figure 2.14).
13. Click **Test Data Source**... to verify connectivity (see Figure 2.15).
14. Click **OK** (see Figure 2.16).

You have now created a file-based DSN (data source name). To check the setting, you can read the file using notepad or a text editor: C:\Program Files\Citrix\Independent Management Architecture\MF20.dsn

15. Click **Next** (see Figure 2.17).

If all of the Windows prerequisites aren't installed, the following pops up: Figure 2.18
Steps 16 through 18 are only required if the Windows prerequisites aren't met.

16. Unmount your XDS_4_0_0_dvd.ISO and mount the Windows 2003 .ISO that was used to install the base operating system, and click **OK** (see Figure 2.18). Windows will then install the components (see Figure 2.19).
17. Remount the XDS_4_0_0_dvd.ISO, and click **OK** (see Figure 2.20).

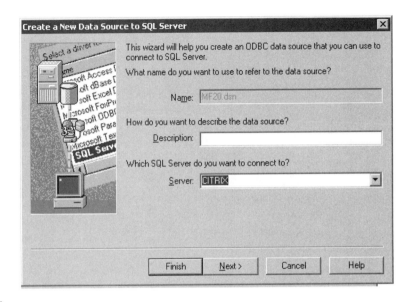

FIGURE 2.11

Creating an ODBC connection.

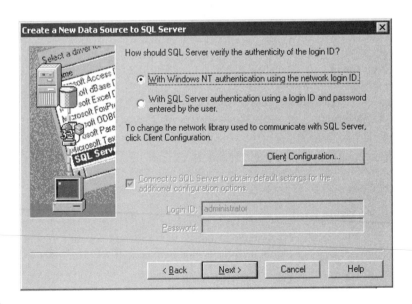

FIGURE 2.12

Configuring database authentication.

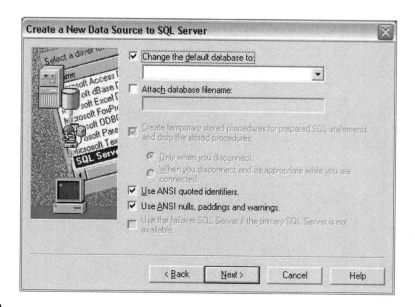

FIGURE 2.13

Database selection.

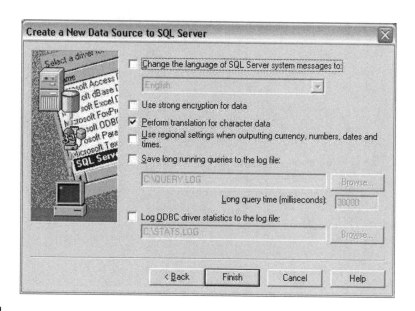

FIGURE 2.14

Finalizing database settings.

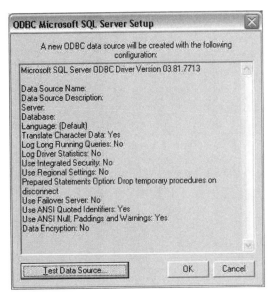

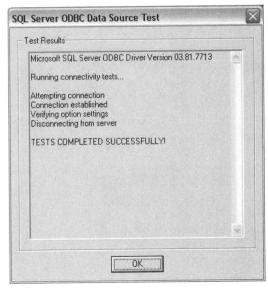

FIGURE 2.15

Testing the data source.

FIGURE 2.16

Test results dialog box.

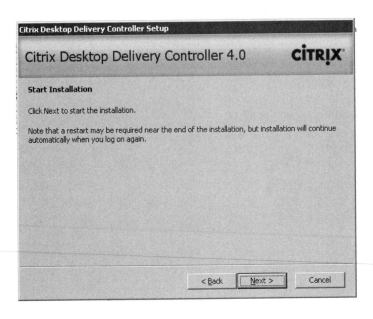

FIGURE 2.17

Initiate installation.

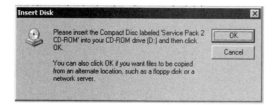

FIGURE 2.18

Windows 2003 media.

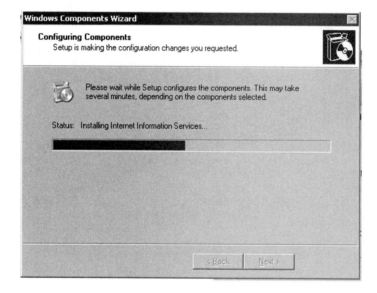

FIGURE 2.19

IIS installation progress.

FIGURE 2.20

Mount XenDesktop media.

18. Click **Yes** to restart the server following the Windows component installation (see Figure 2.21).

You may need to launch the autorun.exe again if it doesn't launch automatically. If you have reached this stage, you may be drumming your fingers on the table waiting for the .Net 3.5 framework to install – yes, it does take a while!

19. The dialog box shown in Figure 2.22 appears six times, click **Continue Anyway** for each. There are three universal drivers (and three hotfixes). The drivers being installed are the Citrix Universal Printer drivers, which have not been digitally signed.

20. The server requires a further restart to complete your installation (see Figure 2.23).

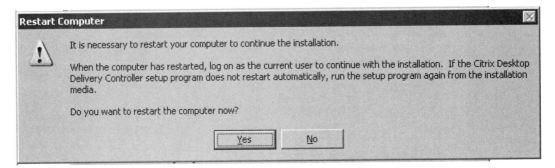

FIGURE 2.21

Restart dialog box.

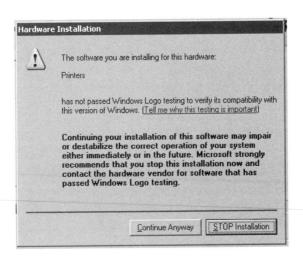

FIGURE 2.22

Unsigned drivers installation.

FIGURE 2.23

Server restart.

DDC Installation Recommendations for Large Farms

IIS running on every DDC will place unnecessary load on the DDC.

Recommendation: For larger farms, run Web Interface on separate load-balanced Web servers.

> **TIP**
>
> To prevent IIS and Web Interface being installed on every server, run the setup.exe program from the command line with the –nosites switch. For example "D:\w2k3\en\setup.exe –nosites"

Recommendation: For performance, it is better to point the Web Interface Servers at the member servers than at the farm master. This reduces load on the farm master.

Dedicated Farm Master for Large Farms

Recommendation: In larger sites, dedicate a server to act as the farm master. Having a dedicated farm master allows it to better process connections.

[E]To configure a farm master, change the following registry keys:

```
HKLM\Software\Citrix\IMA\RUNTIME\UseRegistrySetting
DWORD=UseRegistrySetting
Value=1
```

that enables the use of the registry key, then

```
HKLM\Software\Citrix\IMA\RUNTIME\MasterRanking
DWORD=Value
Value= 1 indicates 'Master',2 indicates 'Backup'3 indicates 'Member', and 4 indicates
'Slave Only'
Set the Value of MasterRanking to "1" and restart the server.
```

In order to offload the work on to the member servers, the registry needs to be changed such that the farm master is responsible for fewer registrations

```
HKLM\Software\Citrix\DesktopServer\MaxWorkers
DWORD=Value
```

[E]See Citrix Knowledge Base Article CTX117477 for more details.

Set the value to a lower number than the member servers. This can be set to zero such that it doesn't process any registrations, but caution should be exercised; you must understand that you are disabling it from processing registrations, and if you only have two DDCs, this could give you a resiliency issue.

Recommendation: Set this value to zero – if you have two or more member servers in addition to the farm master.

ACTIVE DIRECTORY INTEGRATION

The Active Directory Wizard can be used to integrate your XenDesktop Farm with Microsoft Active Directory.

The question most often asked is "Why?" XenDesktop uses Active Directory to present a list of DDCs to the virtual workstations. If any one of the DDCs were to fail, the workstations could query Active Directory and attach to an alternative DDC within a matter of seconds. This is a high availability mechanism that means your broker is highly resilient.

The second question is that of risk, the Active Directory Administrator in any environment wants to be absolutely sure that this will not have an adverse effect on Active Directory. The most important point to convey is that it does *not* update the Active Directory Schema. So what does it do? It creates a number of objects in a designated organizational unit (OU) of your choice.

Inside the OU it creates a Controllers Security Group, which contains the machine accounts of all the DDCs. The Controllers Security Group is used for security purposes, virtual desktops will only register with servers in this group. It creates a Service Connection Points (SCP) object[F] called "Farm SCP" (see Figure 2.24). This contains the name of the farm. If your organization has more than one XenDesktop environment, when installing the Virtual Desktop Agent, you will have an option of which farm the desktop belongs to. It also creates a container called "RegistrationServices" – whenever a new DDC is added to the farm; its objectGUID is added to the RegistrationServices container. That's a lot of information; however, you will no doubt have to give it to the Active Directory Administrator before you are allowed to run the Active Directory Wizard.

The Active Directory Configuration Wizard could either be run by a domain administrator (using runas, for example) or the domain administrator could delegate you permission to the parent OU – you need CreateChild permissions on the parent OU.

AD Integration – Step by Step

1. Launch the Active Directory Configuration Wizard: **Start | Programs | Citrix | Administrative Tools | Active Directory Configuration Wizard** (see Figure 2.25).
2. Click **Next** (see Figure 2.26).

[F]SCP objects are Service Connection Points. SCP objects are used to publish services in Active Directory. They are used to locate services or information about services. Microsoft Exchange and Microsoft SQL can also make use of SCP objects.

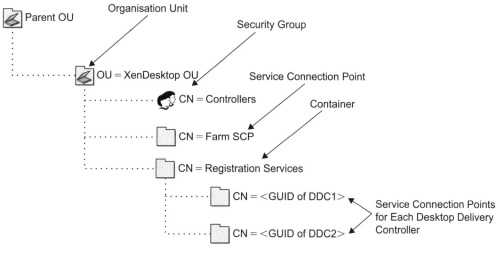

FIGURE 2.24

Active Directory XenDesktop farm objects.

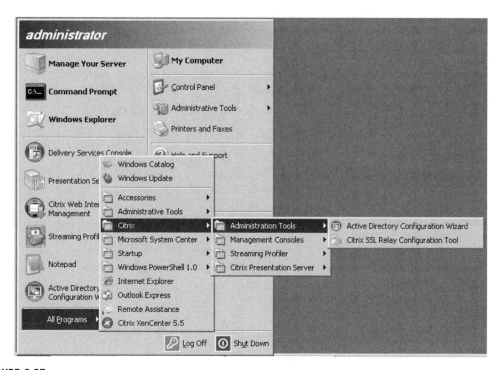

FIGURE 2.25

Active Directory Configuration Wizard start menu item.

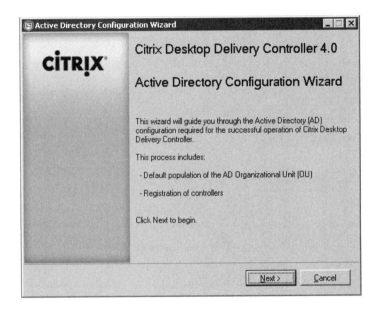

FIGURE 2.26

Active Directory Configuration Wizard.

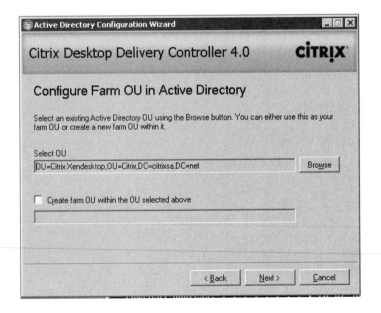

FIGURE 2.27

Active Directory OU selection.

3. Click **Browse** to navigate to the correct location within the Active Directory. If the OU you have been assigned has already been created, select the OU and click **Next** (see Figure 2.27).

4. If the OU has not been precreated, and if you have sufficient permissions, you can select the check box **Create farm OU within the OU selected above** and create the OU in the required location. Enter the OU name and click **Next** (see Figure 2.28).

5. Click "**Add Local Machine**" and click **Next** (see Figure 2.29).

TIP

If you need to change the OU for any reason, you will need to select all the DDCs in your farm and the wizard will reconfigure the settings for all the DDCs.

---

6. Click **Finish** (see Figure 2.30).

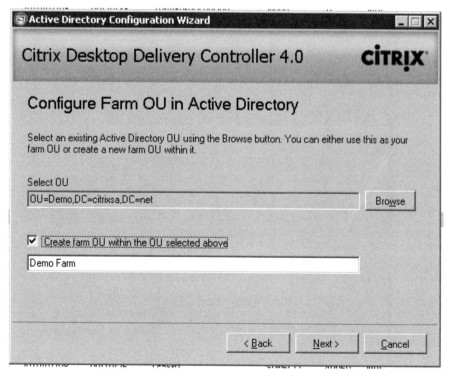

FIGURE 2.28

Create a farm OU.

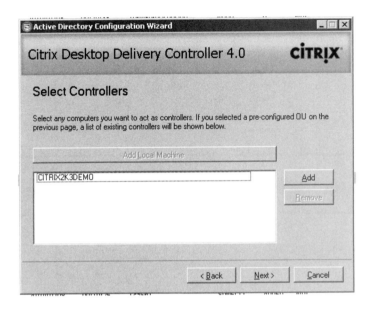

FIGURE 2.29

Add Desktop Delivery Controllers to the farm.

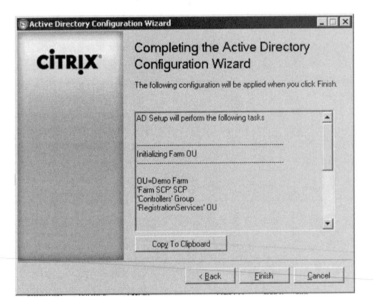

FIGURE 2.30

AD setup verification.

Common issues are as follows:

1. Insufficient permissions will result in the Active Directory Wizard failing.
2. Computer account – If the DDC is configured as a VM, check the event log for domain type errors. If neccessary, re-add the DDC to the domain.
3. Time sync – The VM should be time syncing to the domain, not to the hypervisor (XenServer/Hyper-V/VMware).

SUMMARY

In this chapter, we dived straight into the installation of the Citrix Virtual Desktop broker. We briefly covered how the DDC mechanism actually works, and then we looked at the practical installation steps. The integration of the DDC with Microsoft Active Directory ties the broker to the authentication mechanism. We covered how the Active Directory integration works, and then we stepped through the process of integrating XenDesktop with the Active Directory.

Configuring the Desktop Delivery Controller

INFORMATION IN THIS CHAPTER

* Basic Configuration Settings

The configuration section is separated into two parts, the basic settings are enough to get you to the stage of being able to remotely attach to a virtual desktop, the advanced settings covers configuration that may or may not be necessary depending on your environment.

Some of the advanced configuration settings have dependencies on the interaction with the hypervisor. Consequently, I have structured this such that we perform the basic configuration settings first, and then install a virtual instance on the hypervisor of choice, then subsequently address some of the more advanced settings.

After the XenDesktop software has been installed, you may have noticed two errors in the event logs, the first regarding the configuration of the Active Directory OU (Organizational Unit), which we dealt with in the previous section, and the second error regarding the license server, which we deal with in this section. The Citrix License Server should be familiar to a lot of readers who are already working with Citrix technology.

BASIC CONFIGURATION SETTINGS

The following configuration tasks are all that is required to do a very basic connection to an individual desktop. It is preferable to confirm the functionality of the Desktop Delivery Controller (DDC) at this stage, before we introduce the hypervisor layer. It is also simpler to troubleshoot any issues with a very basic setup.

This section also serves as a template for those wanting to do a very basic demonstration of how a virtual desktop functions.

Performing an Initial Discovery – Step by Step

The first task we have to perform is to check that the software is functioning correctly.

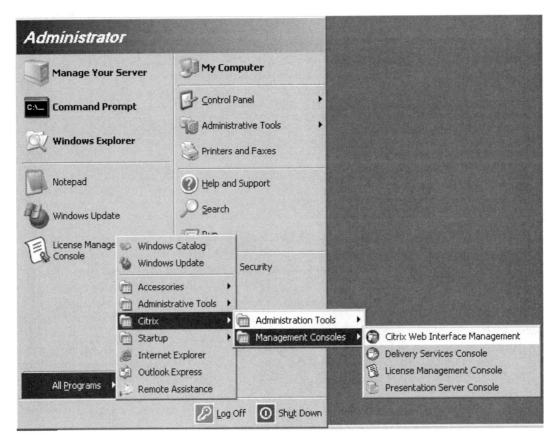

FIGURE 3.1

Checking the software.

1. To do this, select **Start | All Programs | Citrix | Management Consoles | Delivery Services Console** (see Figure 3.1).

> **NOTE**
> The Delivery Services Console is the new name for the Access Management Console (see Figure 3.2).

2. Click **Next** (see Figure 3.2)
3. Click **Next** (see Figure 3.3).
4. Click **Add Local Computer** – this will add the machine you are working on to the discovery list.

   If you have only one Desktop Delivery Controller, jump to Step 7.

5. Click **Add** (see Figure 3.4).

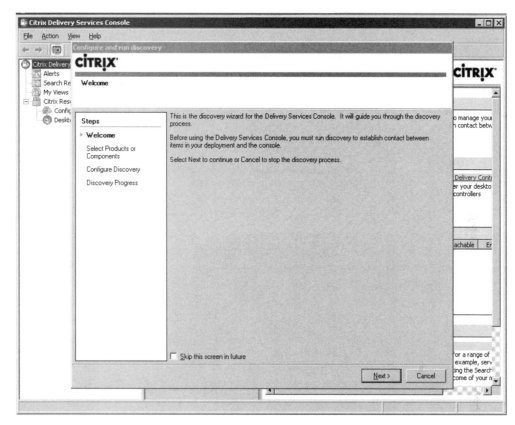

FIGURE 3.2

The discovery wizard for the Delivery Services Console.

6. Enter the hostname(s) of the other Desktop Delivery Controllers, and Click **OK** (see Figure 3.5).
7. Click **Next** – The discovery will now start (see Figure 3.6).
8. Click **Finish** – Any errors would appear in the Description Pane (see Figure 3.7).

NOTE

The discovery is automatically performed each time you open the Delivery Services Console. There will be the facility to cache this information in the following version of the product.

TIP

There are two main reasons that a discovery might fail. First, confirm the name you are trying to discover is correct. If you execute a ping <servername> and the name doesn't resolve correctly, then you need to check the DNS (Domain Name System) settings. Second, check whether all the Citrix Services on the target Desktop Delivery Controller are functioning, and if necessary, start the services.

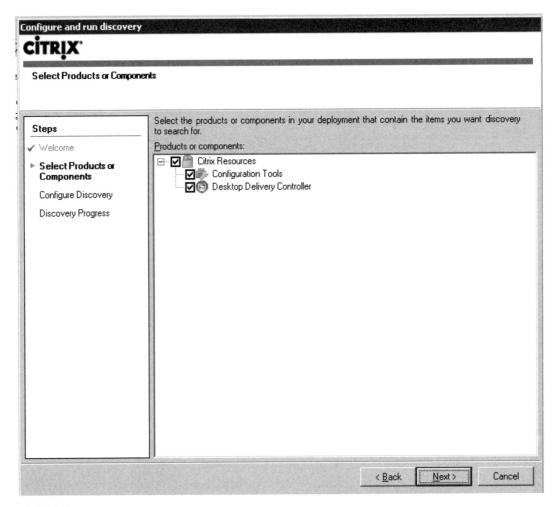

FIGURE 3.3

Selecting products or components.

This console should have a very familiar look and feel to Citrix engineers (see Figure 3.8). It is based on the old Access Management Console, but instead of publishing applications, you are now publishing desktops. The Access Management Console has now been renamed the Delivery Services Console within XenApp 5 too, so as to better align the products.

Configure the XenDesktop License Server – Step by Step

This section steps through adding your license file to your license server. If you haven't as yet obtained your license file, see Chapter 12, "Implementing Virtual Profiles into the Virtual Desktop," for details.

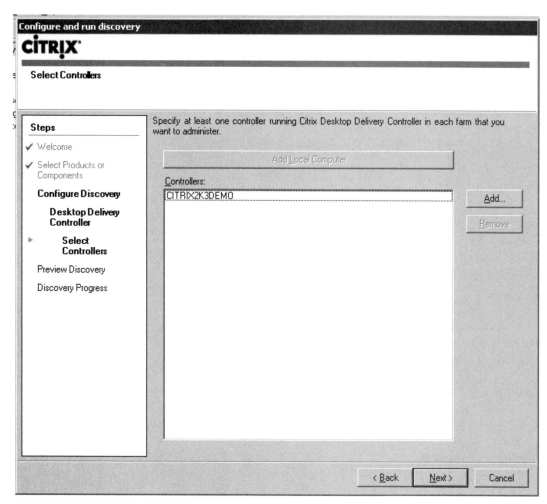

FIGURE 3.4

Selecting a controller.

FIGURE 3.5

Add Controller dialog box.

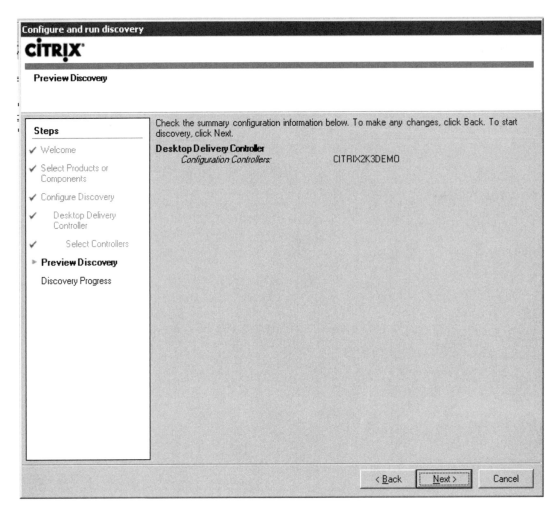

FIGURE 3.6

Preview Discovery.

> **NOTE**
>
> The License Console interface is being completely redesigned, and this will affect the next version of XenDesktop. The new license server is covered in the appendices.

1. Select **Start | All Programs | Citrix | Management Consoles | License Management Console** (see Figure 3.9).
2. Click **Configure License Server** (see Figure 3.10).
3. Select **Copy License file to this license server** (see Figure 3.11).

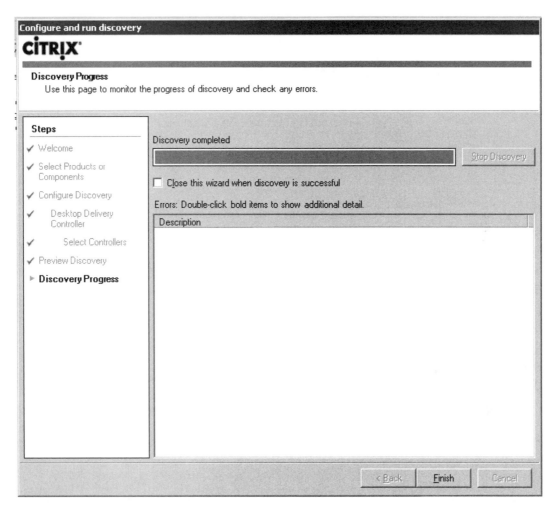

FIGURE 3.7

Discovery progress.

4. Browse to the location of your license file. Click **Open**, and then click **Upload** (see Figure 3.12).

Overdraft is a new addition to the License Console (Figure 3.13). This column shows you if your licenses are "overdrawn." Citrix has added an overdraft to the license model to leave 10% headroom to allow for staff churn (leavers and joiners).

5. Open the Desktop Delivery Controller. Right-click on your **Farm name | Modify farm properties | Modify license server properties** (see Figure 3.14).
6. Specify the License Server Name or IP (Internet Protocol) Address, and click **OK**. Using a hostname is preferred while using a clone in a disaster recovery site (see Figure 3.15).

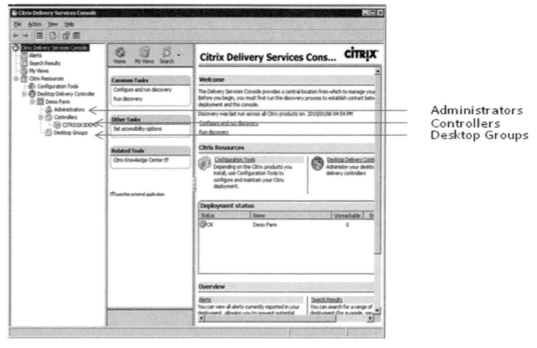

FIGURE 3.8

Delivery Services Console.

FAQ

How long can the license server be off before my servers leave the grace period? The grace period is now either 720 h or 30 days. It is, however, not a desirable state to have your farm in, as it could potentially cause issues. New servers need to register with a license server at least once before they can enter a grace period. I would recommend having HA (High Availability) enabled on the license server if it is a virtual machine, and for disaster-recovery scenarios, a cold standby clone (i.e., same hostname) that is an exact copy of the license server – perhaps with the exception of the IP address if the disaster recovery site uses a separate subnet.

Install the Virtual Desktop Agent on a Test Workstation – Step by Step

You require at least one test workstation to test the functionality of your Desktop Delivery Controller. I advise installing this on a laptop or a desktop that is part of the target domain. I like to install the agent on an existing machine as it is already part of the domain and has the end users applications already installed – but mostly because it makes a really nice demo.

If you do not have a suitable workstation available, skip forward to Chapter 4, "Installing the Virtual Desktop," and install a suitable workstation on the hypervisor of your choice.

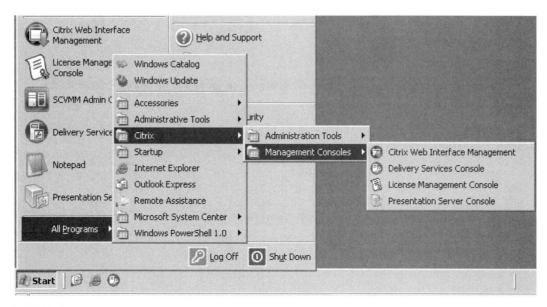

FIGURE 3.9

Selecting the License Management Console.

> **NOTE**
> You will need administrative rights on the workstation in order to install the agent.

1. If you have cut the XDS_4_0_0_dvd.ISO to a physical DVD, you can just place that in the DVD drive of the workstation. If necessary click on the **autorun.exe** on the root of the DVD. The autorun automatically detects the guest operating system and launches the correct .msi file (see Figure 3.16).

Otherwise, it is perhaps simpler to copy the relevant "XdsAgent.msi" file to your workstation. Navigate to the DVD mounted on the Desktop Delivery Controller.

If your workstation is 32 bit, copy **<driveletter>:\w2k3\en\VirtualDesktop\XdsAgent.msi** (if you are unsure whether it is 32 or 64 bit, use this file), to your workstation.

If your workstation is 64 bit, copy **<driveletter>:\x64\en\VirtualDesktop\XdsAgent.msi** to your workstation.

2. If the .NET Framework 3.5 SP 1 is not yet installed, it will automatically detect and prompt you to install it. Click **Install** (see Figure 3.17).

> **NOTE**
> The .NET 3.5 Framework can take a long time to install – don't assume it has hung, it will eventually finish!

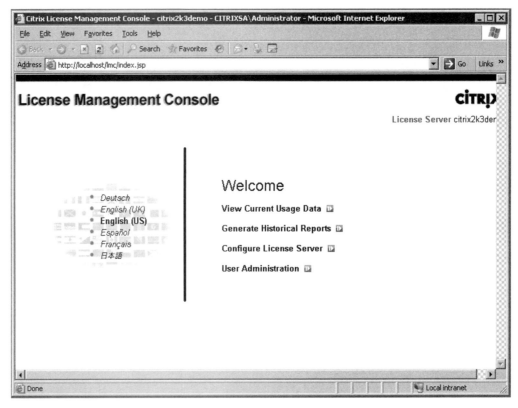

FIGURE 3.10

The License Management Console welcome screen.

3. Click **Next** (see Figure 3.18).
4. Toggle the radio button to accept the license agreement, and click **Next** (see Figure 3.19).
5. Click **Next** to accept the defaults (see Figure 3.20).

NOTE

Sometimes it is necessary to change the Desktop Delivery Controller listener port from 8080 to another number (normally if the port is in use by another application) – this dialog box gives you the opportunity to change the workstation to match the server port.

---

6. Select **Next** to let the wizard automatically configure the Windows Firewall (see Figure 3.21).

If your desktop standard includes a third-party firewall, this will need to be manually configured.

The Microsoft Firewall can be configured through a Group Policy. The Policy settings are located under – **Computer Configuration | Administrative Templates | Network | Network Connections | Windows Firewall**. The Microsoft recommended settings are to allow the use of Local

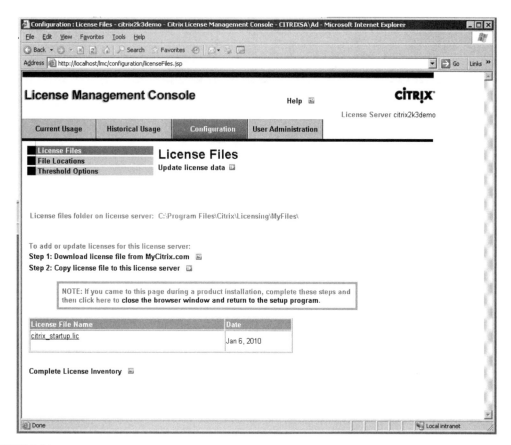

FIGURE 3.11

Citrix License Management Console.

Port exceptions; however, some organizations may have stricter policies that will override your local settings. If you find that communication is being blocked, it may be worthwhile running a Resultant Set of Policy using the Microsoft Group Policy Management Console to ascertain which settings are being applied, and where they derive from.

7. Select the correct XenDesktop Farm[A] from the drop-down list, and click **Next** (see Figure 3.22).

> **NOTE**
>
> There may be a requirement for separate farms for different divisions or departments. It is also a good idea to keep your development/test farm completely separate from any live/production farms.

[A]The setup wizard queries Active Directory for the farm SCP (Service Connection Point) objects, and it returns all the XenDesktop farms.

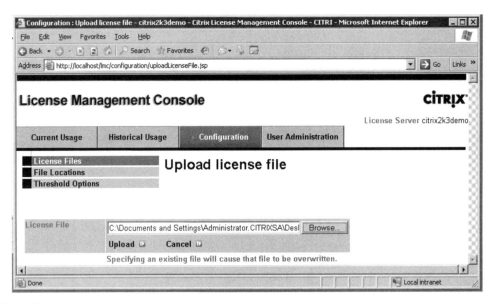

FIGURE 3.12

Citrix License Management Console – upload license file.

8. Click **Install** (see Figure 3.23).

9. As with the Desktop Delivery Controller, the printer drivers haven't been signed. This pop-up box will come up more than once; click **Continue Anyway** (see Figure 3.24).

NOTE

These are the Citrix Universal Print Drivers, which can be used in conjunction with the client-based printers.

---

10. Click **Yes** to restart (see Figure 3.25).

TIP

Scan the Application Event Log of the workstation after the reboot. The logging is quite verbose and (unlike some products) the event messaging is pretty good at finding problems. Most common issues are around the communication between the workstation and the Desktop Delivery Controller.

Check:

- The virtual desktop computer account
- The time on the virtual desktop and the Desktop Delivery Controller – this must be in sync. Make sure that the virtual desktop is using the Domain Controller to set its time and *not* the Server Virtualization Platform. Citrix recommends using NTP (Network Time Protocol) for the virtual desktops and Desktop Delivery Controller.

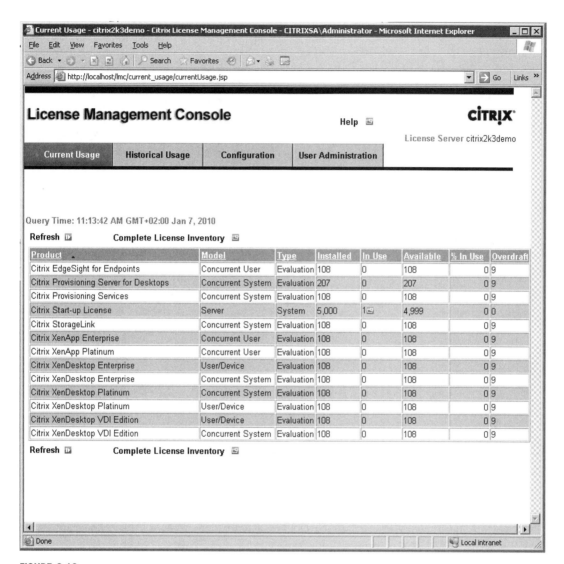

FIGURE 3.13

Citrix License Management Console – click **Current Usage** tab to view your license allocation. Confirm that you have the correct product(s) listed.

- DNS, check that you can resolve the fully qualified domain name (FQDN) of the virtual desktop from the Desktop Delivery Controller and vice versa.
- Confirm that port 8080 (or the configured port) is open for communication. The command line *netstat* will show connections to hosts, and the ports in use.
- XDPing /host <hostname> (CTX123278).

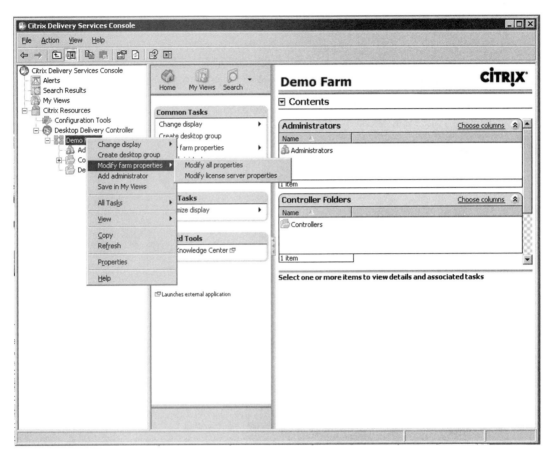

FIGURE 3.14

Citrix Delivery Services Console – farm menu.

Successful registration with the Desktop Delivery Controller is what you are looking for in the event log (see Figure 3.26).

Virtual Desktop Group Creation – Step by Step

Now that we have a test workstation, we can set up a test Desktop Group. Return to the Desktop Delivery Controller and open the Citrix Delivery Services Console.

1. Right-click on **Desktop Groups | Create Desktop Group** (see Figure 3.27).
2. Click **Next** (see Figure 3.28).
3. Leave the Default selection at **Pooled** and click **Next** (see Figure 3.29).

Pooled – All users draw from a common pool of workstations, workstations are randomly assigned and the user will (most likely) get a different computer name at each logon.

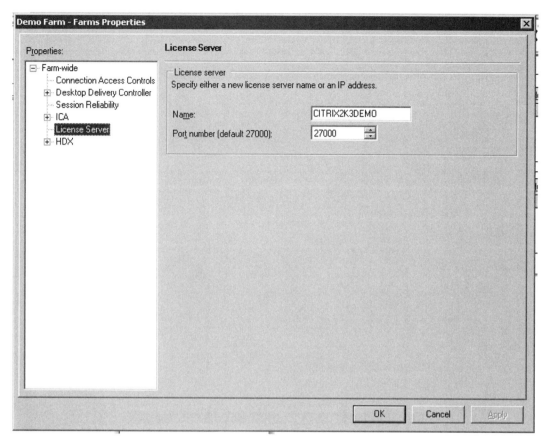

FIGURE 3.15

Farm properties – license server.

Assigned – The user always gets the same workstation. Sometimes, this is useful if the user requires a specific machine name or IP address for some applications such as a Cisco softphone, for example.

There are two types of assigned desktops:

Assign on first use – Sometimes called "sticky," the first workstation you draw becomes the one you always use, and no other user will receive the workstation.

Preassigned – The administrator decides explicitly which user receives which desktop.

> **TIP**
>
> Try to use Pooled wherever possible. It is far simpler to manage a generic pool of common use devices. User uniqueness can almost always be achieved through a combination of virtual applications and Virtual Profiles.

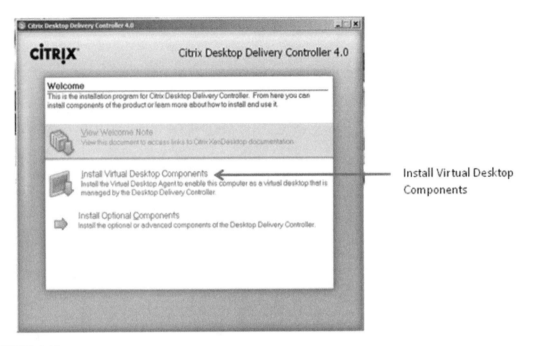

Install Virtual Desktop Components

FIGURE 3.16

Citrix Desktop Delivery Controller 4.0 installation program.

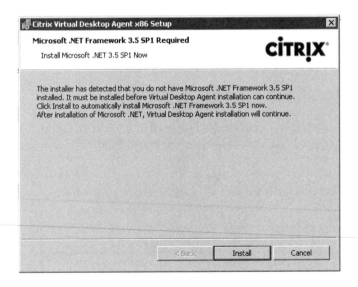

FIGURE 3.17

Microsoft .NET Framework install dialog box.

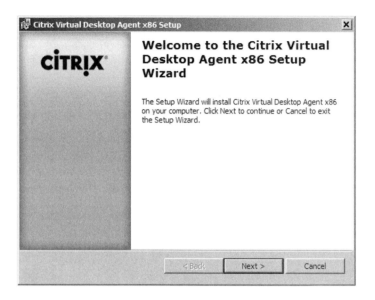

FIGURE 3.18

Virtual Desktop Agent setup wizard.

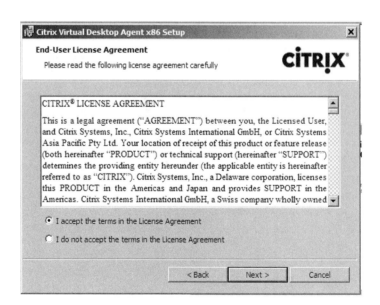

FIGURE 3.19

License agreement.

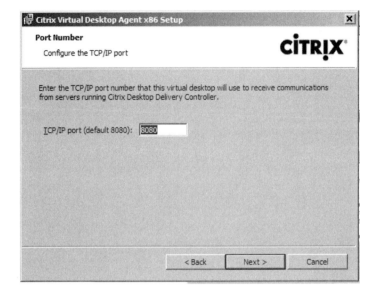

FIGURE 3.20

TCP/IP port number.

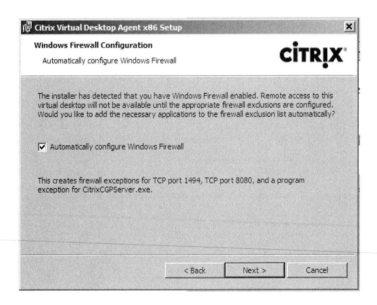

FIGURE 3.21

Firewall configuration.

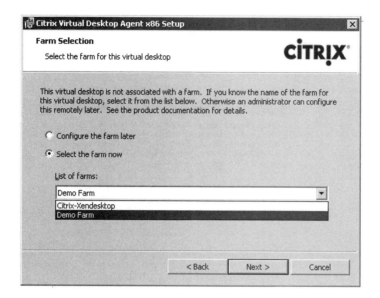

FIGURE 3.22

Farm selection.

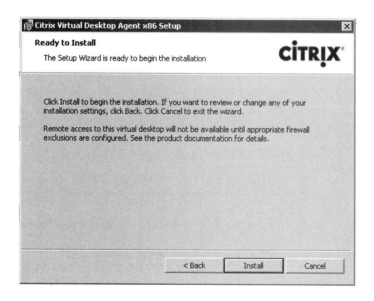

FIGURE 3.23

Ready to install.

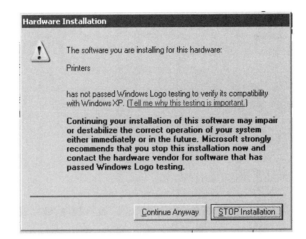

FIGURE 3.24

Windows logo warning.

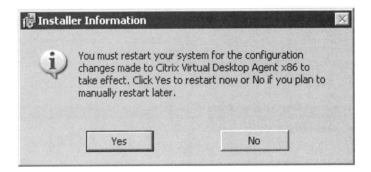

FIGURE 3.25

Restart dialog box.

4. In this example, we are attaching to a simple workstation on the network, so the hosting infrastructure we should choose is **None** (see Figure 3.30).

> **NOTE**
>
> If you have in fact installed your test workstation on a hypervisor, at this stage choose **None** – the workstation will function normally, but you will lose some of the hypervisor integration features. The integration of the Desktop Delivery Controller and the hypervisors will be discussed in the next chapter.

5. Click **Add** – to add a computer account from Active Directory (see Figure 3.31).
6. The selector is a standard Microsoft one, find your computer name in Active Directory and click **OK** (see Figure 3.32).

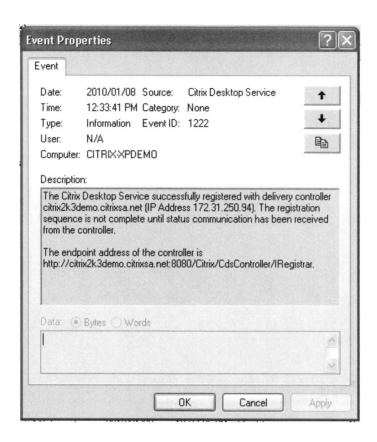

FIGURE 3.26

Event log entry.

TIP

In larger organizations, where the Active Directory tree structure is large, it is often simpler to enter
<DOMAINNAME>\<COMPUTERNAME> and click **Check Names**. In my example, the syntax would be as follows:
citrixsa\citrix-xpdemo. This tip is also applicable to the User Selector in the next step.

---

7. Click **Next** (see Figure 3.33).

8. To add users, click **Add** – again this is a standard Microsoft selector, add the required group or
test user (see Figure 3.34).

9. Click the **Check Names** button to verify the username or group and then click **OK** (see
Figure 3.35).

10. Click **Next** (see Figure 3.36).

11. Give your Desktop Group an appropriate name, and click **Next** (see Figure 3.37).

12. Click **Next** (see Figure 3.38).

13. Click **Finish** (see Figure 3.39).

FIGURE 3.27

Delivery Services Console.

FIGURE 3.28

Create Desktop Group.

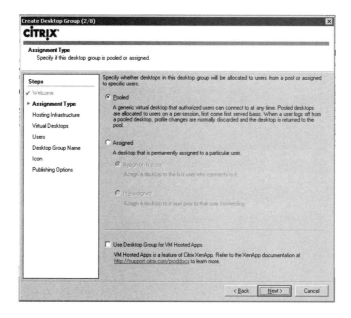

FIGURE 3.29

Assignment type.

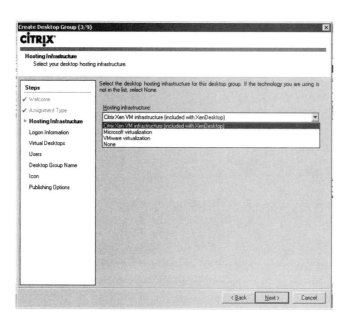

FIGURE 3.30

Hosting infrastructure.

FIGURE 3.31

Virtual desktops.

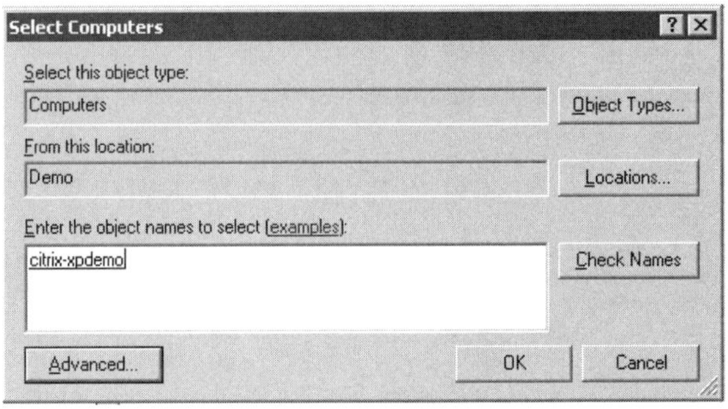

FIGURE 3.32

Select computers.

Open your Desktop Group and view the status of the machine that you have added.

The desktop should appear as "Idle" if it is ready for use (see Figure 3.40). If the Desktop State reads *In Use*, log off any user on the machine. If the Desktop State reads *Not Registered*, hit **F5** to refresh the console. If it remains *Not Registered*, try restarting the "Citrix ICA Service" on the workstation – and check the event log to see if it is registering correctly.

The specific details of virtual Desktop Group creation for XenServer, Hyper-V, and VMware are also covered in detail in Chapter 4, "Installing the Virtual Desktop."

FIGURE 3.33

Virtual desktops.

FIGURE 3.34

Add users.

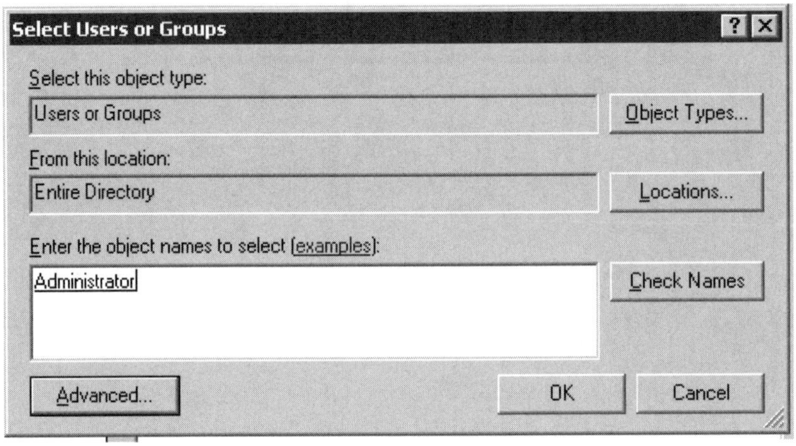

FIGURE 3.35

Select users or groups.

FIGURE 3.36

Add users.

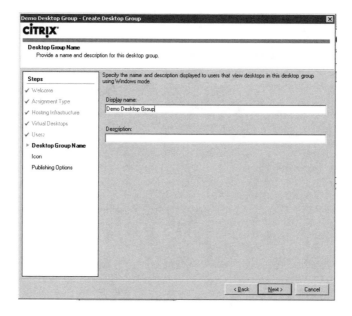

FIGURE 3.37

Desktop Group name.

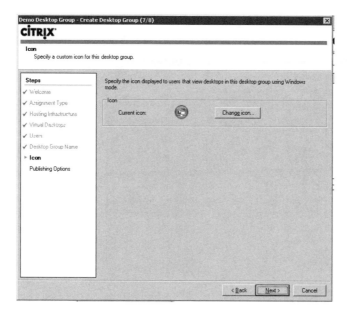

FIGURE 3.38

Select icon.

FIGURE 3.39

Publishing options.

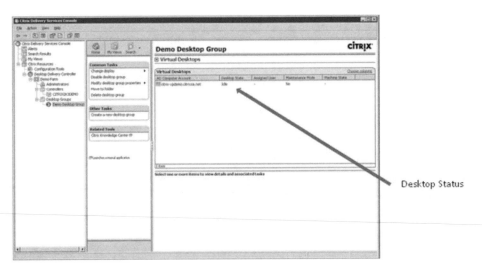

FIGURE 3.40

Virtual desktop status.

Connectivity to a Single Desktop

By default the Desktop Delivery Controller automatically installs the Web Interface component, so nothing further is required to perform the testing. Connectivity can be tested by connecting to the autoinstalled Web site.

1. Type the hostname or IP address into the Web browser on your laptop/PC, you will be automatically redirected to the logon page. Enter the test username, password, and the domain name in the fields and click **Log On** (see Figure 3.41).

   The Desktop Delivery Controller will now prompt you to install the Citrix client.

2. Click the information bar to allow the Citrix Helper Control to run add on (see Figure 3.42).

> **NOTE**
>
> In the event that you have an earlier version of Citrix client, you do have the option to bypass this by clicking **Already Installed**. The earlier versions of Citrix clients do not include some of the newer HDX features. The latest version of the client adds a handy toolbar at the top of the screen, which allows configuration of various client settings.

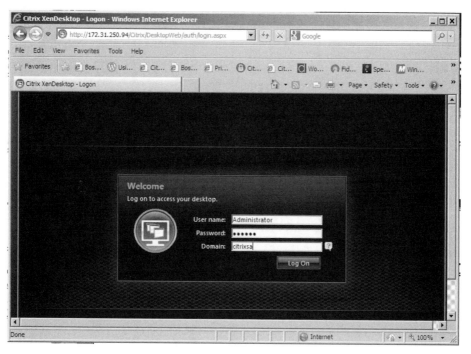

FIGURE 3.41

Web interface portal.

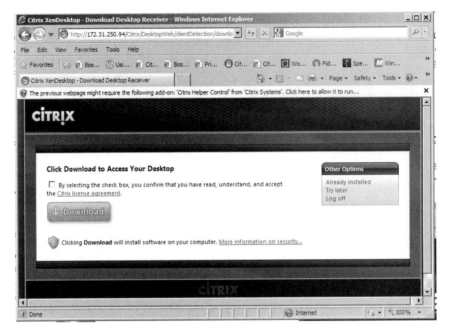

FIGURE 3.42

Citrix client installation.

3. Click **Run** – The Helper Control will try to detect if the Citrix client is installed (see Figure 3.43). If you already have a Citrix client, you can either choose to upgrade the Citrix Receiver or skip past and upgrade later. This will take you to Step 7.
4. Select the checkbox to agree with the Citrix License Agreement, and then click **Download** (see Figure 3.44).
5. Click **Run** to install after downloading (see Figure 3.45).
6. Click **Run** to execute (see Figure 3.46).

   The "CitrixOnlinePluginWeb" will automatically uninstall previous Citrix client versions.

7. Click **OK** (see Figure 3.47).
8. If necessary click the **click to connect** tab inside the Web page (see Figure 3.48).

   If you add the Web site to the Trusted Sites Zone, then by default if your user belongs to one Desktop Group, then the desktop will autolaunch. This may be something you wish to do through a Microsoft Group Policy for the Live/Production Web Interface site.

   The virtual desktop will now launch as shown in Figure 3.49.

NOTE

The native USB (Universal Serial Bus) redirection will only work once you have rebooted the workstation running the Citrix Receiver.

FIGURE 3.43

Run ActiveX control.

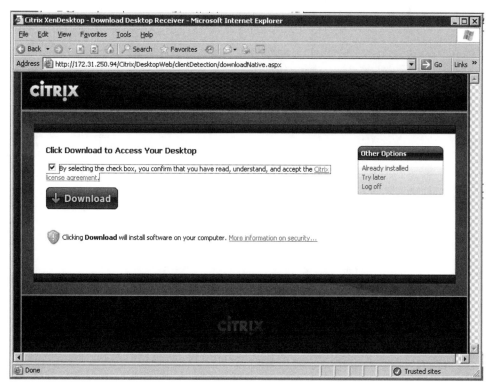

FIGURE 3.44

License agreement and download page.

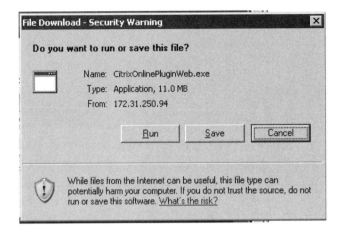

FIGURE 3.45

Citrix online plugin.

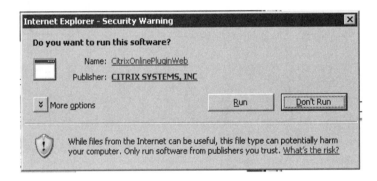

FIGURE 3.46

Run online plugin executable.

FIGURE 3.47

Successful installation.

FIGURE 3.48

Desktop connection page.

FIGURE 3.49

Citrix desktop viewer.

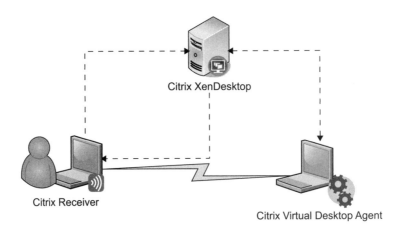

Citrix XenDesktop

Citrix Receiver

Citrix Virtual Desktop Agent

FIGURE 3.50

XenDesktop connection demonstration.

Checkpoint 1 – **Connectivity Demonstration**

You should have reached this stage during the first day – if all the prerequisites were met – if you spent a few hours waiting for IP addresses or security for the OU creation, you may well be into your second day of this project. It is, however, significant because you can already show some tangible results. Because the XenDesktop architecture comprises many components, it is useful to show the individual component functionality in isolation from each other to clarify how each component functions.

This is a good time to get all the interested parties gathered around for a mini demonstration.

Here is the picture:

During this demonstration, you will show the connectivity from one workstation to another, with the Desktop Delivery Controller brokering that connection. If possible use a whiteboard to draw the picture shown in Figure 3.50. What is important to note is that the session established is a direct one, from one workstation to another, with the Desktop Delivery Controller purely brokering the connection.

The user experience with XenDesktop is simply flawless; demonstrate how the local user experience on the local desktop is identical to working on the remote desktop. It is at this point that you achieve buy-in from both technical and nontechnical parties. If possible run a small video clip on the remote desktop, YouTube is a good option; the performance of video streaming from the remote desktop never fails to impress the audience. It never fails to amaze me how, no matter how many meetings you may have before this stage, the physical demonstration clarifies what you are trying to achieve.

TIP

Ask for a USB memory stick from one of those watching, plug it in, and demonstrate how the local peripheral seamlessly redirects to the remote desktop.

SUMMARY

This section aims to draw together the most basic functions of the XenDesktop broker. To that end, we first ran the initial configuration of the Desktop Delivery Controller, we added a license to the license server, and added the XenDesktop agent to a test machine. This "virtual desktop" was then associated with the Desktop Delivery Controller by adding it to a Desktop Group.

The connectivity demonstration is included for both you and the project sponsors to crystallize the concept of what we are trying to achieve.

Installing the Virtual Desktop

INFORMATION IN THIS CHAPTER

- Virtual Desktop Recommendations
- Citrix XenServer
- Microsoft Hyper-V
- VMware vSphere
- Blade Hardware

Installing the base virtual desktop onto a hypervisor is one of the simplest tasks, and also it has no dependencies up until you start integrating it with the provisioning server, which is discussed in Chapter 7, "Fundamental Configuration of the Citrix Provisioning Server."

> **TIP**
> Perform this task when waiting for a network change, a DHCP (Dynamic Host Configuration Protocol) scope to be created, or an OU (Organizational Unit) to be created, and so on.

This section makes the assumption that the hypervisor layer is already in place, and we cover how to perform the virtual desktop installation on these hypervisors.

Hypervisor integration is an important feature of XenDesktop. This extends the reach of the Desktop Delivery Controller (DDC) to interact with virtual machine power settings. The Desktop Delivery Controller can thus power on or off virtual desktops as required, and it also provides the end users with the ability to perform a "physical" reboot of their virtual desktop.

VIRTUAL DESKTOP RECOMMENDATIONS

This section covers some general resource recommendations for the virtual desktops that you will be provisioning to your users.

Memory

Windows XP – At least 512 MB, preferably 1024 MB.
Windows 7 – At least 1024 MB, preferably 2048 MB.

vCPU

Normally one vCPU (virtual CPU) is sufficient. Processor-intensive applications – if you are running multiple multithreaded applications, you may benefit from adding further vCPUs.

> **NOTE**
>
> Adding additional vCPUs doesn't necessarily improve performance – rule of thumb – start with one, if the CPU bottlenecks, then test with two.

Disk

Rule of thumb, assign a 15GB disk for Windows XP, or 25GB disk for Windows 7.

> **TIP**
>
> Calculate the space that your applications consume on your physical desktops. Remember if you are using a shared virtual disk (vDisk), the consumption of SAN (Storage Area Network) space is minimal.

Network

A single network card is sufficient. Multihomed does work, but the connection will only take place over the network card, which registers the machine on the Desktop Delivery Controller.

It is highly recommended that the virtual desktops be placed on a separate VLAN (Virtual LAN). Desktop virtualization is introducing users' desktops into your datacenter; traffic that these machines generate is best isolated from your servers. PXE (Preboot Execution Environment) and DHCP may be required by the virtual desktops. DHCP and PXE requirements are discussed in Chapter 6, "Installation of the Citrix Provisioning Server."

Hyper-V – Synthetic adapters perform better and incur less processor overhead; however, they don't support PXE. We recommend using two adaptors, one synthetic and one legacy. The legacy adaptor can be used by the VM at boot time and the synthetic adaptor will be used by the VM once booted (synthetic has network priority).

For the purposes of a POC (Proof of Concept), a single legacy adaptor is recommended; this will function sufficiently well and is simpler to configure.

Active Directory

Domain member: Disable machine account password changes.

This can be done through a Local Computer Policy, or through a Domain Group Policy (see Figure 4.1).

Instead of the computer account password changes being initiated from Active Directory, they will be managed from the provisioning server.

> **TIP**
>
> It is not necessary to do this manually if you will be using the provisioning server to provide the vDisk. The XenConvert Optimizer will automatically perform this function.

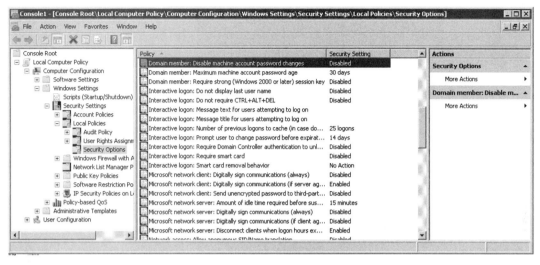

FIGURE 4.1

Security policy – disable machine account password changes.

Your base build machine must be added to the domain.

Use a computer name that you won't use in your target pool. For example, use something generic like "BaseBuildMachineWin7." You will use provisioning server to assign the computer names according to your corporate standards.

Microsoft License

Microsoft volume license editions are recommended. Windows 7 will try to reactivate the software if it detects that the hardware has been changed. This is resolved by using a volume license edition.

General Performance "Tweaks"

The XenConvert Optimizer performs many of the best practice "tweaks" for you, and it can be run on your virtual machine before you upload your base build desktop to a vDisk.

There are a large number of "tweaks" that you can apply. Most of these settings are configurable through Citrix or Microsoft policies. I have included below some of the more common settings, please refer to Chapter 5, "Desktop Delivery Controller – Advanced Configuration Settings," for more details on configuring these settings.

Graphics

The general rule is the less graphical "features" you use, the less traffic you incur. Changes like this should be done judiciously. The Citrix optimizations over the last few years means that the difference in network traffic is actually relatively small. Some simple changes can be made with very little impact to the user experience.

Disable Menu Animations

Disable window contents while dragging – this just drags a frame, and not the window contents, the contents are only displayed when the window is released.

A good rule of thumb is to keep a "Desktop" like graphical experience for LAN (Local Area Network)/Metro LAN type connections and to scale back when displaying virtual desktops over WAN (Wide Area Network) links. The Citrix Policies section will cover policies that have preset settings for connection types.

Audio

Disable System Beep while printing
Use the "No Sounds" Sound Scheme

TIP

Don't assume that users don't use audio, a large amount of user training, and increasingly corporate "webinars," require sound.

Windows Vista and 7

Disable UAC (User Account Control) when logged in as an administrator.

CITRIX XENSERVER

The Desktop Delivery Controller connects natively to Citrix XenServer, without requiring any add-ons. The only "gotcha" around this is that multiple hosts should be specified, using the **Options** button to prevent having a single point of failure.

Installation

1. Connect to the Citrix XenCenter – **Start | Programs | Citrix XenCenter 5.5**.
2. Select one of the XenServers in the left-hand pane, right-click – **New VM…** (see Figure 4.2).
3. Select your desktop operating system, and click **Next** (see Figure 4.3).
4. Give the machine a display name and description (see Figure 4.4).
5. Place the DVD in the physical server as shown in Figure 4.5, or mount the .ISO file to the XenServer. See Chapter 13, "Advanced XenDesktop Client Settings – Audio and Video and Peripherals," for more information on creating an .ISO share on Citrix XenServer.
6. Select **Automatically select a host server with available resources** and then click **Next** (see Figure 4.6). If you want to select a specific host, then select **Use this server as the VM's host server** and select the desired host server.
7. Select one vCPU and 1024 MB of RAM (see Figure 4.7).

   You may choose to increase the amount of RAM for users who require more memory.

8. Click **Add…** to add a virtual disk, add a 20GB disk to your VM (see Figure 4.8).

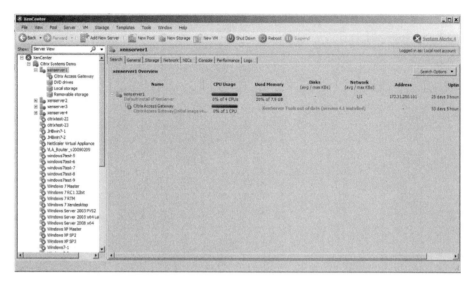

FIGURE 4.2

Citrix XenCenter.

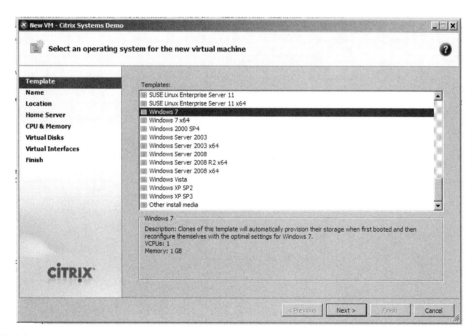

FIGURE 4.3

New VM operating system selection.

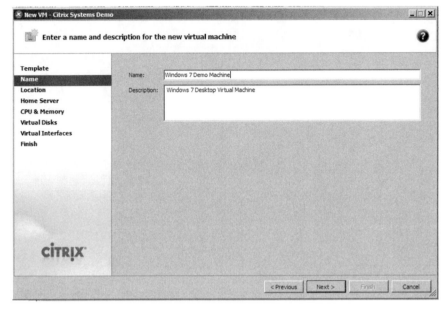

FIGURE 4.4

Name and description.

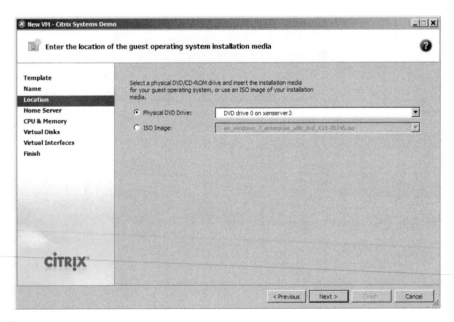

FIGURE 4.5

Location of installation media.

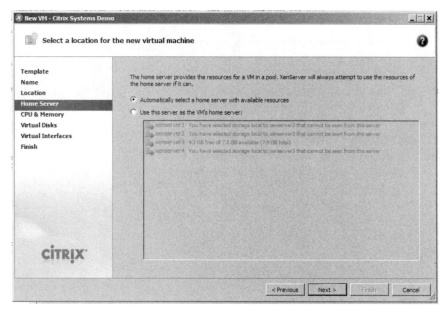

FIGURE 4.6

Home server selection.

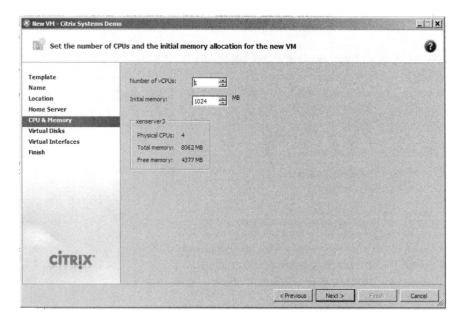

FIGURE 4.7

CPU and memory.

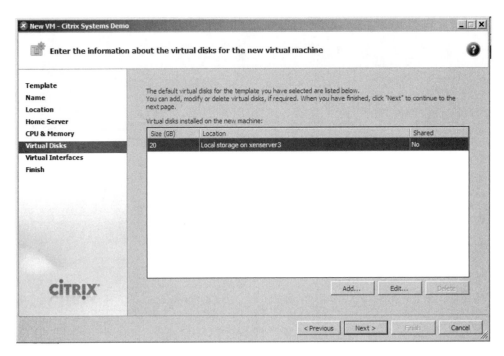

FIGURE 4.8

Virtual disks.

   9. Add a network card, from the drop-down box select the correct network for it to attach to (see Figure 4.9).

   If the XenServer is multihomed, you will have multiple networks to select from. For example, Network 0, Network 1, Network 2, and Network 3. Bonding is often used to create a single resilient interface.

10. Click **Finish** (see Figure 4.10).
11. The installation will now be performed through the XenCenter Console. As shown in Figure 4.11, the installation follows the normal procedure as on a physical host.
12. Right-click on the new virtual machine in the left-hand pane, select **Install XenServer Tools** (see Figure 4.12).
13. Click **Run xensetup.exe** (see Figure 4.13).
14. If UAC is enabled, you will receive the dialog box shown in Figure 4.14, click **Yes**.
15. Select **I accept the terms in the License Agreement**, and click **Next** (see Figure 4.15).
16. Click **Install** (see Figure 4.16).
17. Click **Finish** (see Figure 4.17).
18. Add the VM to the domain.
19. Install the Virtual Desktop Agent on the XenServer virtual machine. See Chapter 3, "Configuring the Desktop Delivery Controller," for step-by-step instructions.

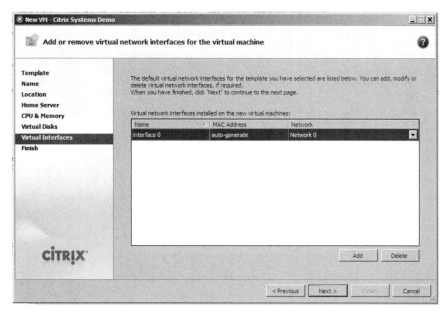

FIGURE 4.9

Virtual interfaces.

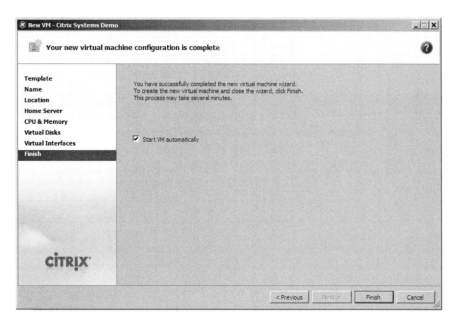

FIGURE 4.10

Successful completion dialog box.

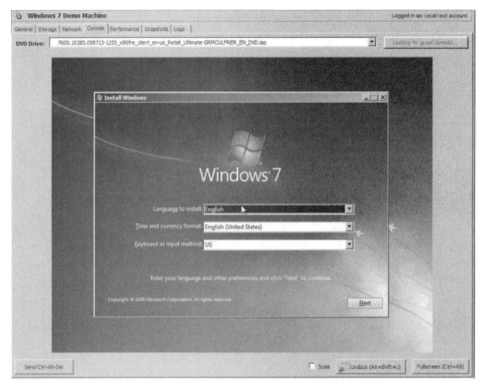

FIGURE 4.11

Virtual machine console.

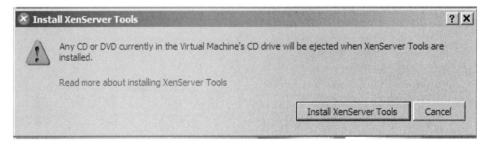

FIGURE 4.12

Install XenServer tools.

Integration

In this section, we return to the integration of the Desktop Delivery Controller with the hypervisor.

Following the same procedure as in Chapter 3, "Configuring the Desktop Delivery Controller," we are adding a Desktop Group for Citrix XenServer.

FIGURE 4.13

Run xensetup.

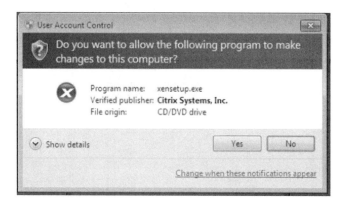

FIGURE 4.14

User account control.

1. Choose Citrix Xen VM infrastructure (see Figure 4.18).
2. For XenServer HA Pools, click **Options**... – (otherwise skip to step 3).
   Enter in the field:

   ```
   Address=[HTTP://<IP of XenServer1>;HTTP://<IP of XenServer2>] (see Figure 4.19).
           XenServer1          XenServer2
   ```

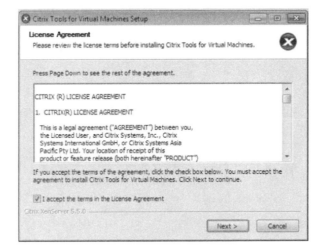

FIGURE 4.15

Citrix license agreement.

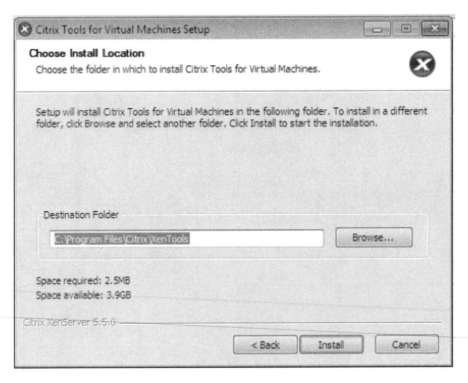

FIGURE 4.16

Choose install location.

FIGURE 4.17

Reboot dialog box.

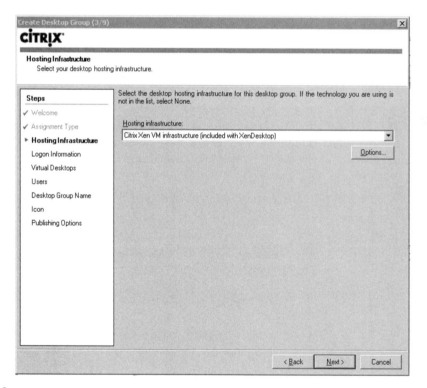

FIGURE 4.18

Hosting infrastructure – Citrix Xen VM infrastructure.

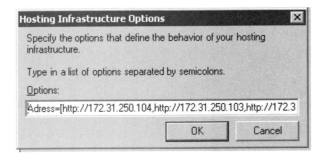

FIGURE 4.19

Hosting infrastructure options.

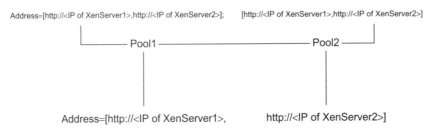

FIGURE 4.20

Selecting multiple pools.

Take care when specifying the XenServer hosts in your pool. Bear in mind if the servers listed are unavailable, the Desktop Delivery Controller will have no means of communicating with the XenServer farm. For larger implementations, multiple XenServer pools can also be addressed. Separate pools are delimited with square brackets and a semicolon (see Figure 4.20).

3. Enter the IP address of a XenServer in your pool, and enter the username and password (see Figure 4.21).
4. Click **Add**… (see Figure 4.22).

The Desktop Delivery Controller enumerates all the VMs running on the servers, and you are given the option to select one or more VMs to add to the Desktop Group.

5. Select all the virtual machines that you want to add to your Desktop Group, and then click **OK** (see Figure 4.23).

Figures 4.24 and 4.25 show two scenarios: in the first (Figure 4.24), the computer account was found automatically – this is normally the case and in the second (Figure 4.25), the computer account wasn't discovered automatically. This is generally due to DNS (Domain Naming System) issues. To circumvent this problem, select the computer in the Virtual Machine Column and click **Edit**…, you are presented with a standard Microsoft Active Directory account selection dialog box; select your computer account to manually associate the correct computer account with the virtual machine.

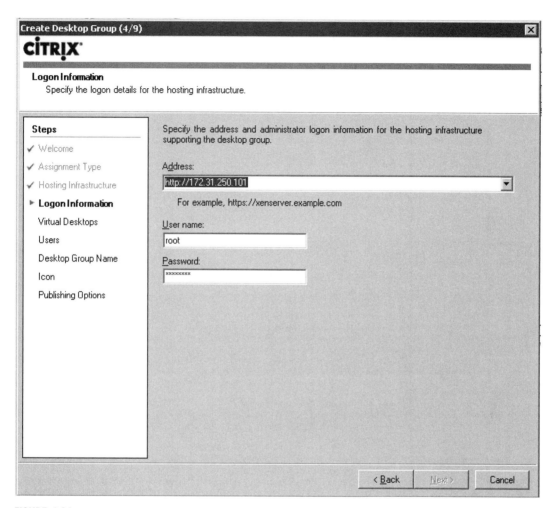

FIGURE 4.21

Logon information.

6. Click **Next**

> **TIP**
>
> If you receive a little red error icon in the Citrix Delivery Services Console, then hover the mouse over the red icon to read a descriptive message (see Figure 4.26).

Add users, and assign a Desktop Group name following the steps you performed earlier in Chapter 3, "Configuring the Desktop Delivery Controller."

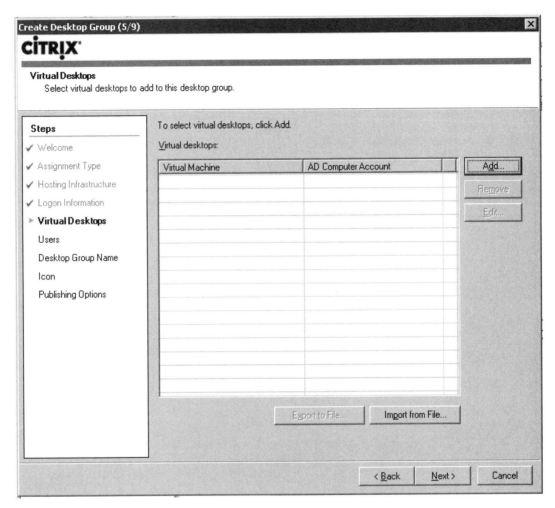

FIGURE 4.22

Virtual desktops.

MICROSOFT HYPER-V

XenDesktop virtual desktops can be hosted on any hypervisor. The hypervisor integration features for Hyper-V require the use of Microsoft System Center Virtual Machine Manager.

Installation

The installation of a virtual desktop can be done through the Hyper-V Manager Console, or the System Center Virtual Machine Manager. In this example, I have created a new Windows 7 virtual desktop using the System Center Virtual Machine Manager.

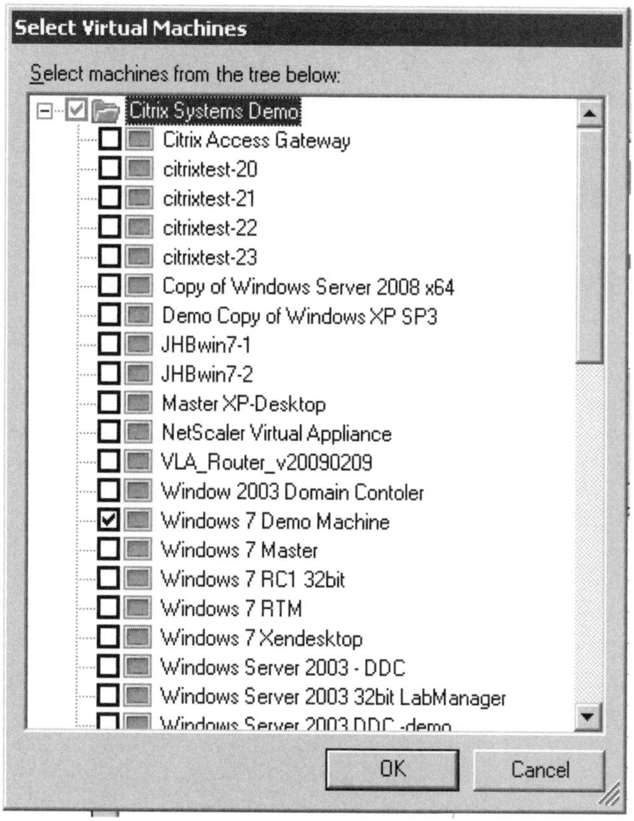

Select Virtual Machines

Select machines from the tree below:

☑ 📁 Citrix Systems Demo
  ☐ ▢ Citrix Access Gateway
  ☐ ▢ citrixtest-20
  ☐ ▢ citrixtest-21
  ☐ ▢ citrixtest-22
  ☐ ▢ citrixtest-23
  ☐ ▢ Copy of Windows Server 2008 x64
  ☐ ▢ Demo Copy of Windows XP SP3
  ☐ ▢ JHBwin7-1
  ☐ ▢ JHBwin7-2
  ☐ ▢ Master XP-Desktop
  ☐ ▢ NetScaler Virtual Appliance
  ☐ ▢ VLA_Router_v20090209
  ☐ ▢ Window 2003 Domain Contoler
  ☑ ▢ Windows 7 Demo Machine
  ☐ ▢ Windows 7 Master
  ☐ ▢ Windows 7 RC1 32bit
  ☐ ▢ Windows 7 RTM
  ☐ ▢ Windows 7 Xendesktop
  ☐ ▢ Windows Server 2003 - DDC
  ☐ ▢ Windows Server 2003 32bit LabManager
  ☐ ▢ Windows Server 2003 DDC -demo

[OK]   [Cancel]

FIGURE 4.23

Select virtual machines.

Due to the PXE requirements of provisioning server, I have selected the network adaptor to be an "Emulated" network adaptor, rather than the default "Synthetic" adaptor. If installing using the Hyper-V Manager Console, change the option to be a legacy network adaptor. Microsoft uses two different terms in the two consoles.

> **NOTE**
>
> Synthetic network adaptors do perform better, but don't support PXE. For the purposes of a POC, a single legacy adaptor is recommended; this will function sufficiently well and is simpler to configure.

1. Open Microsoft System Center Virtual Machine Manager.
2. Click **New virtual machine** (see Figure 4.27).
3. Change the radio button to **Create the new virtual machine with a blank virtual hard disk** (see Figure 4.28).

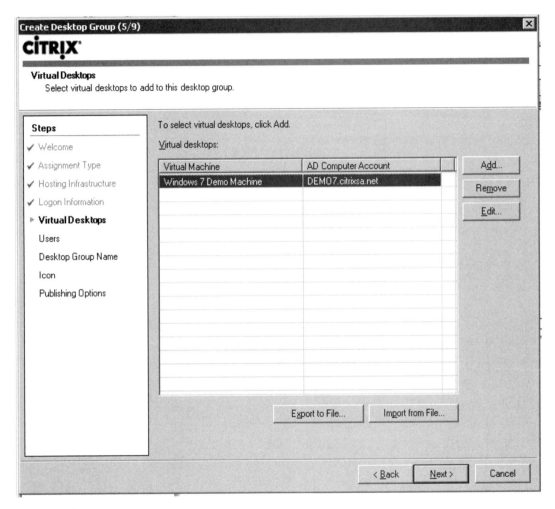

FIGURE 4.24

Scenario 1.

4. Enter a name for the virtual machine, and click **Next** (see Figure 4.29).
5. Select **Memory** and change to 2048 MB, select **Virtual DVD Drive** (see Figure 4.30).
6. Click **Browse** – (or mount the DVD in the physical DVD on the Hyper-V server; see Figure 4.31). In this example, you will browse to an ISO image.

TIP

Select **Share image instead of copying it**, otherwise SCVMM (System Center Virtual Machine Manager) will make a copy of the ISO and store it with the VM.

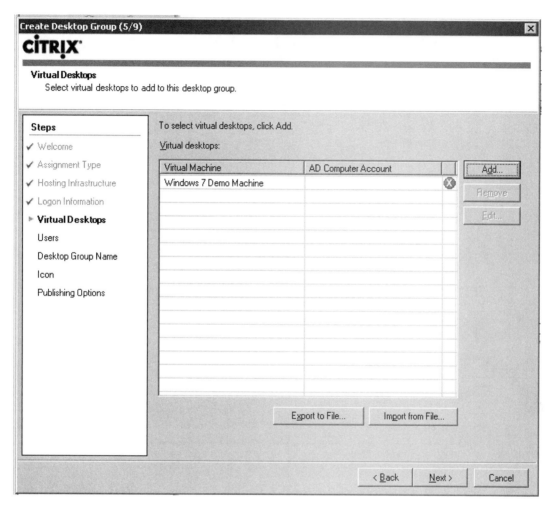

FIGURE 4.25

Scenario 2.

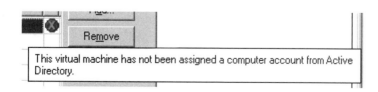

FIGURE 4.26

Virtual machine error.

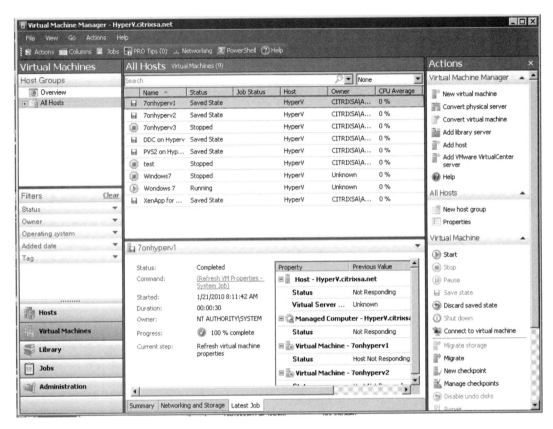

FIGURE 4.27

System Center Virtual Machine Manager.

Using ISO images is simpler than mounting physical DVDs, especially if your physical host is in the datacenter. Inside the SCVMM, select **Library | Add library server**. Using this procedure, you can add a server share that contains your ISO images.

7. Select the ISO image and click **OK** (see Figure 4.32).
8. Select the virtual disk and change the size to 25 GB (see Figure 4.33). Change the disk type to "Fixed."

Fixed disks offer far better performance. Dynamic disks save disk space, but use more CPU cycles growing the disk and have higher overhead on the disk subsystem due to the way the VHD (Virtual Hard Disk) is aligned.

9. If your network adaptor is "Emulated," click **Next**. If the network adaptor is marked as "Synthetic," you will need to remove it using the **Remove** button, and add an emulated adapter using the **Network Adapter** button (see Figure 4.34).
10. Click **Next** (see Figure 4.35).

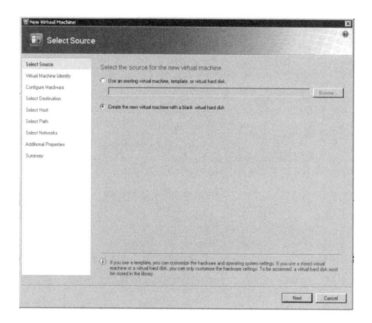

FIGURE 4.28

Select source.

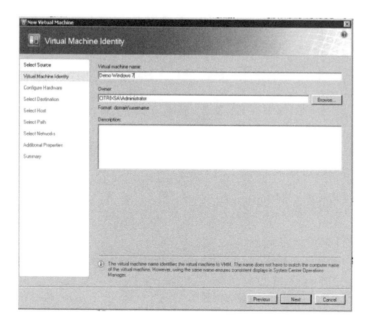

FIGURE 4.29

Virtual machine identity.

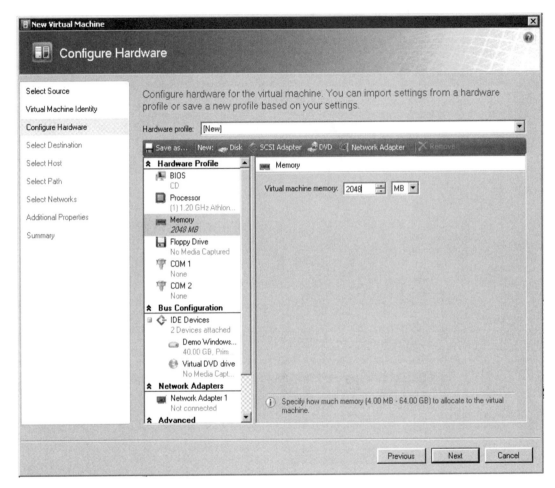

FIGURE 4.30

Configure hardware – memory.

Microsoft uses a library mechanism for the centralized storage of standardized virtual machines and standard templates. We, however, want to deploy a virtual machine to a host.

11. Click **Next** (see Figure 4.36).

System Center Virtual Machine Manager gives you a placement option for when you are managing multiple Hyper-V servers.

12. Change the path if you wish to place the virtual hard disk in an alternative location, and click **Next** (see Figure 4.37).

13. Select the network adapter to connect your virtual machine to the network. Click **Next** (see Figure 4.38).

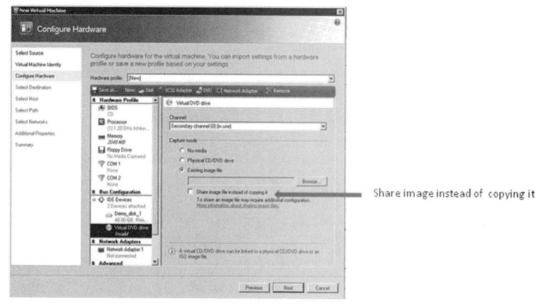

Share image instead of copying it

FIGURE 4.31

Configure hardware – virtual DVD drive.

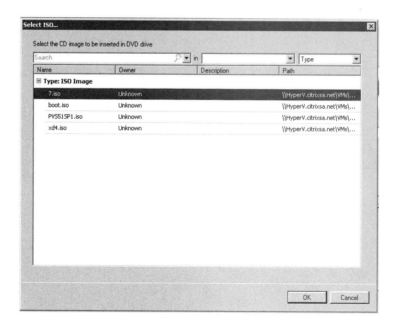

FIGURE 4.32

Select ISO.

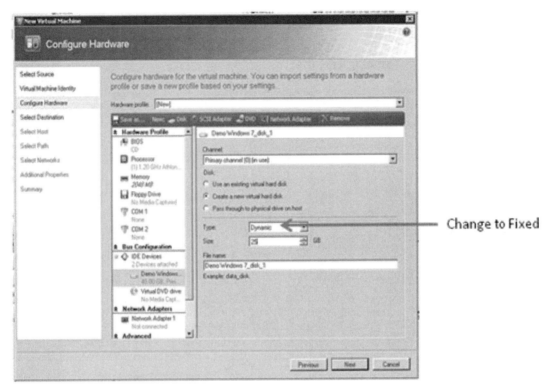

Change to Fixed

FIGURE 4.33

Configure hardware – disk.

14. Change the "Operating system" dropdown to reflect the Guest Operating System – in this case, Windows 7 (see Figure 4.39).
15. Click **Create** (see Figure 4.40).

When you now start the virtual machine, you can install Windows 7 – as you would on a physical hardware (see Figure 4.41).

16. Hyper-V Integration Services. Right-click on your virtual desktop and select **Install virtual guest services** (see Figure 4.42).
17. Add the VM to the domain.
18. Install the Virtual Desktop Agent on the Hyper-V virtual machine as you did in the previous section. See Chapter 3, "Configuring the Desktop Delivery Controller," for step-by-step instructions.

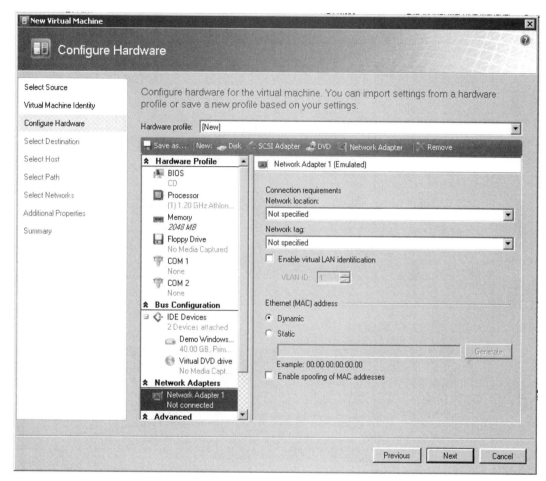

FIGURE 4.34

Configure hardware – network adaptor.

NOTE

Windows 7 is an "Enlightened" operating system, which gives it performance benefits when running virtualized. "Enlightened" is a term coined by Microsoft that means the operating system is aware of the fact that it is running virtualized. In fact, testing[A] on Hyper-V shows Windows 7 outperforming Windows XP by a significant margin.

[A]Performed with LoginVSI Scripts from www.loginconsultants.com.

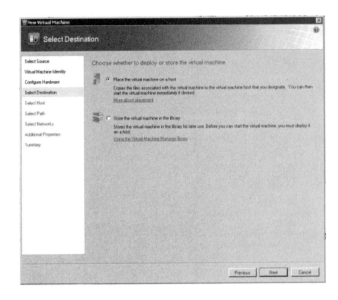

FIGURE 4.35

Select destination.

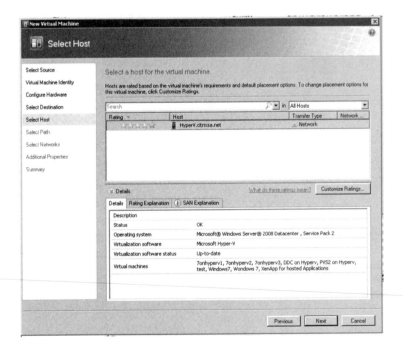

FIGURE 4.36

Select host.

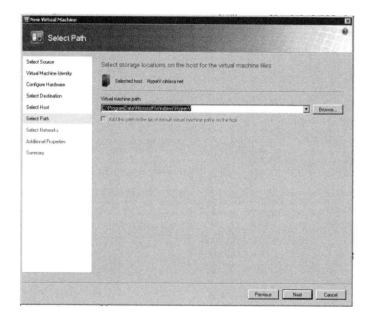

FIGURE 4.37

Select path.

FIGURE 4.38

Select networks.

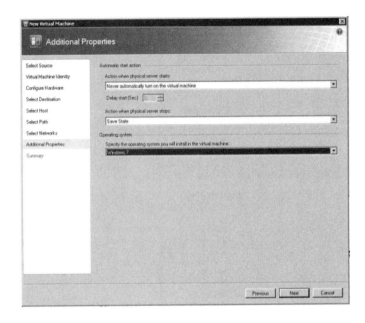

FIGURE 4.39

Additional properties.

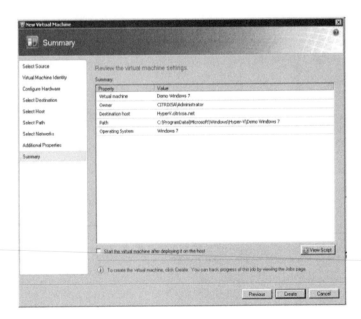

FIGURE 4.40

Summary dialog box.

FIGURE 4.41

Virtual machine viewer.

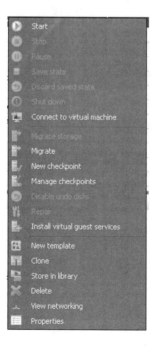

FIGURE 4.42

Virtual machine options.

Integration

This section discusses the process of adding a virtual desktop hosted on Hyper-V to Citrix XenDesktop.

Following the same procedure as in Chapter 3, "Configuring the Desktop Delivery Controller," we are adding a Desktop Group for Microsoft Hyper-V.

1. Choose **Microsoft virtualization** (see Figure 4.43).
2. Enter the name of the System Center Virtual Machine Manager server and a username and password, with sufficient permissions to administer the SCVMM (see Figure 4.44).

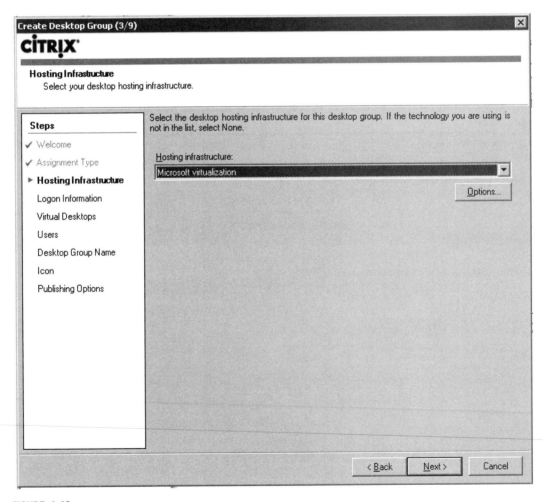

FIGURE 4.43

Hosting infrastructure.

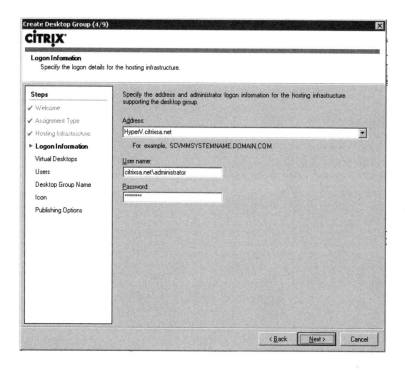

FIGURE 4.44

Logon information.

> **TIP**
>
> Use the format <domainname>\<username>, and use the FQDN (Fully Qualified Domain Name) if you find that you are unable to authenticate.

3. Click **Add**… (see Figure 4.45).
4. Select the virtual machine that you want (see Figure 4.46).
5. Click **Next** (see Figure 4.47).

Add users, and assign a Desktop Group name following the steps from Chapter 3, "Configuring the Desktop Delivery Controller."

VMWARE VSPHERE

Where the Microsoft SCVMM software is used to connect to a Microsoft SCVMM server, with VMware we connect to the vCenter (previously referred to as the Virtual Center). Specifically, we connect to the software development kit (SDK) component on the vCenter Server. The SDK is an integration point for other vendors to plug their software into the vCenter. The communication between the Desktop Delivery Controller and the vCenter is done using either HTTP or HTTPS.

FIGURE 4.45

Virtual desktops.

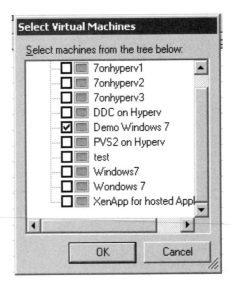

FIGURE 4.46

Select virtual machines.

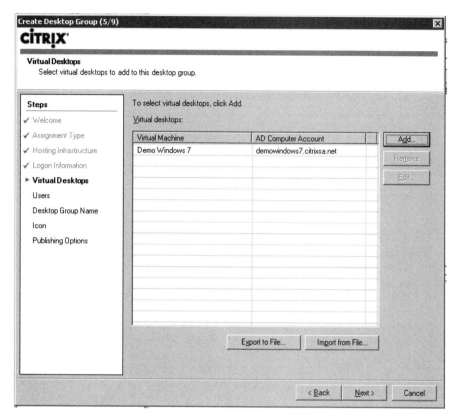

FIGURE 4.47

Virtual desktops.

As with Microsoft's free Hyper-V product, VMware's free ESXi product can be used to host the virtual desktop.

The VMware integration includes support for vSphere, VMware ESX 3.5, and ESX 3.0.

It is more secure to conduct the communications using HTTPS than HTTP. It is, however, much simpler to enable HTTP access. I would recommend using HTTP for a proof of concept type of environment.

Installation

The installation of the virtual desktop can be performed using the vSphere Client. The vSphere Client is connected to either an individual ESX instance, or to the vCenter Server. In this example, I will connect to a vCenter Server, but the process would be identical on a stand-alone ESX Server.

1. Open the vCenter Console.
2. Right-click on your physical host, and select **New Virtual Machine** (see Figure 4.48).

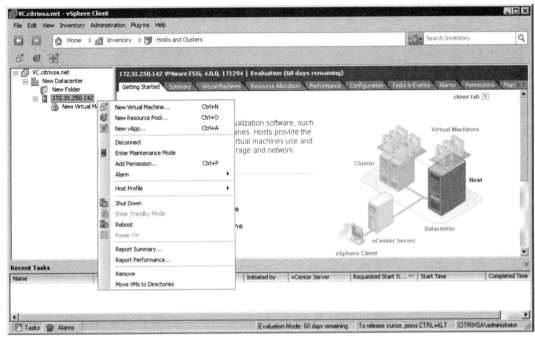

FIGURE 4.48

vSphere Client.

3. Leave the default at **Typical**, and click **Next** (see Figure 4.49).
4. Specify a machine name and an Inventory Location (see Figure 4.50). Select the correct Resource Pool.

NOTE

Use of a dedicated Resource Pool is recommended.

---

5. Select the storage you would like to use, and click **Next** (see Figure 4.51).

NOTE

In this example, I am only presented with one storage option. In most production environments, there will be storage which is dedicated to production, and some (often cheaper storage) dedicated to development. Choose the appropriate assigned storage.

---

6. Select the Guest Operating System (see Figure 4.52).
7. Set the disk size to 25 GB (see Figure 4.53).

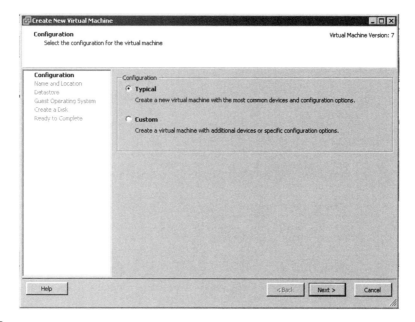

FIGURE 4.49

Create new virtual machine.

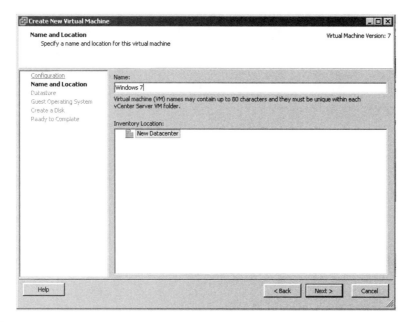

FIGURE 4.50

Name and location.

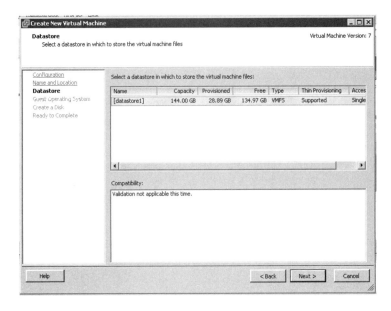

FIGURE 4.51

Datastore.

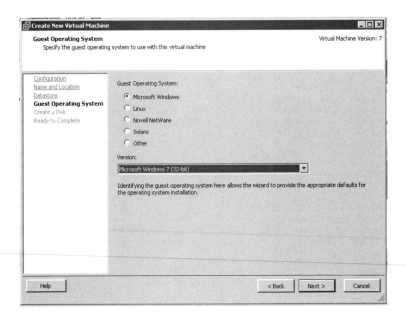

FIGURE 4.52

Guest operating system.

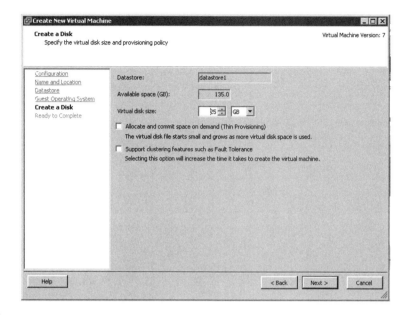

FIGURE 4.53

Create a disk.

> **NOTE**
>
> Thin Provisioning is useful in scenarios where provisioning server is not being used to provide a common vDisk.

8. Click **Finish** (see Figure 4.54).

9. Select your virtual machine, and click **Edit virtual machine settings** in the right-hand pane (see Figure 4.55).

10. First select **CD/DVD Drive**, select the **Device Type**, and **Connect at power on** (see Figure 4.56).

> **NOTE**
>
> Using a **Client Device** will be the slowest, you effectively mount your local CDROM to the virtual machine. The **Host Device** option requires that you have physical access to the server – or something like Integrated Lights Out/DRAC (Dell Remote Access Card) to have a "virtual" physical on the server. A **Datastore ISO File** is most often the most elegant solution. Uploading an ISO file to a datastore is useful, as you can very easily remount the ISO to the machine or other machines.

11. The installation will now be performed through the vCenter Console. As shown in Figure 4.57, the installation follows the normal procedure as on a physical host.

12. Select the virtual machine, right-click and select **Guest | Install/Upgrade VMware Tools** (see Figure 4.58).

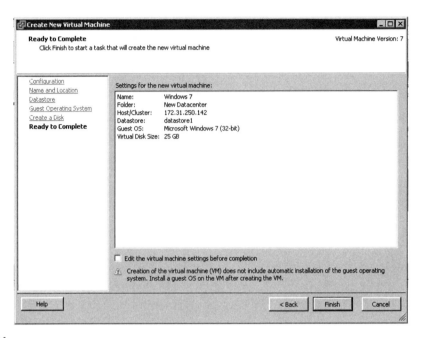

FIGURE 4.54

Ready to complete.

FIGURE 4.55

vSphere Client – virtual machine settings.

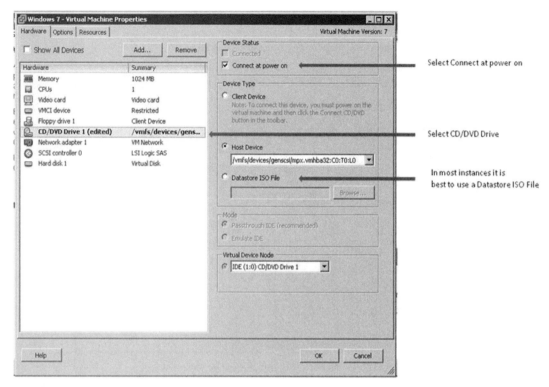

FIGURE 4.56

Virtual machine properties.

13. Click **OK** to acknowledge the warning (see Figure 4.59), click **Run setup.exe** when autoplay launches the VMware Tools setup program (see Figure 4.60).

14. Click **Next** to install the VMware Tools (see Figure 4.61).

15. Select **Typical** and click **Next** (see Figure 4.62).

16. Click **Install** (see Figure 4.63).

17. Click **Finish** (see Figure 4.64).

18. Click **Yes** (see Figure 4.65).

19. Add the VM to the domain.

20. Install the Virtual Desktop Agent on the VMware Virtual Machine. See Chapter 3, "Configuring the Desktop Delivery Controller," for step-by-step instructions.

Integration

This section discusses the process of adding a virtual desktop hosted on VMware vSphere to Citrix XenDesktop.

Following the same procedure as in Chapter 3, "Configuring the Desktop Delivery Controller," we are adding a Desktop Group for VMware vSphere.

FIGURE 4.57

vSphere Client – guest console.

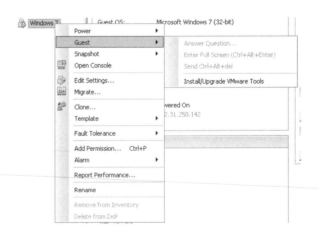

FIGURE 4.58

Virtual machine options.

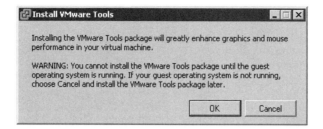

FIGURE 4.59

Install VMware tools.

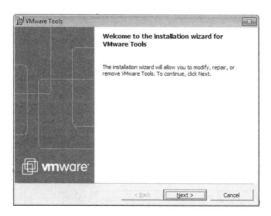

FIGURE 4.60

VMware tools – setup.

FIGURE 4.61

VMware tools – installation.

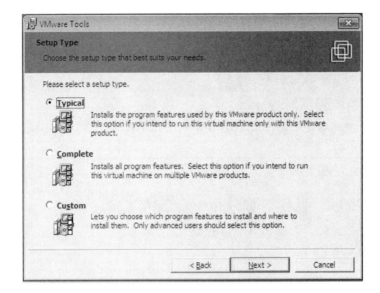

FIGURE 4.62

VMware tools – setup type.

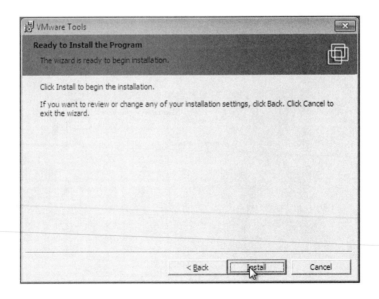

FIGURE 4.63

VMware tools – ready to install.

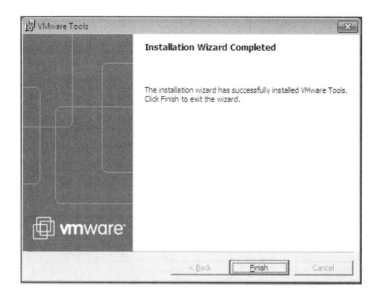

FIGURE 4.64

VMware tools – installation wizard completed.

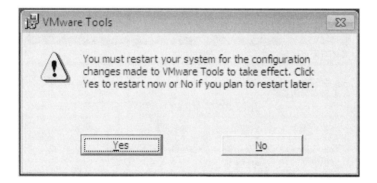

FIGURE 4.65

VMware tools – restart.

1. Select **VMware virtualization** and click **Next** (see Figure 4.66).

The interaction between the Desktop Delivery Controller is done through the vCenter SDK. The SDK is built into the vCenter, and is normally accessible only through HTTPS. Please see the appendix "VMware SDK Integration" for details.

2. Enter the path to the vCenter SDK – for example, HTTP://<vCenterhostname>/sdk or HTTPS://<vcenterhostname>/sdk. Enter a username and password to attach to the vCenter (see Figure 4.67). Remember when using HTTPS, the hostname string must match the certificate, i.e., the FQDN includes the full domain path – mymachine.mydomain.com. The username and password must

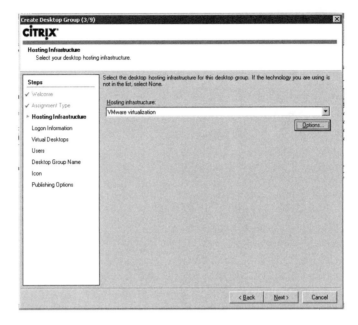

FIGURE 4.66

Hosting infrastructure.

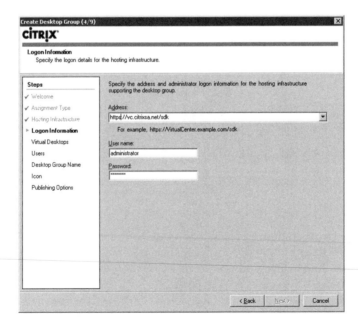

FIGURE 4.67

Logon information.

have the correct rights assigned to connect to the vCenter. This is an area to flag, changing the password or rights of the login account will have an adverse affect to the interaction between the Desktop Delivery Controller and the vCenter.

TIP

Having insufficient permissions is a common problem when integrating with VMware.

---

3. Click **Add…**, and this will enumerate the desktops from the datacenter (see Figure 4.68).
4. Browse your virtual infrastructure (see Figure 4.69).

NOTE

Citrix XenDesktop supports the use of VMware "Resource Groups." In fact I would recommend using a dedicated Resource Group; it is a good way to isolate you environment from other VMware guests – you can leverage having dedicated resource allocations, and also has the security benefit that you can isolate it as a separate security entity.

---

5. Click **Next** (see Figure 4.70).

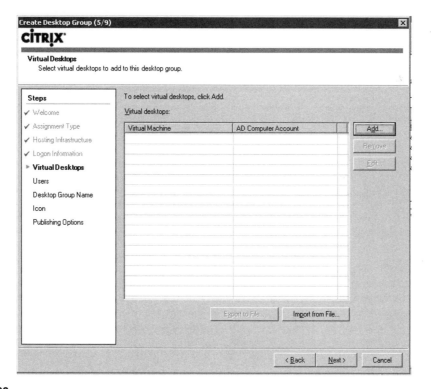

FIGURE 4.68

Virtual desktops.

FIGURE 4.69

Select virtual machines.

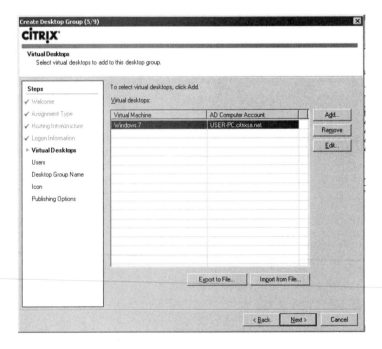

FIGURE 4.70

Virtual desktops.

6. Add users, and assign a Desktop Group name following the steps from Chapter 3, "Configuring the Desktop Delivery Controller."

BLADE HARDWARE

Installation onto a blade hardware would be done in exactly the same way as installing onto a standard PC hardware.

This hardly warrants a section on installation; however, I do wish to highlight that this is a valid option.

Blade hardware solutions are obviously more expensive because you are dedicating a blade to every single user. It will most likely only be relevant to some organizations, and even then to a subset of their users.

The main areas of application would be high-end users with massive resource requirements. Financial brokers in banks are a good example of users this may be relevant to. Additionally, some financial applications can't tolerate, from a business or security point of view, the very small time drift that one gets by placing a desktop on a hypervisor.

A blade hardware solution can also be used in conjunction with provisioning server. We add an extra layer of resilience, the user can utilize any one of the physical blades with their vDisk thus removing the dependency on a single piece of hardware.

SUMMARY

In this section, we discussed the installation of the virtual desktop onto the server infrastructure. We first discussed some general sizing and specification guidelines for the desktop operating systems. We then covered the installation and integration onto XenServer, Hyper-V, and VMware hypervisors – step-by-step installation on the hypervisors, and then the tying together of the hypervisor layer to the Desktop Delivery Controllers. Lastly, we briefly addressed the option of using individual blade servers for each user.

Desktop Delivery Controller – Advanced Configuration Settings

INFORMATION IN THIS CHAPTER

- Delivery Services Console
- Web Interface Configuration for the Integrated Web Site
- XenDesktop Policies and Printing
- Bandwidth

This chapter discusses some of the more advanced configuration settings. We will go into some detail covering the configuration settings. This chapter has a change in pace and focus from the preceding chapters; although most of the chapters discuss the details required to get an implementation working, this chapter deals in fairly granular detail with the console options of the core component. Depending on your implementation (and the available time you have), you may decide to skim through this chapter, or you may spend more time studying the details.

This chapter has been specifically placed after Chapter 4, "Installing the Virtual Desktop," which discusses hypervisor installation. Some of the advanced settings, like idle pool settings, use the hypervisor integration functionality to control the virtual machines.

DELIVERY SERVICES CONSOLE

The majority of XenDesktop settings are configured through the Delivery Services Console. The exceptions to this are the Citrix Policies that are configurable through the Presentation Server Console, which will be discussed in the following section.

In terms of ongoing operational tasks, the Delivery Services Console is an interface that an administrator will almost always have opened.

What follows is a "walk-through" of the Delivery Services Console. Ideally, you should follow this section with a Delivery Services Console opened in front of you, as this will be the easiest way to familiarize yourself with it. If you have used the Citrix XenApp consoles, you will notice many commonalities between this console and that of XenApp.

Open the Delivery Services Console – **Start | All Programs | Citrix | Management Consoles | Delivery Services Console** (Figure 5.1).

Nodes in the left-hand pane:

Alerts – Any warnings or errors are reported under the **Alerts** node.

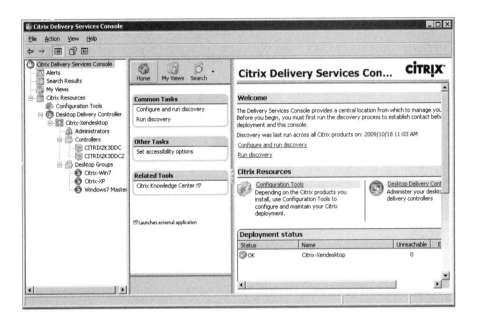

FIGURE 5.1

Delivery Services Console.

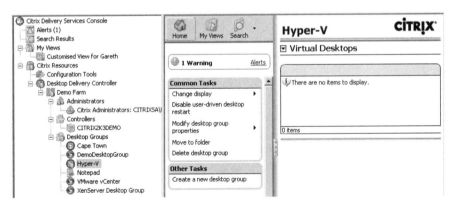

FIGURE 5.2

Locating alerts in the console.

The alerts mechanism is quite intuitive. In the above example, I created an alert by removing all the virtual desktops from a Desktop Group. This creates a Warning Alert under the **Alerts** node informing the administrator that there aren't any virtual desktops configured in the Desktop Group. It also creates a breadcrumb trail, which you can follow from **Desktop Delivery Controller | Demo Farm | Desktop Groups | Hyper-V**, (Figure 5.2) which is the Desktop Group with the problem.

> **NOTE**
> Warnings are denoted with an orange alert, whereas errors are denoted with a red alert.

Search Results – Right-clicking on this node gives you the option to search for items in the XenDesktop farm.

Run new advanced search (Figure 5.3).

You have options to search by:

- Sessions By User (Figure 5.4)
- Desktop Groups By User
- Discovered Items

The **Browse**… button allows you to search a subset of the discovered items. This is the simplest mechanism to find objects in your XenDesktop farm.

Rerun search (Figure 5.3) – runs the same search again if you need to find changes to the search.

Save In My Views (Figure 5.3) – saves the current search in the My Views folder.

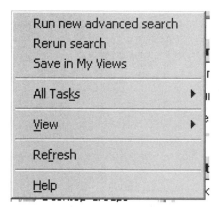

FIGURE 5.3

Search results menu.

FIGURE 5.4

Search dialog box.

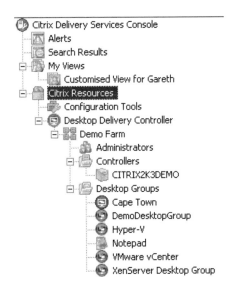

FIGURE 5.5

The Citrix Resources node.

My Views (Figure 5.5) – the **My Views** option is used to provide a view of a specific object or folder in the XenDesktop farm. You can create a custom folder with contents that you wish to view regularly.

My Views is really only useful in implementations where you have created a large number of objects, and it saves time to be able to quickly navigate to a subset of these objects.

The **Citrix Resources** (Figure 5.5) node contains the XenDesktop farms that you have "discovered" when you first opened the Console.

Select **Citrix Resources** and **Configure and Run Discovery** to add Desktop Delivery Controller servers you wish to query in order to add their farm information to console. The **Run Discovery** option simply reruns the discovery against the Desktop Delivery Controllers that you have already added.

The Citrix Resources – **Configuration Tools** (Figure 5.5) node simply gives you options to run a discovery of objects in your XenDesktop farm.

The Citrix Resources – **Desktop Delivery Controller** (Figure 5.5) node contains the XenDesktop farm (or farms) that have been discovered.

The farms that have been discovered are a subnode of the **Desktop Delivery Controller** node.

In order to configure farm settings, right-click on the farm that you created in Chapter 2, "Installation of the Broker – Desktop Delivery Controller."

Select the **Properties** option (Figure 5.6).

Connection Access Controls (Figure 5.7) – Radio button option, either set to **Any connection** or to **Citrix Access Gateway connections only**. Citrix Access Gateway is the Citrix SSL VPN (Virtual Private Network), and this setting would make the farm available to all users or only to those remote users tunneling in through the VPN.

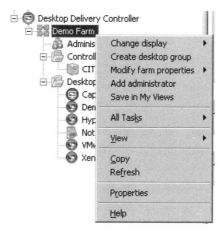

FIGURE 5.6

Farm options menu.

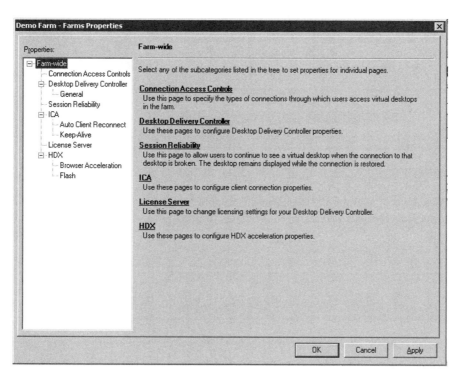

FIGURE 5.7

Farm properties dialog box.

Desktop Delivery Controller – General (Figure 5.7)

- **XML Service DNS resolution** – a tick box enabling the Citrix XML services to return the FQDN (DNS hostname) to the clients; in other words, the Desktop Delivery Controller sends the machine name to the end point rather than an Internet Protocol (IP) address.
- **Enable 32-bit icon color depth** – a tick box that enables high color depth of the icons displayed to the user in Web Interface or through the XenApp Services (PN Agent) client.
- **Session Reliability** – This is a tick box that enables you to enable or disable session reliability. Session reliability assists by freezing the current screen – should the connection drop – and then it automatically attempts to reconnect in the background. You also have the option to change the default port from 2598 to a different port.

> **NOTE**
>
> The primary port used by the XenDesktop client is 2598. I don't recommend changing it unless there is a very compelling reason. There is a further option to change the time the sessions are kept active from 60 s to a different number. This could be increased if you are running over unreliable/slow links – like a VSAT (Satellite) connection.

ICA (Figure 5.7)

- **Auto Client Reconnect** (Figure 5.7) – this option sets how the Citrix Client must respond to interrupted ICA (HDX) sessions. There are two options: **Require User authentication** – when sessions reestablish you need to reauthenticate. **Reconnect automatically** – the reconnection doesn't require reauthentication. There is also a tick box option to log automatic reconnection.

> **TIP**
>
> The default is **Reconnect automatically** and not to log events – the default is recommended. Reauthentication should only be required in "high security" environments, and the logging can create a lot of events if your links are bad.

- **Keep-Alive** (Figure 5.7) – ICA keep-alives are not enabled by default as their functionality overlaps with that of session reliability. If you are using session reliability, you won't need keep-alives and if you aren't, then you can enable this setting. The keep-alive maintains the session for 60 s (by default) if a disconnection is detected. This – like session reliability – stops the session from being dropped immediately if it is interrupted. The keep-alive timeout can be increased for high latency networks.

> **NOTE**
>
> If **Session Reliability** is disabled, port 1494 will be used by the ICA client to connect.

> **TIP**
>
> Use session reliability, if possible, as it provides a more intuitive experience for the user.

License Server (Figure 5.7) – Set the license server hostname and port number for the entire farm.

HDX (Figure 5.7)

- **Browser Acceleration** – By default enabled, this accelerates Web browser traffic within the XenDesktop session. There is a further option to "Compress JPEG images to improve bandwidth" and the levels can be set to **Low**, **Medium**, or **High** through a drop-down list; the higher the compression, the lower the bandwidth. This may be useful in WAN scenarios. **Variable image compression** check box will automatically adjust the setting based on the user's available bandwidth.
- **Flash** – Tick box to "Enable Adobe Flash Player." This will redirect flash content to play directly to an "Adobe Flash Player" installed on the client rather than through the virtual desktop.

> **TIP**
>
> Flash redirection is great for LAN links, giving the user the Flash rendering locally on their physical device. This does require Flash Player on their device, and thus only works with "Windows" type end points.

The **Administrators** (Figure 5.5) node: Citrix Resources – Desktop Delivery Controller – <Your Farm> – Administrators. This node gives you the option to add administrators to your XenDesktop farm.

Right-click on the **Administrators** node, or select **Add Administrator** in the central pane. You can allocate *delegated administration* or *full control privileges* to a user or group.

Delegated administrators can view everything in the Delivery Services Console. Delegated administrators can perform maintenance tasks on the user and machine objects such as logging off users, sending them messages, and stopping or starting virtual desktops. Delegated administrators can't do farm level tasks like changing Desktop Groups.

> **TIP**
>
> After installation, only the account that executed the installation is an administrator for the farm. This represents a single point of failure. Should that account be deleted, disabled, or be otherwise unavailable, you will not be able to administer the XenDesktop farm. Add an Administrative Group and grant it full control over your farm. You can also add the "Local Administrators" group, which will grant the rights to all users who are local administrators on the Desktop Delivery Controller.

The **Controllers** (Figure 5.5) node has an option for you to "Create Folder." In larger environments this would help you to sort your Desktop Delivery Controllers into groups.

Right-click on the Desktop Delivery Controller you have created. Select **Properties**.

License Server (Figure 5.8) – Use farm setting set the server to automatically inherit the settings you set at a "farm level." Deselect, and you could assign a separate license server and port number for an individual Desktop Delivery Controller.

> **TIP**
>
> If you are using some "Device licenses" and some "User licenses," you would need to use different license servers to host these licenses, and then use the Desktop Delivery Controllers to service different Desktop Groups.

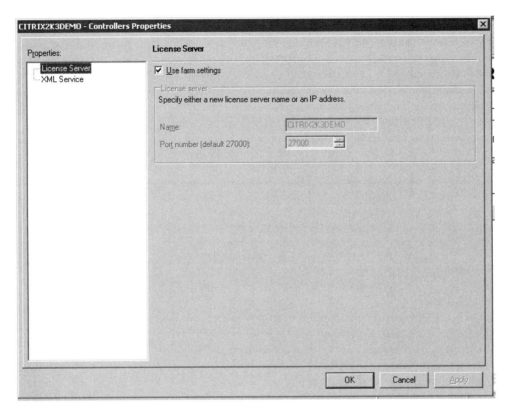

FIGURE 5.8

Desktop Delivery Controller properties dialog box.

XML Service (Figure 5.8) – The XML service can be set to "Trust requests sent to the XML Service" – the default is to verify the requests first, but this can be enabled if you have put other security (like IPSEC etc.) in place first.

The XML port can also be altered here – if it is not being shared with IIS.

> **TIP**
>
> Either use port 80 or port 8080 if possible. These are the "standard" ports. To set the port to 8080 if it is currently sharing with IIS, use the command
> ```
>     ctxxmlss /U
> ```
> This will unregister the XML service, and reboot the server.
> ```
>     ctxxmlss /R8080
> ```
> This will register the port to 8080.

Select **Desktop Groups** (Figure 5.9).
Shown above is the Desktop Group created on Citrix XenServer.

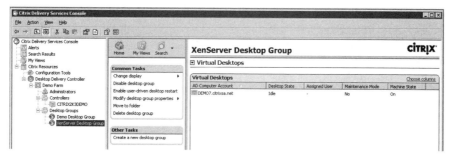

FIGURE 5.9

Viewing Desktop Groups.

FIGURE 5.10

Desktop Groups view menu.

Note that the machine state column is only available through integration with the hypervisor. The Desktop Delivery Controller interrogates the hypervisor for the current machine state and displays the information in the Delivery Services Console.

The central task pane contains some of the "Common Tasks."

Change display – gives you a drop-down list (Figure 5.10) allowing you to change the information displayed in the right-hand pane. Most of the nodes only have the options to View Information or Alerts, but at the Desktop Group level, we are able to select various views to display in the right-hand pane.

The default view is "Virtual Desktops" which is the view shown above.

- **Information** – This option displays basic details of the Desktop Group.
- **Alerts** – This option displays warning (orange)/error (red) messages.
- **Configured Users** – This option displays the groups and users configured to use this Desktop Group.
- **Read-Only Properties** – This option displays the current settings that have been set through the properties dialog box. (The **Farm** node also has a "Read Only" option.)
- **Virtual Desktops In Use** – This option displays those desktops that are currently connected.
- **Virtual Desktops** – This option displays all virtual desktops in the Desktop Group, and the virtual desktops' current state.

Disable Desktop Group (Figure 5.9) – This option disables the selected Desktop Group. This renders the Desktop Group inaccessible to the users. This setting will also stop the Desktop Group icon being presented to the user through Web Interface.

Enable user-driven Restart (Figure 5.9) – This setting adds a **restart** button to the Users Web Interface page (Figure 5.11).

This setting only works if your desktop is running on an "integrated" hypervisor because the actual restart action is an instruction sent from the Desktop Delivery Controller to the hypervisor – XenServer, the VMware SDK, or System Center Virtual Machine Manager.

Move to Folder (Figure 5.9) – allows you to move the Desktop Group to a subfolder. Subfolders can be created at the node above the Desktop Groups; it is useful in more complex environments to arrange your Desktop Groups according to structural (development/test/production) or business (Sales/Marketing/IT etc.) needs.

Delete Desktop Group (Figure 5.9) – allows you to delete a Desktop Group, and **Create a new Desktop Group** – as you would expect – allows you to create a new Desktop Group.

Click on **Modify desktop group properties | Modify all properties** (Figure 5.12).

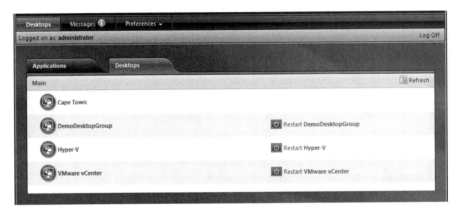

FIGURE 5.11

Web Interface – "Restart" button.

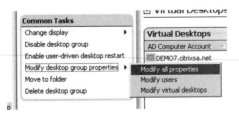

FIGURE 5.12

Desktop Group modification menu.

Basic (Figure 5.13)

- **Desktop Group Name** – The name and description of the Desktop Group can be amended. The Desktop Group can additionally be enabled or disabled from this menu, through a checkbox – **Disable Desktop Group**.
- **Assignment Type** – This is for viewing whether the assignment type is Pool/Assigned – Assigned on first use and so on, and whether the Desktop Group is being used for VM-hosted apps or not.

> **NOTE**
>
> These settings cannot be changed after the Desktop Group has been created. You would need to delete and re-create the Desktop Group.

- **Hosting Infrastructure** – Like the Assignment Type, this is a read-only setting. Under this, you can view the Hosting Infrastructure: XenServer – "Citrix Xen VM infrastructure," VMware – "VMware virtualization," Microsoft – "Microsoft virtualization," or without integration – "None."

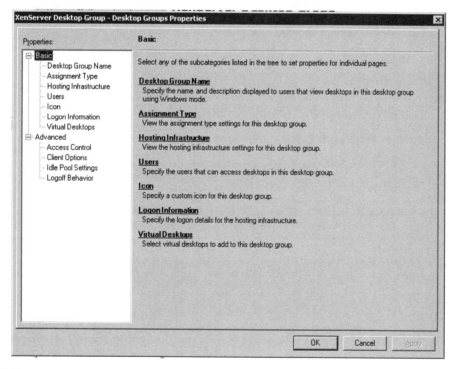

FIGURE 5.13

Desktop Group properties dialog box.

- **Users** – View and modify the users and groups assigned this Desktop Group. Add and remove buttons to modify users and groups.
- **Icon** – Displays the current icon used to represent the Desktop Group to the users. The **Change icon…** button allows you to browse for an alternative, or your own custom icon.
- **Logon Information** – View and modify the logon information for the hosting infrastructure. Here, you can edit the hostname/IP address of the server you are interfacing with, and the logon information.

TIP

If the vCenter/SCVMM/XenCenter logon changes, this is where you would need to edit it on the Desktop Groups.

- **Virtual Desktops** (Figure 5.14) – View and modify virtual desktops assigned to your Desktop Group.

TIP

The "Export to File" can be handy if you want to create (or recreate) a Desktop Group using the same group of virtual desktops.

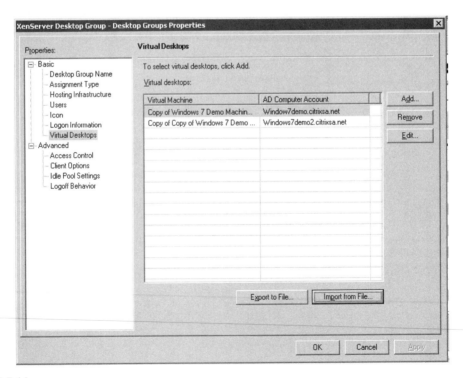

FIGURE 5.14

Modify virtual desktops.

Advanced (Figure 5.14)

- **Access Control** – Access control is used in conjunction with Citrix Access Gateway, and this can be used to only allow users connecting through the Access Gateway and even with certain Access Gateway filters to access the Desktop Group. The default is to allow all connection types. The finer details of Access Gateway is outside the scope of this manual. The filters can allow you to do things like only allow users access if, for example, they have a certain antivirus package installed.
- **Clients Options**
  - **Appearance** – Change the color depth; choose from 16 colors, 256 colors, high color (16 bit), and true color (24 bit). The default is true color.
  - **Connection – Encryption** – Choose the encryption level of the ICA protocol from Basic up to 128-bit(RC5).
  - **Connection Protocols** – Currently ICA and Microsoft RDP are available. You can add the RDP protocol. By default only the ICA protocol is available.

> **NOTE**
>
> You will lose ICA/HDX functionality if you choose the RDP protocol.

- **Idle Pool Settings** (Figure 5.15) – The Idle Pool Setting deserves specific emphasis. The Desktop Delivery Controller takes over managing the powering on or off of virtual desktops. This can be somewhat disconcerting for those who are familiar with managing this through a hypervisor management tool.

Select Idle Pool Settings in the left-hand pane (Figure 5.15). Set the number of virtual desktops you would like to remain powered on.

The idle desktops are virtual desktops that are powered on and waiting for a user to connect to them. In order to give users an "instant on" experience, as users log on, the Desktop Delivery Controller starts additional virtual desktops. The idle pool must be big enough such that the number of idle desktops isn't depleted before the additional virtual desktops become available. If the idle pool is depleted, the user must wait until a virtual desktop becomes available. Having a larger idle pool during peak times is advisable.

This can be used in conjunction with power management capabilities at the hypervisor level – XenServer Power Management (5.6) and VMware DPM. Intelligent powering off of virtual desktops can translate to significant power saving in the datacenter.

- **Business days** – Select days that a pool of machines should be kept powered on for connection.
- **Day start** – Specify the start of the business day, or the time from which your users start working.
- **Peak end** – The peak start is automatically taken as the "Day start," the peak end is the time before which the bulk of your users have logged on.
- **Day end** – Specify the end of the business day, or the time after which your users have finished work.
- **Idle Desktop Count** – Specify the number of idle desktops that should be running during: Business hours, Peak time, and Out of hours.

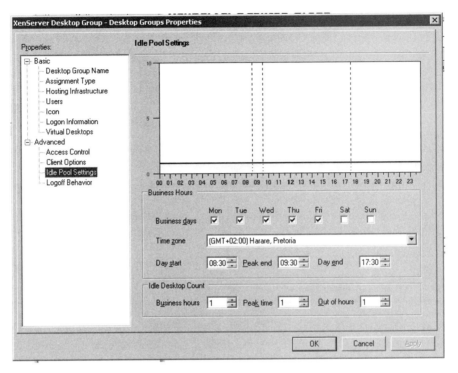

FIGURE 5.15

Modify Idle Pool Settings.

During the initial installation and configuration phase, I recommend leaving all of the virtual desktops powered on. Institute the Idle Pool Settings in a production environment.

NOTE

Booting multiple virtual desktops simultaneously can place a load on the hypervisor (the physical servers). Additionally, it is recommended[A] to stagger booting of virtual desktops in large environments, as this prevents placing an undue load on the physical servers.

[A]Best practices for Citrix XenDesktop with provisioning server.

The booting of virtual desktops can be throttled by altering the number of concurrent commands that may be executed. Limiting the concurrent commands prevents the Desktop Delivery Controller from starting too many virtual desktops simultaneously. Each environment differs from the next; the performance of the server hardware and the number of physical hosts across which the load will be spread should be considered when considering how many virtual desktops should be started at one time – basically you will need to test this, but you can try a "MaximumTransitionRate" of 20 as a starting point.

Edit the file "C:\Program Files\Citrix\VmManagement\CdsPoolMgr.exe.config."

Add the line in bold and italics text.

```
<?xml version="1.0" encoding="utf-8" ?>
<configuration>
<appSettings>
<add key="LogToCdf" value ="1"/>
<add key="LogFileName" value ="C:\cdslogs\VMManager.log"/>
<add key="LogDebug" value="1"/>
<add key="MaximumTransitionRate" value="20"/>
</appSettings>
</configuration>
```

> **TIP**
>
> Be aware that through hypervisor integration, the Desktop Delivery Controller will automatically shut down any desktops in your Desktop Group that exceed the number in the idle pool. If you want to power off the virtual desktops, change the idle pool to zero, or change it to one to boot an individual instance. Alternatively, disabling the Desktop Group will also disable the Desktop Group from being powered on or off by the Desktop Delivery Controller.

Logoff Behavior (Figure 5.16)

Set the behavior of the virtual desktop – Restart on logoff, or Do nothing – i.e., leave the virtual desktop powered on.

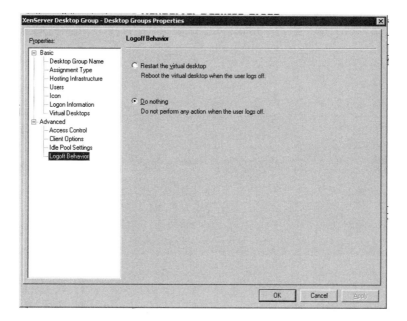

FIGURE 5.16

Modify logoff behavior.

TIP

To save your having to wait for virtual desktops to power up, during the installation and configuration phase, set the Desktop Group to "Do Nothing" at logoff.

Restart at logoff can, however, be very handy in a production environment. When using provisioning server to assign a virtual disk (vDisk) to the virtual desktop, a new updated vDisk can be assigned to the virtual desktop and the change will automatically only take place when the virtual desktop is restarted – which in this case would be at logoff.

The "Do nothing" setting is also often used in call center/shift worker type environments because it prevents a "reboot storm" between shifts. Rebooting the entire pool of virtual desktops can place significant load on the servers hosting the virtual desktops, and the time required to reboot the entire pool can potentially be an issue.

WEB INTERFACE CONFIGURATION FOR THE INTEGRATED WEB SITE

Citrix XenDesktop automatically installs Web Interface as part of the default installation. The configuration of Web Interface has been moved out of the Delivery Services Console into its own console in this version of the product.

Click **Start | Programs | Citrix | Management Consoles** (Figure 5.17).

One of the most common requirements is to edit the Web site to automatically set the preselect to the active directory domain.

The following configuration is recommended for a single domain environment or an environment where all the users are in the same domain.

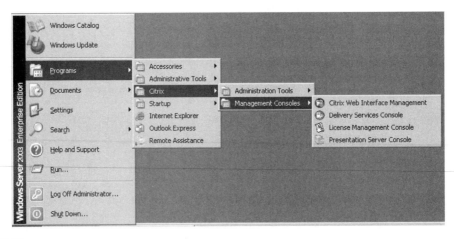

FIGURE 5.17

Launch Web Interface console.

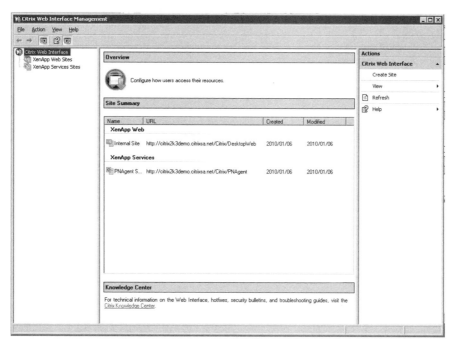

FIGURE 5.18

Web Interface console.

Set the Logon Domain

1. Select the Web Site – somewhat confusingly called "XenApp Web Sites" (Figure 5.18).
The XenApp Service Site is used to integrate with what most Citrix engineers refer to as Program Neighborhood Agent – now called Citrix Applications. The services site is used to populate the users **Start Menu** with the application icons, without requiring the user to log on to the Web site. This is a useful desktop integration tool, which is more applicable to virtual applications.
2. In the right-hand pane, select **Authentication Methods** (Figure 5.19).
3. Select **Properties** (Figure 5.20).
4. In the left-hand pane, select **Authentication Type**, and click **Settings**… (Figure 5.21).
5. Select **Hide Domain box** (Figure 5.22) from the domain list, select **Pre-populated**, and click **Add**…. Insert the required domain name and then click **OK** and **OK** again.

Amending the Web site appearance is another simple task you can perform to customize the Web front end for your XenDesktop.

Click **Web Site Appearance** in the right-hand pane (Figure 5.23).

You can replace the standard Citrix logos with your own corporate logos – using either .gif or .jpg formats.

Add you images to the folder: C:\Inetpub\wwwroot\Citrix\DesktopWeb\media.

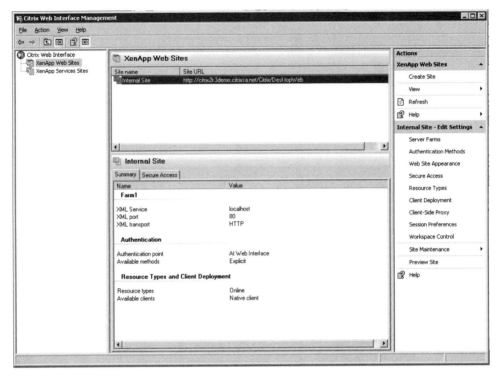

FIGURE 5.19

Web Interface management console.

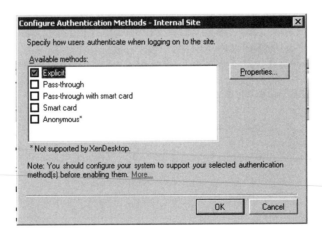

FIGURE 5.20

Authentication methods dialog box.

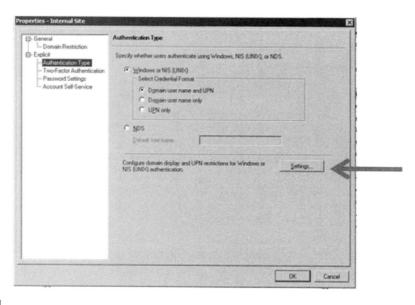

FIGURE 5.21

Authentication properties dialog box.

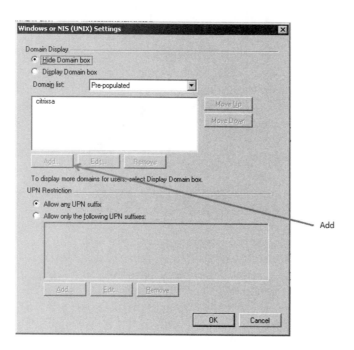

FIGURE 5.22

Domain settings dialog box.

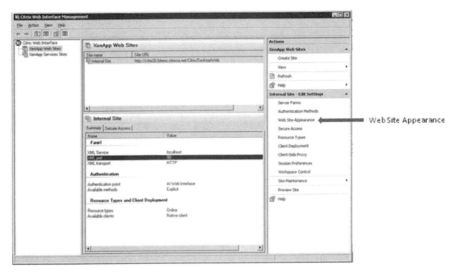

FIGURE 5.23

Amending Web site appearance.

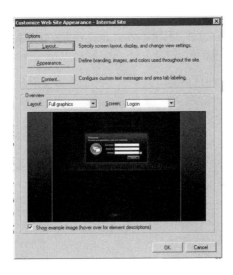

FIGURE 5.24

Web site appearance dialog box.

Amend the paths under "Appearance," for example ".media/mylogo.gif" (Figure 5.24).

Test your Web site by attaching to http://localhost (Figure 5.25) on the Desktop Delivery Controller.

Having successfully tested the Web site from on the server itself, you can now test it from another workstation.

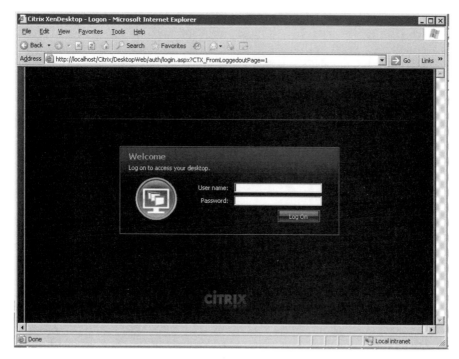

FIGURE 5.25

Web Interface logon page.

FIGURE 5.26

Site maintenance menu.

> **TIP**
>
> If you find that your Web site no longer functions, try the Repair Site from the Site Maintenance in the Actions Pane of the Web Interface Console (Figure 5.26).

Web Interface Installed on a Separate Web Server Step-by-Step

In production environments, it is recommended that Web Interface be installed on a separate server from the Desktop Delivery Controller. As per Chapter 2, "Installation of the Broker – Desktop Delivery Controller," the Desktop Delivery Controller should be installed with the –nosites switch to prevent Web Interface from installing automatically.

In this chapter, we will use a "XenApp Web" site to provide access to the virtual desktops, and later in Chapter 10, you will learn how we use a XenApp services site to provision applications into the virtual desktops. In terms of planning, you can use the same Web Interface site(s), to provision both the virtual desktop and the virtual applications into the virtual desktops.

> **TIP**
>
> The NetScaler VPX Express edition is a free VPX appliance. This makes a great load balancer. You can create multiple Web Interface sites and provide resilience using a NetScaler pair in front on the Web Interface sites. NetScaler VPX falls outside the scope of this book, but is most certainly worth investigating.

Web Interface Prerequisites

- Operating system
  - Windows 2003 SP2 (32 bit or x64)
  - Windows 2008 SP2 (32 bit or x64)
  - Windows 2008 R2
- Components
  - IIS 6, 7, or 7.5 depending on their respective operating systems – with the caveat that Windows 2003 x64 runs in 32-bit mode.
  - NET Framework 3.5 with Service Pack 1, and Visual J#.NET 2.0 Second Edition – These installation files can be found under the support folder on the XenDesktop media.
  - ASP.NET 2.0 – installed and enabled in IIS.

For example on Windows 2008: If IIS is already installed, check whether ASP .NET is enabled. **Server Manager | Roles** – right-click on the Web Server (IIS) and select **Add Role Services** (Figure 5.27).

1. Mount the XenDesktop ISO on the Web Server. Browse to w2k3\en\Web Interface (the file is also located under x64\en\Web Interface, but it is exactly the same executable).
2. Select the preferred language from the drop-down list and click **OK** (Figure 5.28).
3. Click **Next** (Figure 5.29).
4. Toggle the license radio button to **I accept the license agreement**, and click **Next** (Figure 5.30).
5. Accept the default location or click **Browse…** and select the desired folder then click **Next** (Figure 5.31).
6. Change the radio button to **Copy the clients to the computer**, browse the XenDesktop DVD, for example, to D:\w2k3\en\Clients. Then click **Next** (Figure 5.32).

> **TIP**
>
> If you "skip this step," the clients won't automatically deploy and install from the Web site, but will redirect to the Internet and try to download from there. It is much simpler to install the clients at this stage than to add them and edit the deployment settings later.

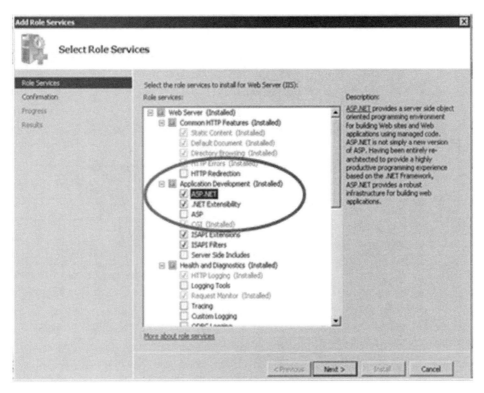

FIGURE 5.27

Select the ASP .NET role service.

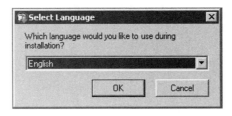

FIGURE 5.28

Language selection dialog box.

7. Click **Next** (Figure 5.33).

8. Click **Finish** (Figure 5.34), and selecting the **Start creating sites now** launches the "Citrix Web Interface Management" console.

9. Click **Create Site** in the right-hand pane (Figure 5.35).

FIGURE 5.29

Introductory setup dialog box.

FIGURE 5.30

License agreement dialog box.

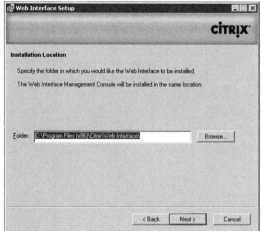

FIGURE 5.31

Installation location dialog box.

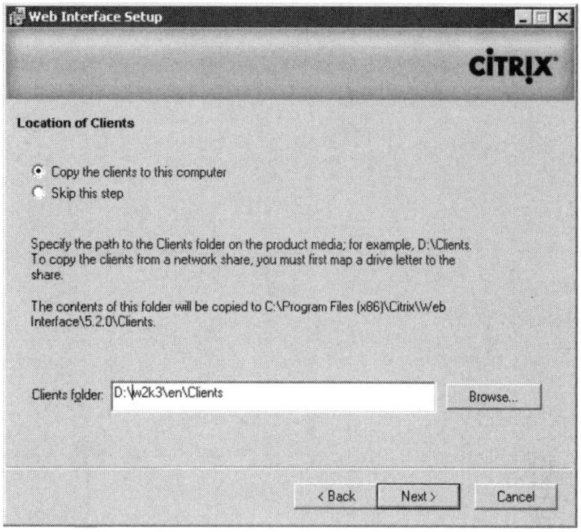

FIGURE 5.32

Client location dialog box.

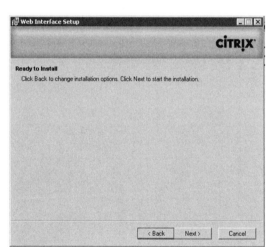

FIGURE 5.33

Installation initialization dialog box.

FIGURE 5.34

Successful installation dialog box.

10. Select **XenApp Web**, and click **Next** (Figure 5.36).

> **NOTE**
>
> XenApp Web is for virtual desktops, XenApp services is for virtual applications provisioned to the virtual desktops.

11. Select the check box **Set as the default page for the IIS site**, and then click **Next** (Figure 5.37).
12. Leave the default to authenticate **At Web Interface** and click **Next** (Figure 5.38).

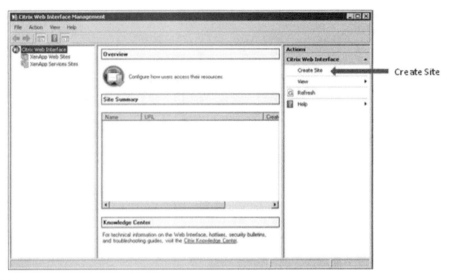

FIGURE 5.35

Creating a site from the management console.

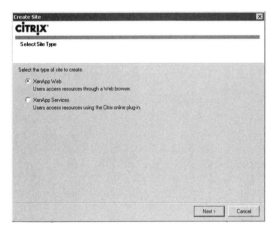

FIGURE 5.36

Site type dialog box.

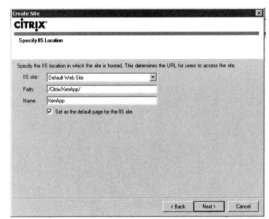

FIGURE 5.37

IIS location dialog box.

> **NOTE**
>
> Web Interface provides various authentication options, including using Microsoft AD Federated Services, Access Gateway (Citrix's SSL VPN appliance), third-party Kerberos or at the Web site. For the purposes of this book, we will assume Active Directory, but you should be aware of the various options.

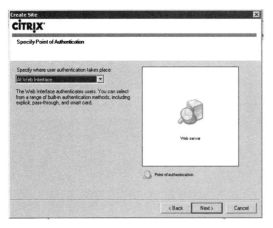

FIGURE 5.38

Authentication point selection dialog box.

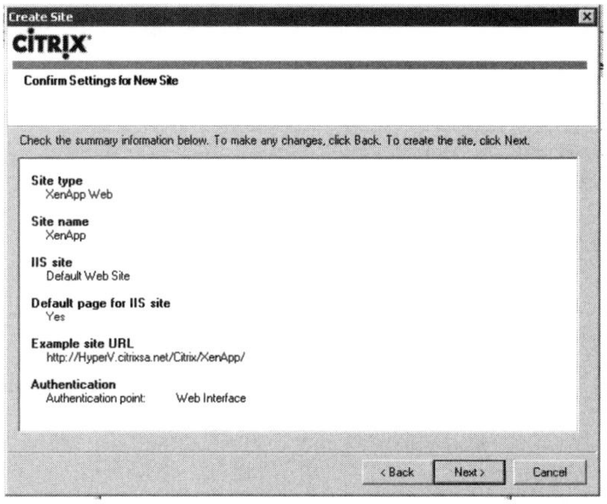

FIGURE 5.39

Summary information checklist.

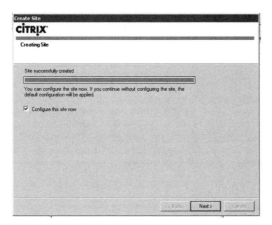

FIGURE 5.40

Site configuration dialog box.

13. Figure 5.39 is a dialog box, which provides a list of the settings you have chosen, check that the selections are correct, and click **Next**.

14. The site is now installed. By default the check box **Configure the site now** is selected. It is simplest to configure the site at install. Click **Next** (Figure 5.40).

15. Enter a "Farm name" – this is a "Display Name" and it is not necessary that it be same as that of the XenDesktop farm; however, for practical purposes, it is advisable to use the same name. Click **Add**... to enter the names (or IP addresses) of your Desktop Delivery Controllers. Move the primary XML server to the top of the list. Click **Next** (Figure 5.41).

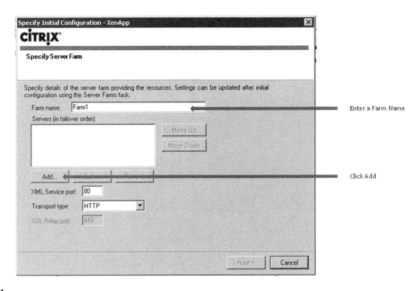

FIGURE 5.41

Specify XenApp server farm dialog box.

> **NOTE**
>
> If there are multiple servers in the farm, it is good practice to add a number of Desktop Delivery Controllers for resiliency. As previously mentioned, larger farms may use a dedicated server to provide XML services, the servers are accessed in order, and consequently the dedicated XML server should be at the top of the list. The Web Interface site will by default use port 80 to communicate with the XML service of the XenApp servers. Remember to change the XML port to match that on the Desktop Delivery Controllers (e.g., 8080).

16. Leave the selection at "Explicit" and click **Next** (Figure 5.42).

> **NOTE**
>
> Explicit authentication is the appropriate authentication type for a Web Portal logon. When using the Web Services (formerly Program Neighborhood Agent), as we will be doing for XenApp applications, Pass-through is often the best option.

17. Click **Add**…, and then enter your domain name, click **OK** and **Next** (Figure 5.43).

> **NOTE**
>
> You can alternatively set up domain customization after this stage using the procedure in the previous section. It is simpler to do the customization during the configuration. In a single-domain scenario, adding the domain name will automatically populate the domain field and hide the domain field from the user. In multidomain environments, where you are using this for security purposes, the user will need to log on using the syntax domain\username, as UPN logons aren't accepted.

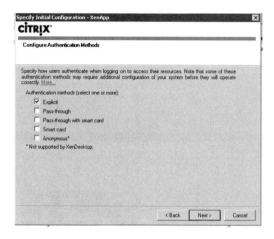

FIGURE 5.42

Configure authentication methods dialog box.

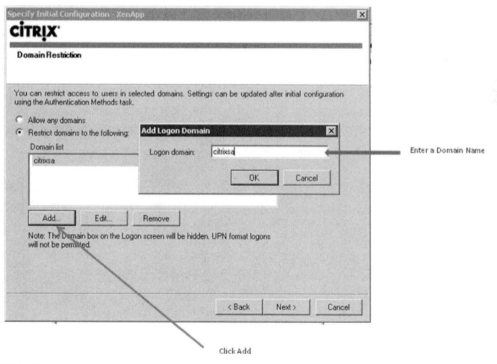

FIGURE 5.43

Domain restriction dialog box.

18. Select your preferred logon screen appearance – (I prefer **Minimal**), and click **Next** (Figure 5.44).
19. Leave the default at **Online** and click **Next** (Figure 5.45).
   Note: For more information on Resource Types, please see Chapter 10, "Configure Citrix XenApp for Application Provisioning."
20. Review your selections and click **Finish** (Figure 5.46).

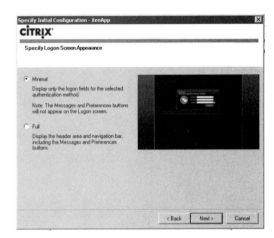

FIGURE 5.44

Logon appearance dialog box.

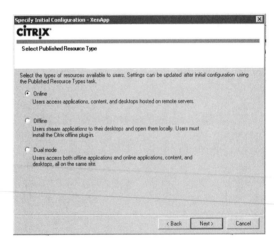

FIGURE 5.45

Published resource type selection dialog box.

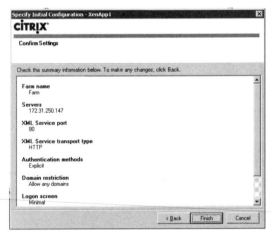

FIGURE 5.46

Settings confirmation dialog box.

Integrating XenDesktop with Access Gateway

A XenDesktop farm may be integrated with the Citrix SSL VPN – the Access Gateway. Selecting Secure Access (Figure 5.47) allows you to

1. Define subnets which will access the virtual desktops through an Access Gateway. Alternatively, define the internal subnets as default (i.e., direct), and the default (i.e., all the rest) as Access Gateway.
2. Specify the FQDN (Fully Qualified Domain Name) of the Access Gateway – this must match the SSL certificate.
3. Specify the Secure Ticket Authorities. The STA functions are integrated into both the Desktop Delivery Controller servers, and XenApp servers.

The full details of configuring an Access Gateway fall outside the scope of this book; however, it is important to underline that this is a significant feature. Using Access Gateway to access your virtual desktop could be used as part of your Disaster Recovery/Business Continuity plan.

The Access Gateway can provide full SSL VPN access, or for heightened security, SSL Proxy access to only their virtual desktop. The concept of providing just SSL proxy access is useful: instead of offering access to the network, you only provide remote access to a single virtual desktop. This is more secure as it dramatically reduces the surface of attack.

> **NOTE**
>
> The Access Gateway VPX appliance is a virtual machine that can be used in place of a physical Access Gateway. The Access Gateway VPX appliance replaces the software-based Citrix Secure Gateway.

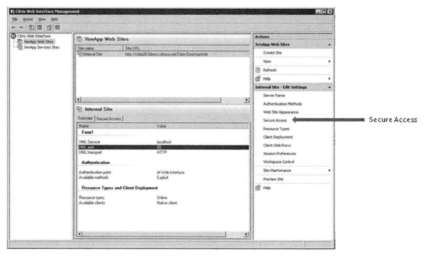

FIGURE 5.47

Use the secure access setting to configure Access Gateway.

Checkpoint 2 – Connectivity to a Virtual Desktop

This is the second milestone in your desktop virtualization project. This demo may be better suited to a technical audience as the demo may be quite similar to what you demoed in the first milestone. A technical audience will better appreciate that the virtual desktop is now running on a hypervisor out of the datacenter and the distinction between that and a physical device.

Here is the basic diagram to sketch out for your audience (Figure 5.48).

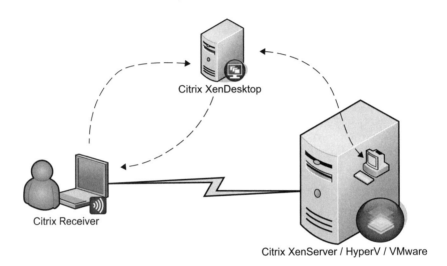

FIGURE 5.48

Connecting to a virtual desktop.

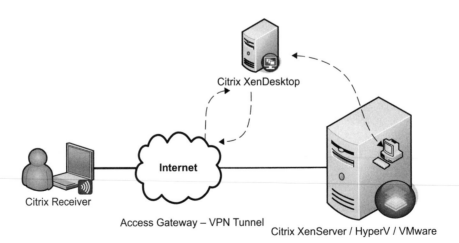

FIGURE 5.49

Connecting to a virtual desktop over a VPN.

The exception to this rule would be if you have set up an Access Gateway or VPN access (Figure 5.49), the demonstration of a laptop connecting externally to a virtual desktop in the datacenter is something both technical and business stakeholders should see.

As with the first demonstration, emphasis on the video, audio, and peripheral (USB /webcams, etc.) capabilities are the aspects that define user experience to be the same if not better than a physical device.

XENDESKTOP POLICIES AND PRINTING

Policies and printing are two areas that are important to plan for, because they become the two areas that operationally will need maintenance – as your users change, or your users' needs change.

These are also both areas that are being updated in the not too distant future, with new enhancements.

Citrix XenDesktop and Policies

There are two types of policies that you can implement in a XenDesktop environment: Citrix Policies and standard Microsoft Policies. Citrix Policies are unique to a Citrix environment; the Microsoft Group Policies are implemented through Active Directory. It is recommended that the virtual desktops have their own Microsoft Policies separate from physical desktops.

Microsoft Policies are an important tool for managing the virtual desktop environment. There are many commonalities between your standard desktop policies and virtual desktop policies. Your existing desktop policies are a good starting point for creating your virtual desktop policies. It is a good idea to keep your virtual desktop policies separate from your standard desktop policies. Don't just link your existing Group Policy Objects (GPOs) to the new virtual desktop OU. The contents and settings of the desktops are very similar, but the physical implementation is obviously very different. We are placing user workstations in the datacenter, so there may well be different security requirements. Operationally, it will simplify your life to keep the policies separate. GPOs are applied by default to organizational units (OUs).

In the current version of XenApp, Citrix Policies are managed through the Advanced Configuration Console; in the next version of XenApp, these settings have been moved into the Delivery Services Console. We can expect these settings to be migrated into the Delivery Services Console in the following version of both XenApp and XenDesktop.

A further enhancement will be that these same policies will also be able to be configured through both a Microsoft GPO and the Delivery Services Console. The new settings will be made available to a Microsoft GPO by adding a custom .adm file to the GPO.

Citrix Printer Options

Printing is an important consideration as we are changing the physical structure of attaching to our printers. Print job routing is important to consider.

There are three different mechanisms by which Citrix virtual desktops can attach to physical print devices.

1. Network printers
2. Session printers
3. Client autocreated printers

Network Printers

Network printers work exactly the same as they would when using a conventional desktop PC. Network printers are mapped in the conventional way using a login script; the login script could be a simple batch file, .vbs or .kix, for example. The important thing to bear in mind with network printers is the location of the print server, the location of the virtual desktops, and the location of the print device.

The print job will spool on the virtual desktop and traverse the network to the print server, and then to the print device. If your VDI project also includes a centralization aspect, the increase in print traffic needs to be considered. In Figure 5.50, you can see how the print job routes to the physical device.

The print traffic flows outside of the ICA stream and is not able to be compressed as it is outside of the ICA protocol. Physical devices like a Citrix Branch Repeater (or Cisco WAAS/Riverbed, etc.) are the best way to compress this type of traffic.

The print server should always be local to the virtual desktops, and this rule is applicable to all the types of printing. The print device and the user can be remote from the virtual desktop, but the print server should be on the same LAN as the virtual desktop.

> **NOTE**
>
> The print server and the virtual desktop must have matching drivers. The Windows print server won't load a Citrix universal driver, and consequently the universal drivers can only be used with Client autocreated direct printing.

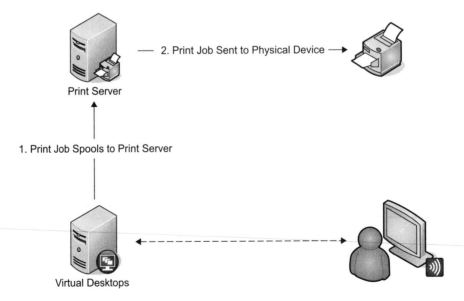

FIGURE 5.50

Network printer's job routing.

Client Side Rendering (CSR) is a new "feature" introduced since Windows Vista. This places the load on the client to perform the rendering rather than the server. I would recommend disabling this on a Windows 2008 print server, as it improves the performance of the virtual desktop.

Session Printers

Session printers work in exactly the same way as a network printer. The differentiator is that the management of the printer mappings is managed using Citrix Policies. Session printers require a print server to work; the Citrix Policies only perform a mapping function. A session printer can be created using the standard filtering of policies. The two most commonly used filters would be to map a specific printer to

1. An Active Directory Group
2. An IP subnet

Active Directory Groups are routinely used to map network printers; mapping to IP subnets, however, opens interesting possibilities. Depending on which subnet you logon to, you could be mapped a printer in that subnet, which could be useful if your users move around a lot.

Client Autocreated

Client autocreated network printers are created on the virtual desktop, by reading the settings on the client device, and remapping the printers to the virtual desktop. The mechanism works by interrogating the print manager on the end point, and relaying that information to the virtual desktop. In effect, all your printers on the end point are automatically created in your virtual desktop.

> **NOTE**
>
> Only client autocreated printers can make use of the Citrix universal print driver mechanism. Network printers and session printers must use native drivers.

There are two types of routing that can be used with autocreated client printers: connect directly or connect indirectly.

Connect Directly

Connect directly (Figure 5.51) can only be used with network printers. The virtual desktop reads the connection details and creates its own connection to the print server.

Connect Indirectly

Connect indirectly (Figure 5.52) means that the print jobs always routes through the client device.

The print traffic to the client flows within the Citrix ICA session. The traffic is then sent to the print server, and from there to the print device.

This can be useful in scenarios where the print server is on a network that is not visible to the virtual desktop, but is visible to the client device (untrusted domains for example). Additionally, if it is unavoidable that the print server is local to the client device, but not to the virtual desktop, you may achieve better compression and management of the print traffic if it is kept within the Citrix Session.

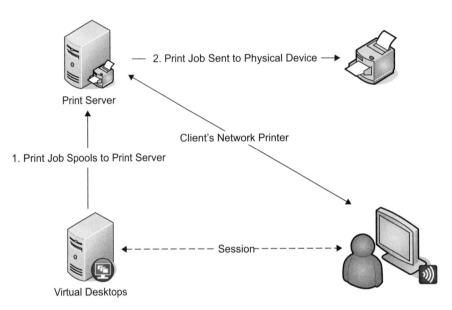

FIGURE 5.51

Autocreated printers using connect directly.

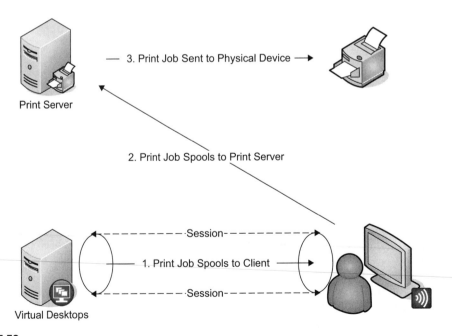

FIGURE 5.52

Autocreated network printers using connect indirectly.

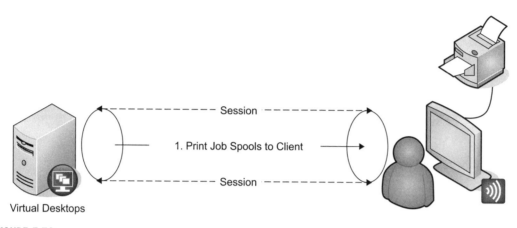

Virtual Desktops

FIGURE 5.53

Autocreated local print devices.

Locally Attached Devices

Locally attached (Figure 5.53) printers by their very nature always connect indirectly. As the physical device is attached to the client device, the print job will always route through the client device. A local print device could be connected through a USB or LPT port.

Create a Citrix Policy Step-by-Step

1. Click **Start | All Programs | Citrix Management Consoles | Presentation Server Console** (Figure 5.54).

   For those who are familiar with Citrix XenApp, you will see that this console is exactly the same as the XenApp Console. The Desktop Groups are even listed under the **Applications** folder. What we are interested in is creating policies to manage the settings in our XenDesktop environment. Select the **Policies** node in the left-hand pane. By default, there are no policies configured.
2. To create a policy, right-click on the **Policies** node.
3. Select **Create Policy** (Figure 5.55).
4. Enter a name for your policy, and click **OK** (Figure 5.56).

TIP

The **Optimize initial policy settings for a connection type** check box allows you to apply the Citrix default recommendations for WAN, Satellite, or Dial Up. Selecting one of these from the drop-down list will create the recommended settings in your policy.

---

5. Right-click on the new policy you have created, and select **Properties** (Figure 5.57).

   The Citrix XenDesktop Policies enable you to configure how your users' sessions are configured. Based on the available bandwidth and your security settings, you can choose how the

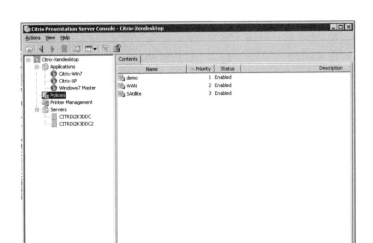

FIGURE 5.54

Citrix Presentation Server Console.

FIGURE 5.55

Policies node menu.

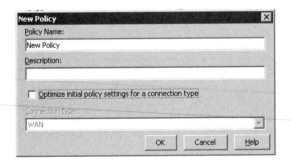

FIGURE 5.56

New policy dialog box.

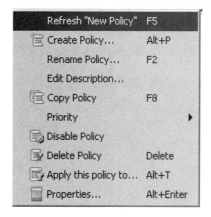

FIGURE 5.57

Policy menu.

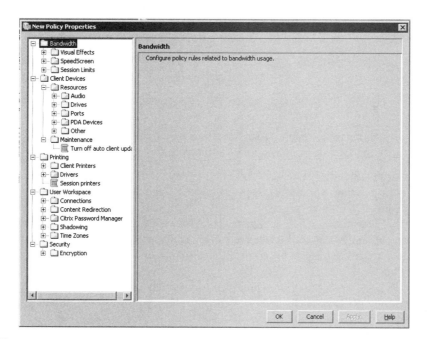

FIGURE 5.58

Policy properties dialog box.

virtual desktop interacts with the end point. You can choose the how graphics get handled, how peripherals like USB devices get mapped from the end point to the virtual desktop.

6. Once you have chosen your settings click **OK** (Figure 5.58).

7. Right-click on your policy again (Figure 5.57), and select **Apply this policy to**….

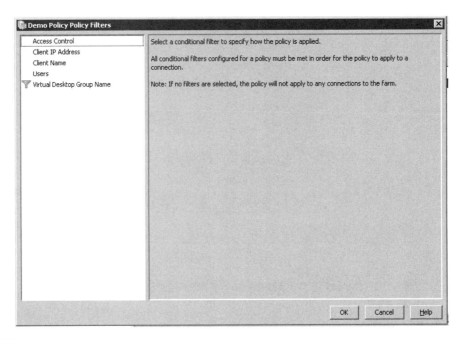

FIGURE 5.59

Policy filters dialog box.

By default your policy will not apply to anyone. There are five different filters that you can apply. If the user matches the filter, the policy applies to the user (Figure 5.59).

- **Access Control** – Based on the Citrix Access Gateway product. Used if the user logs in through a specific Access Gateway Farm, with specific Access Gateway Filters.
- **Client IP Address** – This is particularly useful in XenDesktop environments, if the user logs on from a certain subnet, the policy applies to them. Given that the connectivity links between the XenDesktop and the subnet are known, we can choose appropriate settings.
- **Client Name** – This setting is based on the hostname of the physical end point device; the policy may apply.
- **Servers** – This setting is based on which XenApp server delivers an application; a policy will apply. Useful in DR (Disaster Recovery) scenarios where you may want different settings if you are accessing the failover XenApp servers.
- **Users** – This setting is based on Active Directory – either User or Group membership. Useful for security settings, or enabling peripherals for only a subset of users.
- **Virtual Desktop Group Name** – This setting is based on the Desktop Group Name to which the virtual desktop belongs.

The **Servers** option is only available in the XenApp version of the console, and likewise, the Virtual Desktop Group Name option only exists in the XenDesktop version of the console.

8. Add the appropriate filter and click **OK** (Figure 5.59).

A green tick on the policy icon indicates it is active, an orange line indicates that it is disabled.

TIP

If you suspect that you have an issue with policies, it is preferable to disable policies than delete them.

Citrix XenDesktop Policy Settings Explained

In this section, we will dig into the details of individual Citrix Policy settings. As with the rest of this chapter, only a subset of this information may be relevant to your implementation. I do, however, advise you to at least skim through this section, as you may well "discover" functionality that you were unaware of.

Figure 5.60 is an example of the Policy Console, note the "breadcrumb" mechanism, whereby you can intuitively find where settings have been configured by following the blue arrows to the configured settings.

Most of the policies have the following options (Figure 5.60):

- **Not Configured** – This policy setting is not set.
- **Disabled** – This policy prevents these settings of the rule from being applied.
- **Enabled** – This policy causes the settings of the rule to be applied.

Not Configured and Enabled, are pretty easy to understand, but why the ability to disable a policy setting? Disabling a rule neither enables nor disables the settings; rather it prevents any other lower ranked policies from affecting the default setting. Multiple policies may be applied to a user, and the order in which they have been set will define the user's effective set of settings. Disabling a policy will cause all lower ranked policies for that setting to not be applied.

So, for example, I may have a policy that is enabled to allow USB mapping. I might also decide that I don't want users from a particular subnet to have the USB mapping allowed. This is often the case if you have an area that is publicly accessible – like Internet kiosks. I have set a general policy that I apply to "Domain Users" that allows USB mapping. By default USB mapping is not enabled.

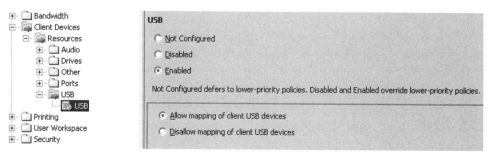

FIGURE 5.60

Client USB mapping policy.

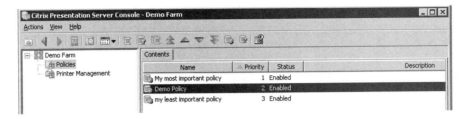

FIGURE 5.61

Setting the ranking of policies.

There are two ways in which I could prevent the subnet from receiving the policy settings.

1. We could create a higher ranked policy that sets this setting as "Disabled" and filter it to only apply to the subnet.
2. We could set a higher ranked policy, where the policy is enabled, but set to **Disallow mapping of client USB devices**, and filter it to only apply to that subnet.

Both of these options will stop the user from mapping USB devices. My preference would be to enable the rule, and set it to **Disallow mapping of client USB devices** because it would be easier for anyone else scrutinizing the policies to understand.

So to reiterate, disabling a rule will have no affect on the settings, it only prevents other rules from affecting these particular settings. A disabled policy is somewhat similar to a Microsoft "No Override" setting, and similarly it should be used sparingly.

Clicking the double arrows makes the policy either the highest priority or the lowest priority. The single arrows move the policy up or down in single increments. Priority "1" is the top priority, and the higher the number, the lower the priority (Figure 5.61).

The Citrix Policies are grouped into the following subsections:

- Bandwidth
- Client Devices
- Printing
- User Workspace
- Security

We will step through each of these sections, with a brief explanation of each policy setting. It would be best to step through this section with the Presentation Server Console open in front of you, if at all possible.

BANDWIDTH

Visual Effects (Figure 5.62)

- **Turn off desktop wallpaper** – this setting not only prevents unnecessary graphics being used, but also prevents the use of desktop wallpaper.

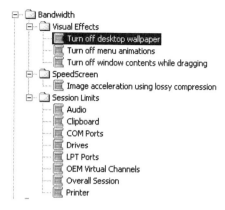

FIGURE 5.62

Citrix Policies – Bandwidth node.

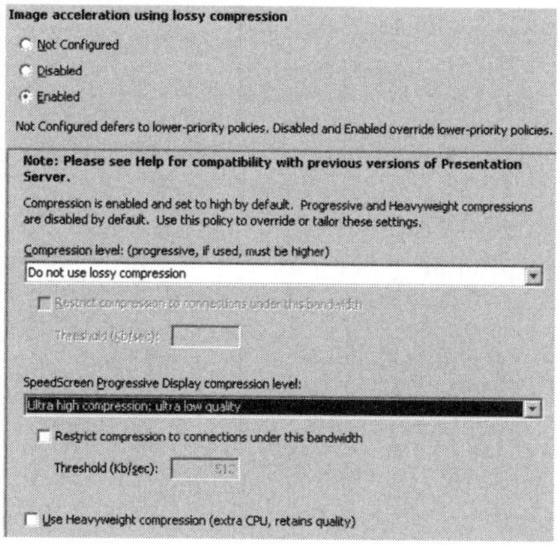

FIGURE 5.63

Image acceleration settings.

- **Turn off menu animations** – this setting prevents start menu components from building out gradually sliding out.
- **Turn off window contents while dragging** – if you move a application window from one part of the screen to another, the frame and contents are normally displayed while its is being moved. This setting moves only an outline frame of the window, and the contents are only displayed when the frame stops moving.

Speed Screen

Image acceleration using lossy compression (Figure 5.63) – this rule contains three settings:

1. **Compression Level** – This setting refers to the level of compression that should be used to display graphics. You can choose to degrade the graphics to decrease bandwidth usage.

2. **SpeedScreen Progressive Display** – This setting applies compression to images that are in motion. In other words, if I were to move a graphic object in my application, the image would degrade while in motion, and then sharpen up once it stops moving.
   A further subsetting on both of these rules is that you can choose that this only be applied to bandwidths lower than the amount you define. This is useful when defining remote users.
3. **Use Heavyweight compression** – This setting retains graphic quality, but increases the load on the processor (CPU) of the virtual desktop.

Session Limits (Figure 5.62)

The ICA protocol assigns virtual channels to different types of traffic sent between the client and the virtual desktop. The administrator can restrict the bandwidth used by virtual channels.

The settings are as follows (Figure 5.64):

- **Not Configured** – Not set in this policy.
- **Disabled** – The policy is disabled.
- **Enabled** – The bandwidth limits specified are applied to the virtual channel.

NOTE

Setting the policy to **Disabled** disables the policy; it does *not* disable the virtual channel.

- **Audio** – Restricts the bandwidth of sounds.
- **Clipboard** – Restricts the bandwidth of clipboard mirroring between the virtual desktop and the physical device.
- **Com Ports** – Restricts the bandwidth of Com Port mapping.
- **Drives** – Restricts the bandwidth of Drive mapping from the physical to the virtual desktop.
- **LPT Ports** – Restricts the bandwidth of LPT Port mapping (for older printer types).
- **OEM Virtual Channels** – Restricts the bandwidth of OEM virtual channels.
  Note: OEM virtual channels can be used with things like smart cards or other third-party hardware.
- **Overall Session** – Total usage per session – this enables you to restrict the total bandwidth usage.
- **Printer** – Restricts the bandwidth of the printer channel, which is responsible for carrying print traffic.

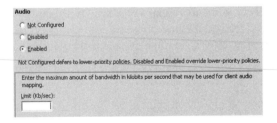

FIGURE 5.64

Session limits for the audio virtual channel.

> **NOTE**
>
> The printer channel only carries "client autocreated" printer traffic. Network printers – such as those mapped using logon scripts or "session printers" – are created using Citrix Policies. Both pass their print network traffic outside of the virtual channels, directly from the print server to the physical print device. This bandwidth setting will thus only affect "client autocreated" printers.

Client Devices

When the **Bandwidth** node is enabled, the administrator can restrict the bandwidth used by the virtual channels, the **Resources** (Figure 5.65) node allows the administrator to disable or enable some of the virtual channels.

1. Audio
    * **Microphones** – turn client microphones either on or off
    * **Sound quality** – set sound quality to one of three settings
        - High sound quality; lowest performance
        - Medium sound quality; good performance
        - Low sound quality; best performance
    * **Turn off speakers** – turn off audio mapping to client speakers
2. Drives
    * **Connection** – enables or disables "Connect client drives at logon"
    * **Mapping** – enables you to disable connection to any or all of the following:
        - Floppy drives
        - Hard drives
        - CD-ROM drives
        - Remote drives
        - USB disk drives

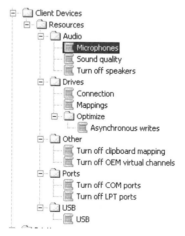

FIGURE 5.65

Citrix Policies – Client Devices node.

3. Optimize
   - **Asynchronous Writes** – enabling this setting can assist writes to client drives over links that are both high bandwidth and high latency.
4. Other
   - **Turn off clipboard mapping** – enabling this setting prevents clipboard contents from being copied both to and from the client device (can be useful in high-security environments).
   - **Turn off OEM virtual channels** – enabling this setting blocks OEM (third-party) applications from using custom virtual channels.
5. Ports
   - **Turn off COM ports** – disables COM port mappings.
   - **Turn off LPT ports** – disables LPT port mappings.
6. USB
   - **USB** – has settings to Allow or Disallow "mappings of client USB devices."

NOTE

By default, client USB devices are *not* mapped.

Printing

This section looks at the configurations covered in the Citrix Print Options earlier in this chapter (Figure 5.66).

Client Printers Client printers are any printers installed on the physical end point. Autocreation is the process of mapping the same printer inside the virtual desktop.

1. **Autocreation**
   - *Autocreate all client printers* – This setting maps all the printers.
   - *Autocreate local (non-network) client printers only* – This setting maps only printers that are physically attached to the client device.

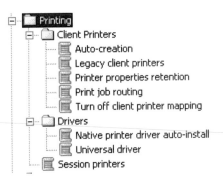

FIGURE 5.66

Citrix Print Policies.

- *Autocreate the client's default printer only* – This setting only creates the default printer of the client physical device.
- *Do not autocreate client printers* – This setting does not map client-side printers to the virtual desktop.

2. **Legacy client printers** – This setting changes how client-side printers appear inside the user session, and is more applicable to how printers are created within XenApp where the user may have multiple sessions.
   - *Create dynamic session-private client printers* – This setting creates client device printers that are linked to the session ID (and under XenApp not visible to other users).
   - *Create old-style client printers* – This setting creates printers linked to the user account (which are visible under XenApp to other users on the same XenApp server).

3. **Printer properties retention** – This setting refers to printer-specific settings, for example, paper size (A4 or Letter), and where the printer options are stored.
   - *Saved on client device only* – This setting saves the settings on the physical end point. This is not possible on read-only client devices. Use this if the settings can't be saved in the profile.
   - *Retained in user profile only* – The printer settings are held in a roaming (or virtual profile). This is a common option in virtual desktop environments, and the one which I recommend.
   - *Held in profile only if not saved on client* – This attempts to save the settings on the end point, and fails back to the profile if the client can't save the settings. This setting also uses extra time and bandwidth to perform this action.

4. **Print job routing** – Print job routing should be planned around the placement of virtual desktops, the print server, and the print device. Please see the previous section on Citrix Printer Options to ascertain the best option.
   - *Connect directly to network print server if possible* – The virtual desktop maps the network printer, and spools directly to the print server.
   - *Always connect indirectly as a client printer* – The virtual desktop spools the print job to the client device which then forwards it to the print server.

5. Turn off client printer mapping
   - *Turn off client printer mapping* – This setting disables all connections to client printers using the autocreated method.

Drivers This section deals with print drivers. Native drivers are those released by the printer manufacturer (e.g., HP, Ricoh, Nashua, Minolta etc.). Print drivers are less of an issue in a virtual desktop environment than they are for Terminal Services/RDS as the drivers have typically been written for the virtual desktop operating system. Issues may still exist when using older drivers, intended for Vista, on Windows 7, so testing is important.

1. **Native print driver auto-install**
   - *Install Windows native drivers as needed* – This policy results in the native print drivers downloading and installing from the print server onto the virtual desktop.

> **NOTE**
> I recommend adding the necessary print drivers to the base image. Setting the driver to autoinstall can potentially result in the drivers installing repeatedly in subsequent sessions as the image is read-only.

- *Do not automatically install drivers* – This setting prevents the drivers from automatically downloading. The printer will then either be mapped with the universal driver if it is enabled, or it will simply be not mapped at all if the universal driver isn't enabled.

2. **Universal driver**
   - *Use universal driver only if the requested driver is unavailable* – This setting results in the native driver being used if it is installed, but failing back to the universal driver if it isn't installed (can be used in conjunction with "do not automatically install drivers").
   - *Use only printer model specific drivers* – This policy only allows the use of the native driver. If the native driver is not installed, then the printer will not map.
   - *Use universal driver only* – This policy prevents the use of native drivers, only the universal driver can be used.

Session Printers (Figure 5.67) If the policy applies to a given virtual desktop, all of the listed session printers are mapped to the users' virtual desktop.

The **Add**... button enables you to add to the list of session printers.

The **Settings**... button (Figure 5.68) enables you to configure default settings for the printer, including paper size, number of copies, print quality (75 dpi to 600 dpi), orientation, and lastly, how the settings are applied. **Apply customized settings at every logon** overrides saving these settings in the profile.

The **Remove** button removes the highlighted printer from the list of session printers.

Choose client's default printer

- *Do not adjust the user's default printer* – This option just adds the session printers to the user's list of printers, and the first printer created is set as the default printer. The default printer of the session is not saved to the profile.

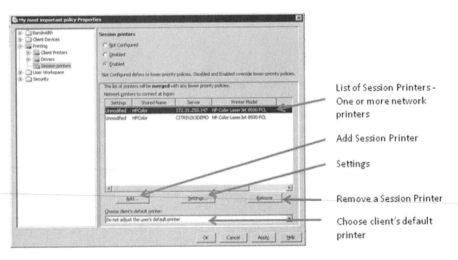

FIGURE 5.67

Session printer configuration.

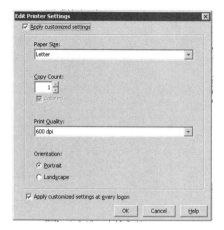

FIGURE 5.68

Print job settings.

FIGURE 5.69

Add printers dialog box.

- *Set default printer to the client's main printer* – This sets the users default printer on the virtual desktop to be whatever is set on the client device.
- *<Session Printer>* – You can also set one of the list of session printers (they are all listed) to be the user's default printer.

Adding a Session Printer Step-by-step:

1. Click **Add**, and to add a network printer (Figure 5.69).
2. Click **New**.
3. Click **Next** (Figure 5.70).
   You can change the connection credentials in the unlikely event that the logged on user account doesn't have visibility of the printer.
4. Type in a UNC path, or browse to a network printer and click **Finish** (Figure 5.71).

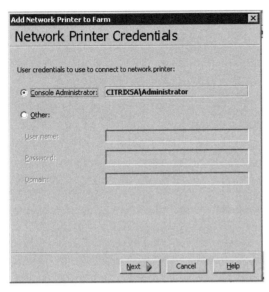

FIGURE 5.70

Connection user credentials dialog box.

FIGURE 5.71

Network printer location dialog box.

User Workspace
- Time Zones – "Do Not Use Clients' Local Time"
Note: By default the virtual desktop automatically assumes the time zone on the client device.

Security
- Encryption – SecureICA encryption – set the ICA encryption level. The encryption levels can be set to – Basic, RC5 (128 bit) logon only, RC5 (40 bit), RC5 (56 bit), RC5 (128 bit).

> **NOTE**
> The default setting of basic is sufficient for most XenDesktop environments. Higher encryption levels will incur a processor overhead.

Microsoft Policy Settings

As previously mentioned, the Delivery Services Console in XenApp 6.0 will integrate the Citrix Policies into it as one console. What will also be introduced will be the ability to manage the Citrix Policies through a Microsoft Group Policy Management Console. The changes within XenApp will no doubt also be introduced into XenDesktop. The standardization of managing all policies through the Microsoft Group Policy Management Console will be welcome news to many organizations.

Broadly speaking, a lot of the policy settings you would use in a Terminal Services/RDS environment are also applicable in a virtual desktop environment. A good recommendation is to redirect user data out of the virtual desktop. Redirect My Documents to a network location, for example, and hide the operating system hard drive. The virtual desktops are commonly pooled between all the users, and in this instance, if the user were to save data to a local hard drive, the information wouldn't persist between sessions.

Enabling loopback processing is a worthwhile concept to consider in a virtual desktop environment. Loopback processing on Microsoft GPOs alters how policy settings are applied. Normally policies are applied in the order Site, Domain, and then OU with machine policies applying at boot and user policies at logon; loopback processing processes the machine policies again after the user policies. Merge Mode applies both user and then machine policies, while Replace Mode only applies GPOs applied to computer account.

TIP

Be aware that the Virtual Desktop Agent uses port 8080 by default to communicate with the Desktop Delivery Controller. Group Policy Objects defining firewall policies could potentially block the communication between the virtual desktops and the desktop.

Delivery Controller

The use of Group Policies to manage Virtual Profiles will also be covered in more depth in Chapter 12, "Implementing Virtual Profiles into the Virtual Desktop."

SUMMARY

This chapter dealt with the XenDesktop Management Consoles in depth. We stepped through the Delivery Services Console studying the settings for managing XenDesktop farms. This was followed by looking at the Citrix Web Interface Management Console, and how this should be configured for presenting virtual desktops to our users. The significant checkpoint covered was a demonstration of using these configurations to demonstrate a connection to a virtual desktop – significantly this includes all the components introduced since the first checkpoint. In the subsequent subsections, we discussed the Presentation Server Console, focusing on the Citrix printer options and Citrix policy settings in depth. Lastly, we briefly looked at how Microsoft Policies can be integrated with XenDesktop.

Installation of the Citrix Provisioning Server

INFORMATION IN THIS CHAPTER

- Prerequisites
- Recommendations
- DHCP Configuration
- Installation of Provisioning Server – Step by Step

Provisioning server (PVS) is the component of a XenDesktop VDI (Virtual Desktop Infrastructure) solution that is typically the least understood. Provisioning server introduces "disk virtualization." In the same way we broke the link between one physical piece of hardware serving one operating system, we can now have one "virtual disk" being accessed by multiple virtual machines.

Provisioning server uses the network to mount the virtual disk to the virtual desktop. The Citrix terminology for this virtual disk is a vDisk.

When you normally create a virtual machine, you would assign memory, virtual CPU(s), network card(s), and disk. The disk would normally be in a VHD (XenServer/Hyper-V) or VMDK (VMware) format. With provisioning server, you only assign memory, CPU, and network resources, and there is no disk mounted for the base operating system. The "ah ha" moment is generally when you open the hypervisor console and show how there is no disk attached, and how the boot order is set to boot from the network.

Typically each virtual desktop is assigned an individual disk (see Figure 6.1).

A single vDisk is mounted to multiple virtual desktops through the network (see Figure 6.2).

FAQ

But how does the same disk boot multiple machines without resulting in conflicts?

The provisioning server injects the virtual desktop "uniqueness" at boot time. The provisioning server uses a database to map virtual desktops to machine names and Security Identifiers (SIDs). Each virtual desktop has a virtual Mac address, which is associated with a virtual desktop computer name. The boot disk is read-only and is used by all the assigned virtual desktops, each virtual machine is additionally assigned "Write Cache," which is Read/Write, the virtual desktop uses this as working space for things like its pagefile, and any other write actions required by the operating system.

A single physical provisioning server "officially" scales to 480 virtual desktops; however, recent updates to the product have raised that number considerably.[A] For practical purposes, the scaling out is more likely to be determined by the redundancy requirement. Two or more provisioning servers can be set up in a High Availability cluster.

[A]Delivering 5000 desktops with Citrix XenDesktop – "ONE physical provisioning server could easily support 3300 desktops."

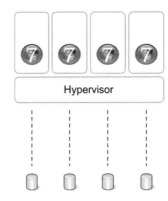

FIGURE 6.1

Virtual desktops without provisioning server.

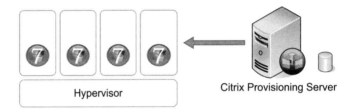

FIGURE 6.2

Virtual desktops with provisioning server.

FAQ

Physical or Virtual?

The provisioning server is a relatively heavy load, especially in terms of network requirements. For a small proof of concept or a pilot, it can be run as a virtual machine on the hypervisor infrastructure. For a production/live environment, one or more physical servers are recommended.

FAQ

Can a vDisk hosted by Citrix Provisioning Server be used across multiple hypervisors?

No, the vDisk will be specific to the hypervisor on which it was created. Each hypervisor presents virtual hardware and the drivers are specific to each hypervisor.

PREREQUISITES

Important considerations:

1. The user account performing the installation must be a local administrator on the provisioning server.
2. An Active Directory Service Account for Citrix Provisioning Server. For proof of concept/pilot type implementations, the local Network Service Account can be used rather than an Active Directory user account.
3. Windows Server 2003 SP2 and Windows Server 2008 and Windows Server 2008 R2 (32 or 64 bit) – all editions are supported for the provisioning server.

   The Installation Guide states "all versions." For a production environment, Windows Server 2008 (64 bit) would be the best choice in terms of performance and scalability. Windows Server 2008 R2 is currently supported in version 5.6.

   SQL Express database is sufficient for a proof of concept. A pilot or production environment should make use of an Enterprise database, which can be easily backed up and restored as required.

4. Requires Microsoft SQL 2005 or Microsoft SQL 2008. Express editions included. Please see Appendix.

TIP

As with the Desktop Delivery Controller, ask the database administrator in your organization to create a database for you.

---

5. Have a separate logical or physical drive location available for virtual disks. SAN (Storage Area Network) storage is recommended if available.
6. The .NET Framework 3.5.1 is required. This is installed on Windows Server 2003, but on Windows Server 2008 R2, you add it as a "Feature" under Server Manager.

RECOMMENDATIONS

The following tuning tips should be used for production environments. If you are running a small proof of concept, you can safely ignore these optimizations.

Windows Server 2008 (64 bit) will give you the best performance. System cache allocations on Windows Server 2008 64 bit are far higher, and consequently your access to the vDisk is quicker.

If you can't use 64-bit Windows Server 2008 or Windows Server 2008 R2 in your organization, then disable Physical Address Extensions for your provisioning server. For Windows Server 2003 SP2 32 bit, use /NOPAE switch in your boot.ini file (NOPAE – No Physical Address Extensions). For Windows Server 2008 32 bit, run the bcdedit utility from the command line:

```
bcdedit /set nx AlwaysOff
bcdedit /set pae ForceDisable
```

For Windows Server 2003, setting performance to be optimized for system cache will improve performance. Windows Server 2003 LargeSystemCache:

Start | Settings | Control Panel | System | Advanced | Performance Section | Settings Advanced | Memory Usage | Select System Cache (see Figure 6.3).

Transmission Control Protocol (TCP) offloading has a detrimental effect on performance. This is a function that moves some tasks from the processor to the network card. The recommended setting is:

```
HKEY_LOCAL_MACHINE\SYSTEM\CurrentControlSet\Services\TCPIP\Parameters\
Key: "DisableTaskOffload" (dword)
Value: "1"
```

Another network optimization is to disable Large Send Offload, for best performance set:

```
HKEY_LOCAL_MACHINE\SYSTEM\CurrentControlSet\Services\BNNS\Parameters\
DWORD = EnableOffload
Value "0"
```

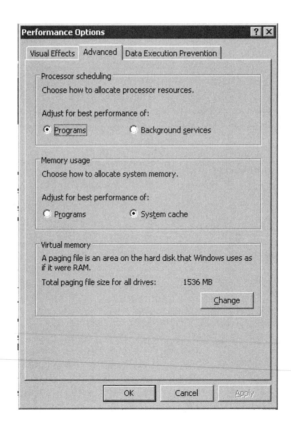

FIGURE 6.3

Setting memory usage to system cache.

On your switches, disable the Spanning Tree Protocol (STP) and enable PortFast. PortFast is the Cisco term, but other vendors have the equivalent functionality.

Teaming your network cards in a provisioning server will also improve your network throughput. For performance, I recommend enabling both HA (High Availability) and load balancing in the NIC (Network Interface Card) teaming settings.

DHCP CONFIGURATION

Citrix Provisioning Server is best used with a Dynamic Host Configuration Protocol (DHCP) server. Although it is entirely possible to use it without DHCP, it does, however, make the solution more complex to manage. Each guest virtual desktop will require an individual IP address and this can be achieved by assigning each machine an IP address out of a pool using DHCP, or a unique boot .ISO file would have to be mounted to each virtual desktop. Each boot .ISO file would have a different IP address, but point to the same Trivial File Transfer Protocol (TFTP) server to mount the virtual disk (vDisk). Clearly having different boot .ISO files for each virtual desktop is an onerous administrative task, and, moreover, it makes it very difficult to change IP ranges of the guests.

> **NOTE**
>
> DHCP can be used with or without PXE (Preboot Execution Environment). A generic .ISO image can be used to define the location of the boot file if used in conjunction with DHCP. Building a boot .ISO is discussed in Chapter 8, "Additional Provisioning Server Configuration Settings."

There are two options for using DHCP: (1) a DHCP server[B] on a separate server is supported or (2) Microsoft DHCP can be installed on the Citrix Provisioning Server. For the sake of simplicity, it is easiest to have it installed on the Citrix Provisioning Server, as the installation wizard will then do the automatic configuration for you. A large number of organizations, however, keep very strict control over DHCP services on their network; in these cases, you will need to integrate into an existing DHCP server.

Create the PXE Scope Options on a Microsoft DHCP Server – Step by Step

Any DHCP server that can support the 66 and 67 scope options can be used. In this example, we will be using a Microsoft DHCP server. These steps are required if the Citrix Provisioning Server and Microsoft DHCP are installed on separate servers.

1. Select the DHCP server, and click **Action** (Windows Server 2003) (see Figure 6.4).

   For Windows Server 2008, right-click on the **IPv4**, select **Set Predefined Options**… (see Figure 6.5).

2. Set Predefined Options (Windows Server 2003) (see Figure 6.6).

   The remaining steps are identical for both Windows Server 2003 and 2008.

[B]Various types of DHCP servers are supported, including Tellurian and Microsoft DHCP.

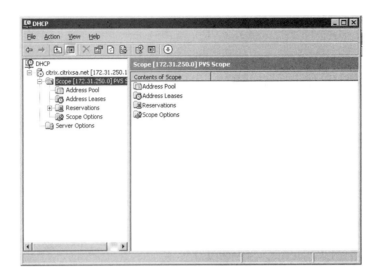

FIGURE 6.4

DHCP on Windows Server 2003.

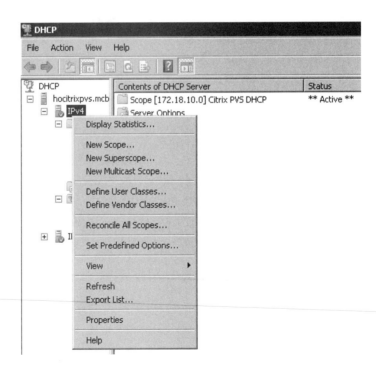

FIGURE 6.5

DHCP on Windows Server 2008.

FIGURE 6.6

DHCP options on Windows 2008.

3. Click **Add**… (see Figure 6.7).
4. Enter **Boot Server Host Name**, change the Data Type to **String**, set Code as **66**, and enter a Description as **TFTP boot server host name**. Click **OK** (see Figure 6.8).
5. And click **Add**… again.
6. Enter **Bootfile Name**, change the Data Type to **String**, set Code as **67**, and enter a Description as **Bootfile Name**. Click **OK** (see Figure 6.9).

The options have now been added to DHCP, and now we can configure them.

7. Select your scope, and select **Scope Options**, and right-click.
8. Select **Configure Options** (see Figure 6.10).
9. Scroll down to scope option 66, and select it. Inside String value, add the IP address of the provisioning server, and if you have more than one provisioning server, then delimit the entries with a semicolon – for example: 192.168.0.10;192.168.0.11 (see Figure 6.11).
10. Scroll down to scope option 67, and select it. Inside the String value, enter the text: **ARDBP32.BIN** (see Figure 6.12).

ARDBP32.BIN is the boot file that we are offering on the PXE server.

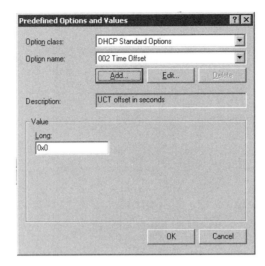

FIGURE 6.7

Predefined options and values.

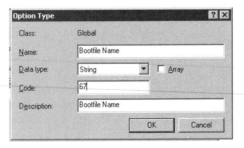

FIGURE 6.8

TFTP option type.

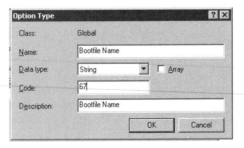

FIGURE 6.9

Bootfile option type.

FIGURE 6.10

Configure scope options.

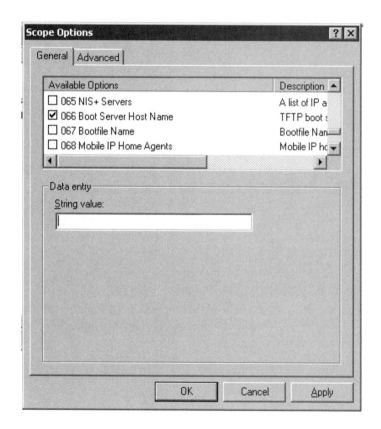

FIGURE 6.11

Scope options – option 66.

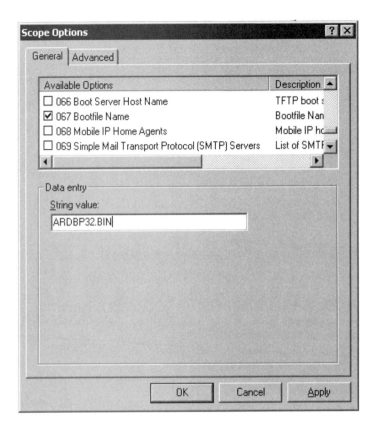

FIGURE 6.12

Scope options – option 67.

INSTALLATION OF PROVISIONING SERVER – STEP BY STEP

Insert Provisioning Server DVD, or mount PVS .ISO if you are using a virtual machine. If autoruns are enabled, you will get the dialog below, otherwise double-click **autorun.exe** on the root of the provisioning server media.

1. Select **Server Installation** (see Figure 6.13).
2. Click **Install Server**[C] (see Figure 6.14).
3. Click **Next** (see Figure 6.15).
4. Toggle the radio button to accept the license agreement, and click **Next** (see Figure 6.16).
5. Enter a User Name and Organization details, and click **Next** (see Figure 6.17).
6. Click **Next** (see Figure 6.18).

[C]The provisioning server will share the same license server that we previously installed for the Desktop Delivery Controller.

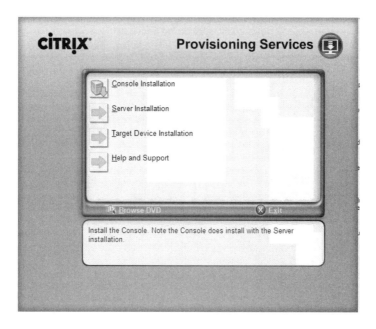

FIGURE 6.13

Provisioning services installation.

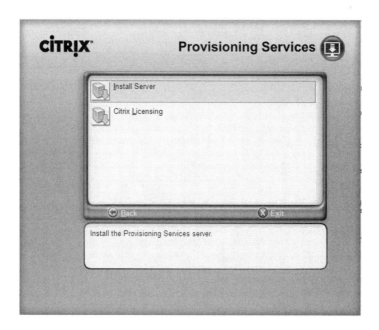

FIGURE 6.14

Server installation.

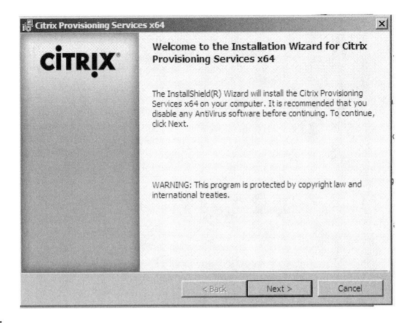

FIGURE 6.15

Provisioning services installation welcome.

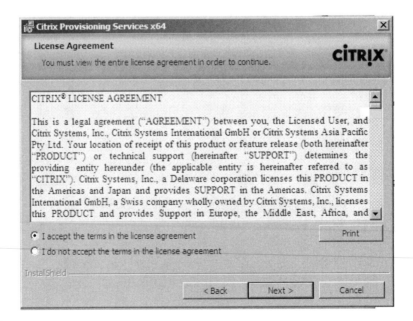

FIGURE 6.16

License agreement.

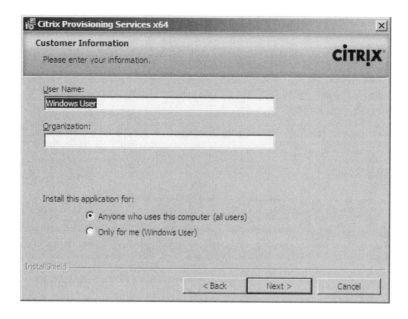

FIGURE 6.17

Customer information.

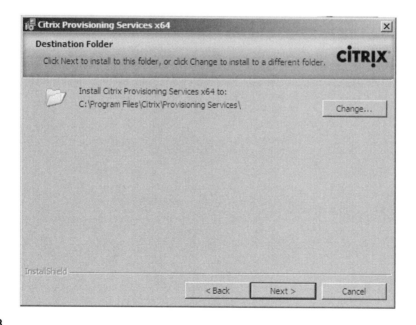

FIGURE 6.18

Destination folder.

You could choose to install your provisioning server on a second logical or physical drive, if you wish to install the operating system and applications on separate drives, click **Change**… and type or browse to the desired location.

 7. Click **Next** (see Figure 6.19).
 8. Click **Install** (see Figure 6.20).
 9. Click **Finish** (see Figure 6.21).

After the installation is complete, the Citrix Provisioning Services Configuration Wizard pops up.

10. Click **Next** (see Figure 6.22).
11. Select the DHCP option that you have chosen (see Figure 6.23 or 6.24).

NOTE

If you want to use locally installed DHCP for a simple proof of concept, you must have installed DHCP before running the configuration wizard, otherwise it won't automatically add the scope options for you.

---

12. Click **Next** (see Figure 6.25).
13. Select **Create farm** for the first Citrix Provisioning Server, join existing farm for subsequent installations, and click **Next** (see Figure 6.26).

Local SQLExpress (see Figure 6.27).
Dedicated SQL Server (see Figure 6.28).

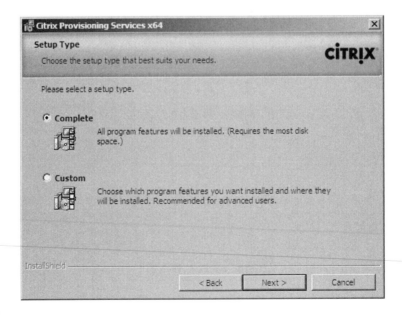

FIGURE 6.19

Setup type.

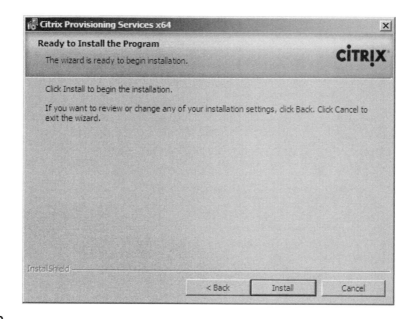

FIGURE 6.20

Ready to install.

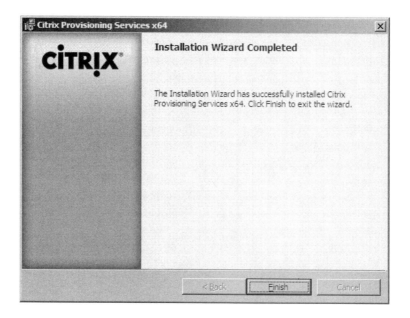

FIGURE 6.21

Successful installation.

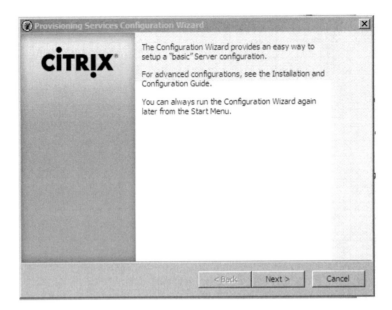

FIGURE 6.22

Provisioning Services Configuration Wizard.

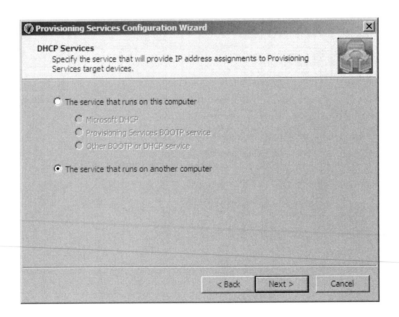

FIGURE 6.23

DHCP services – on another computer.

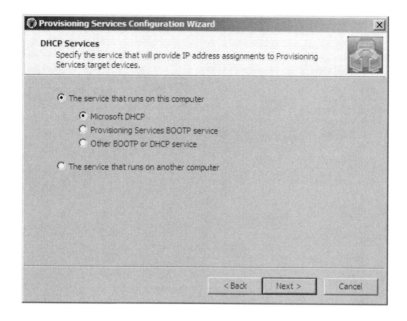

FIGURE 6.24

DHCP services – on this computer.

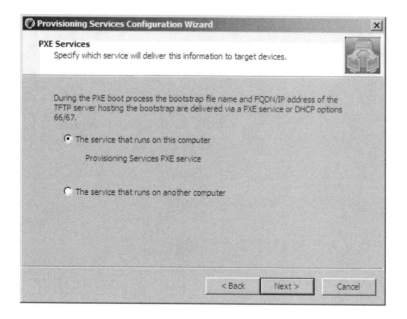

FIGURE 6.25

PXE services.

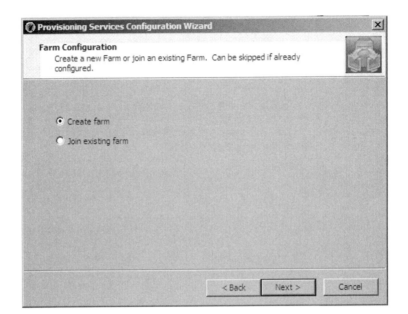

FIGURE 6.26

Farm configuration.

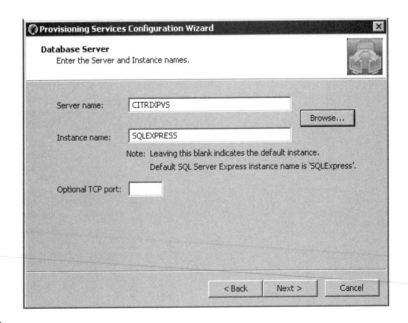

FIGURE 6.27

Database server – SQLExpress.

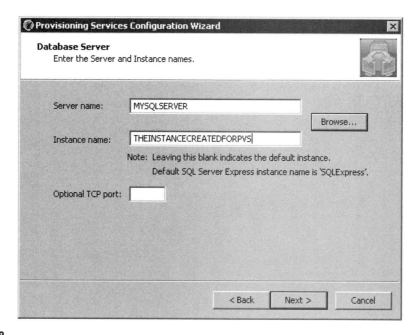

FIGURE 6.28

Database server – SQL Server.

14. For a simple proof of concept, enter your hostname, and "SQLEXPRESS" in the Instance field (Figure 6.27), and for pilot or production systems, connect to a database instance that you have created for this purpose (Figure 6.28).

The way in which we create a back-end configuration database is analogous to the database that we create for the Desktop Delivery Controller.

> **NOTE**
>
> Each Citrix component requires a separate database, first one for XenDesktop Desktop Delivery Controller, second for Citrix Provisioning Server, and a third for Citrix XenApp for Application provisioning. It can be the same database server, but there must be three different databases on the server.

15. Change the farm name to something specific to your environment. If you have more than one site or plan to use more than one site in the future, then enter a locale-specific name. You can use multiple sites for multiple physical locations, and also for high availability[D] or disaster recovery locations (see Figure 6.29).

[D]Citrix Provisioning Server has sophisticated high availability capabilities.

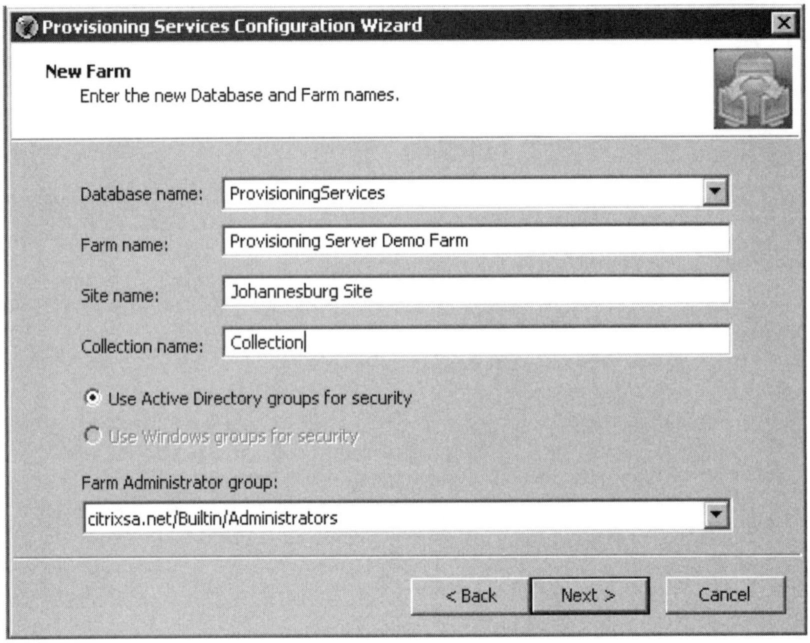

FIGURE 6.29

New farm.

16. Change the license server to point at the Citrix License Server you installed in Chapter 2, "Installation of the Broker – Desktop Delivery Controller," then click **Next** (see Figure 6.30).

Although it is possible to run the licensing locally on the Citrix Provisioning Server, it is recommended that the licensing is run separately. The Citrix Licensing Server provides licenses for all the XenDesktop components. This makes sense in the context of redundancy of all of the components including having multiple Citrix Provisioning Servers.

17. Select the appropriate user account. If in doubt, leave it at the default – **Network service account**, and select the check box **Configure the database for the account** (see Figure 6.31).

A "Specified user account" would be used if the virtual disks are being accessed from a network share. This is typically the case in a multiple Server Provisioning Server environment. Multiple provisioning servers can be used for load balancing and high availability. If using this option, also check **Configure the database for this account**.

The option "Local System Account" is as per the comment for use with a SAN – if your hard drive in the provisioning server is actually mounted from a SAN.

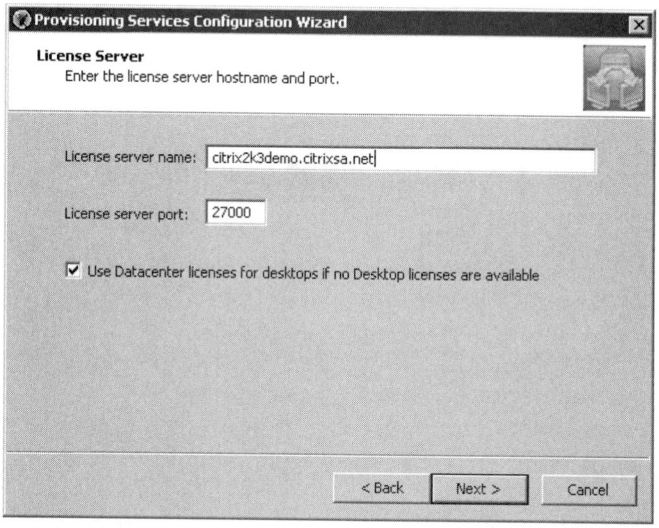

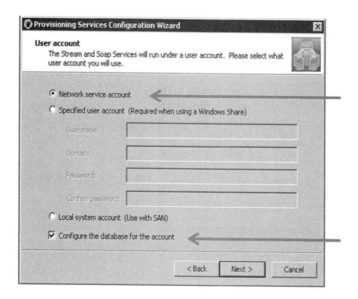

FIGURE 6.30

License server.

FIGURE 6.31

User account.

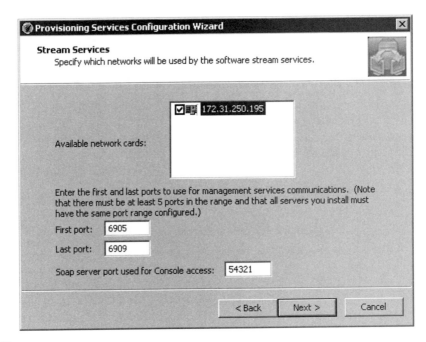

FIGURE 6.32

Stream services.

18. Select the network card that provisioning server will use (see Figure 6.32).

It is possible to configure servers with multiple network cards. Changing your IP address would require that the configuration wizard be run again.

19. Select the check box (by default it is cleared) – **Use the Provisioning Services TFTP service** (see Figure 6.33).

TFTP – Trivial File Transfer Protocol is a UDP-based (User Datagram Protocol) file-transfer mechanism. TFTP is used to download the boot file – ARDP32.BIN – to the virtual desktop.

20. Click **Next** (see Figure 6.34).

In a multiple provisioning server environment, the dialog box above gives the ability to configure multiple PXE boot servers. Simply click the **Add** button to configure multiple servers in your provisioning server farm with the PXE capability.

21. Click **Finish** (see Figure 6.35).

If your Windows Firewall is enabled, the installation dialog box may prompt you to either disable it, or open the relevant ports. See the Appendix for Citrix Communication Ports.

22. Click **Done** (see Figure 6.36).

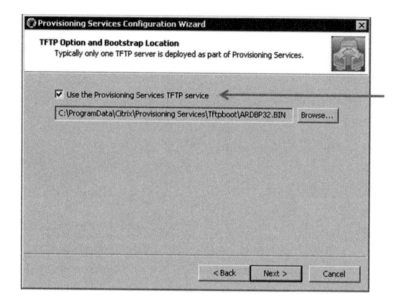

FIGURE 6.33

TFTP option and bootstrap location.

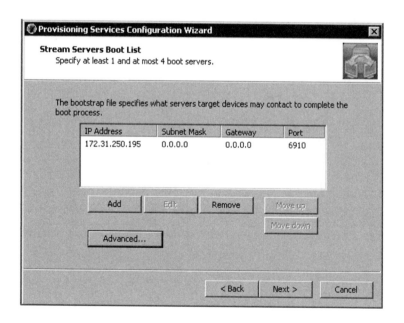

FIGURE 6.34

Stream servers boot list.

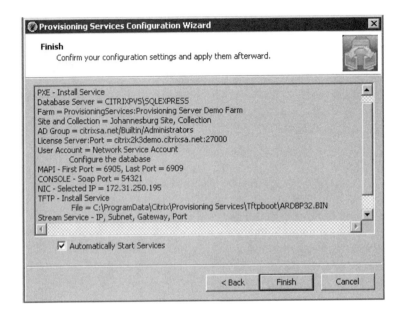

FIGURE 6.35

Confirm your configuration settings.

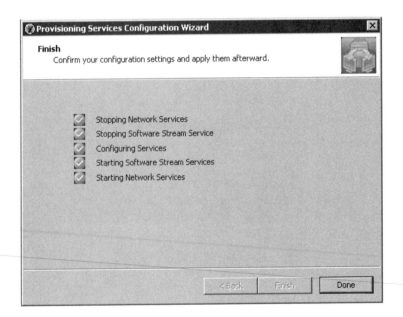

FIGURE 6.36

Successful installation.

SUMMARY

This chapter discussed a basic introduction into how Citrix Provisioning Server functions. We then covered the software and hardware prerequisites. The Citrix Provisioning Server has fairly high resource requirements, so tuning recommendations were then addressed to achieve best performance. It is simplest to use DHCP to deliver the provisioning server settings to the virtual desktop; we discussed the DHCP configuration for a basic implementation. This chapter then explained in detail how to perform an installation of Citrix Provisioning Server.

Fundamental Configuration of the Citrix Provisioning Server

INFORMATION IN THIS CHAPTER

- The vDisk Store
- The vDisk
- Create a Base Target Device

This chapter introduces you to the fundamentals of using Provisioning Server in a XenDesktop environment.

The primary tool used to manage provisioning server is the Provisioning Services Console. The Provisioning Services Console (see Figure 7.1) allows us to manage how we provision virtual disks (vDisks) to workstations (Target Devices).

The **Sites** node (see Figure 7.2) allows us to configure:

Servers	Configure the provisioning servers in the farm.
vDisk Pool	These are bootable vDisks that we assign to machines. We can configure various aspects of how the vDisk functions.
Device Collections	Group our Target Devices so we can assign vDisks to these groups. The Target Devices are defined by their MAC addresses.
User Groups	Granular permission assignment.
Views	Customized views for groups.

The **Stores** node is used to configure the storage locations for the vDisks. It is important that all the provisioning servers in a farm can access the same vDisks to enable fail over and load balancing of the vDisks among provisioning servers in the farm.

The next three sections will deal with creating the vDisk Store, then creating a vDisk in the Store, and finally with assigning the vDisk to a Target Device.

THE VDISK STORE

The first step required, before we can provision vDisks, is to create a storage location to store the vDisks and write cache.

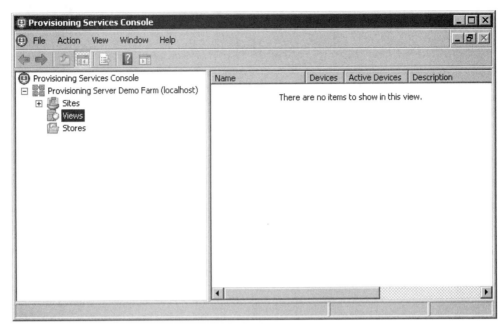

FIGURE 7.1

Provisioning Services Console.

FIGURE 7.2

Sites node.

Design Decisions – vDisk and Write Cache Placement

The vDisk component is always mounted through the provisioning server, which can store the vDisk in one of two places: on a local hard disk or on shared storage[A] (see Figure 7.3).

[A]Shared storage referred to in this section could be Fiber Channel Storage Area Network or iSCSI.

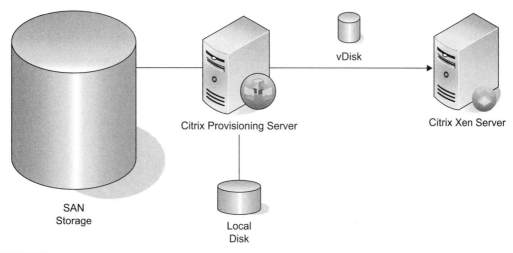

FIGURE 7.3

vDisk storage options.

Using a distributed or clustered file system, multiple provisioning servers can attach to the same shared storage. Shared storage is, however, not a requirement for high availability. In a design using multiple provisioning servers, you can also simply copy the vDisk onto local storage on all the provisioning servers; because the vDisk is read only, this does not affect the ability to fail over. Deciding factors between the two would be the number of provisioning servers and the number of vDisks, and at a certain point, it would become desirable to maintain vDisks in one location.

vDisk Recommendation

Local storage is recommended for smaller implementations, larger Enterprise implementations can equally use local storage or Storage Area Network (SAN) attached storage. SAN storage may, however, be useful in larger environments where the benefits around the replication of the vDisks outweigh the costs.

> **NOTE**
>
> Never place a vDisk on a Common Internet File System (CIFS) share (standard Windows share). Microsoft Windows will not cache data reads from a share to memory. A local disk or SAN-attached disk will cache to memory, resulting in requests from multiple virtual desktops to the vDisk being read from memory. Memory access will always be faster than disk.

The vDisk is attached from the provisioning server, the write cache could also be stored on the provisioning server or a Network share, or the write cache could be mounted directly at the hypervisor layer (see Figure 7.4).

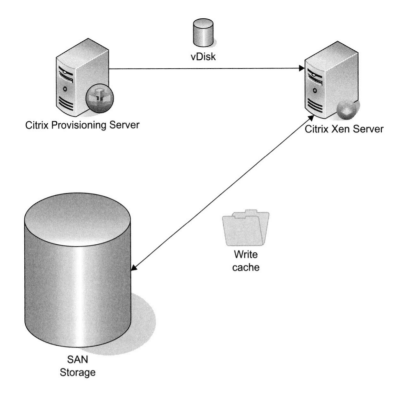

FIGURE 7.4

Write cache placement.

The locations for write cache include[B] the following:

- **Via the provisioning server** – on the provisioning server local hard drive, or on shared storage attached to the provisioning server.
- **At the hypervisor layer** – on the local hard drive of the hypervisor (XenServer, vSphere/ESX or Hyper-V) or on shared storage (SAN/iSCSI) attached to the hypervisor layer.

Via the provisioning server is a simple solution, but it doesn't give the best performance. Caching to the local provisioning server hard disk is the simplest option, and as such useful for proof of concept implementations.

Write cache mounted at the hypervisor level will give the best performance. Write cache is used for all write operations and having this mounted locally will improve disk access speeds. The write cache could be written to local hard disk; however, this would prevent dynamic placement of virtual machines as it is utilizing a local resource, i.e., no XenMotion/VMotion or intelligent VM placement (SCVMM etc.). Shared storage at a hypervisor layer gives good performance and flexibility.

[B]Provisioning server also has a cache to RAM option, but it isn't a good fit for VDI implementations.

There is an additional option of encrypting the write cache. Encryption will have a performance impact. Encryption is not recommended unless explicitly required.

Write Cache Recommendation

Shared storage at the hypervisor layer.

NOTE

Using the write cache disk for more that write cache is not uncommon. The system disk is read only in many designs. The write cache disk is persistent, so it is a good location for things like EdgeSight logs. Other uses can be for applications that update regularly – clearly the applications file will need to be redirected to the "D: Drive." The write cache disk size recommendation of 1 GB would obviously need to be reviewed under these circumstances. User configuration settings are best managed using Virtual Profiles; the write cache disk is not the best place for these types of settings.

TIP

For a proof of concept or pilot environment, it may be sensible to store the write cache on the provisioning server. This serves two purposes: first is that it is simpler, and second is that it allows you to easily and accurately gauge how large all the write cache disks are growing – which is dependent on the applications decisions you may have taken. Should the write cache fill up, it would negatively impact performance.

Create the Store – Step by Step

For the sake of simplicity, this section covers placing the vDisk and the write cache on the local disk of the provisioning server – Target Device shared storage.

It is recommended that the store be on disk with high access speeds. The location could be a SAN-mounted disk. The store could also reside on a network share.

Create a share on a separate drive to host your vDisks. You could, for example, create a P: drive and create a vDisk folder to contain the vDisks, create a second folder called WriteCache.

1. Right-click on the **Stores** node, and select **Create Store** (see Figure 7.5).
2. Enter a name for your store, and select your site from the drop-down box (see Figure 7.6).
3. Select the **Servers** tab – check the box next to your provisioning server(s) (see Figure 7.7).

NOTE

You would specify multiple servers if you wish the vDisk to be highly available.

---

4. Select the **Paths** tab.
5. Enter the path for the vDisk store, and click **Add**... and enter a path for write cache (see Figure 7.8).

In this example, I have placed the vDisk and write cache on the provisioning server. If you are placing the write cache on the Target Devices hard disk, you can leave the default write cache path blank.

FIGURE 7.5

Create store.

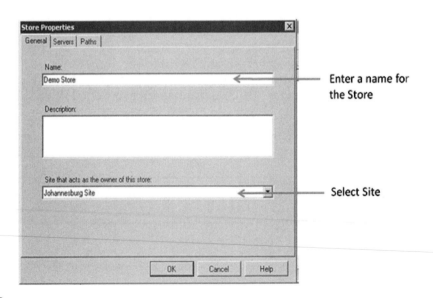

FIGURE 7.6

Store properties – General.

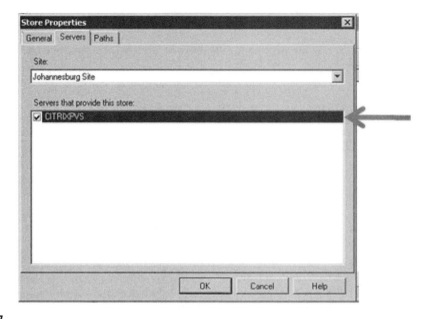

FIGURE 7.7

Store properties – Servers.

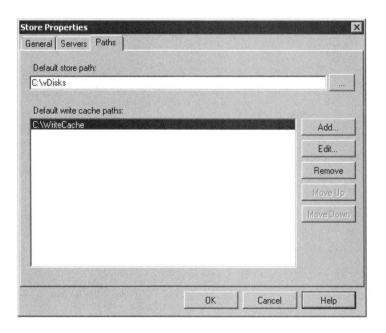

FIGURE 7.8

Store properties – Paths.

THE VDISK

The vDisk is the fundamental element of provisioning server, which could be categorized as a "Virtual Disk" technology.

Design Decisions – vDisk Mode – Private or Standard

Provisioning server has two disk modes for Citrix XenDesktop. The first is Private mode; this is as the name suggests a private individual disk for each and every virtual desktop. The second is Standard mode; a Standard mode vDisk is a shared common disk image for multiple virtual desktops.

The Private mode vDisks are Read/Write disks and the user's settings and changes are saved in the user's individual disk. There is a 1:1 relationship between virtual desktops and vDisks (see Figure 7.9).

So, for example, in the scenario above, 100 vDisks have unique mappings to 100 virtual desktops.

This vDisk architecture is very similar to a normal distributed desktop environment. Over time the virtual desktop builds will drift from a standard build, with uniqueness held in each vDisk.

The storage requirements are an important aspect of virtual desktop infrastructure (VDI). If the vDisks are assumed to be 25 GB in size, then the storage requirements are as follows:

$$25\,GB \times 100 = 2500\,GB = 2500/1024 = 2.44\,TB$$

There are a small number of scenarios where it is desirable for the users' desktops to utilize Private mode vDisks. An example would be for software developers.

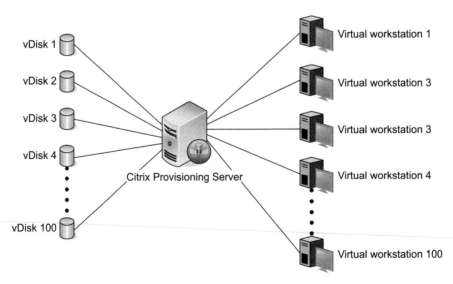

FIGURE 7.9

Utilizing Private mode vDisks.

The Standard mode vDisks are read-only disks and the uniqueness required in the session is stored in a write cache. Write cache is a delta to the base vDisk. The user's settings and changes are saved in the user's Virtual Profile (see Figure 7.10).

So, for example, in the scenario above, 100 virtual desktops share one vDisk, and use a separate write cache for each virtual workstation.

The provisioning server injects required machine uniqueness into the write cache at logon. Details like the computer name are held in the provisioning server database. These required unique machine settings are associated to the MAC address of the virtual desktop.

This vDisk architecture is a complete redesign of the desktop architecture. This approach utilizes multiple virtualization technologies in order to build out the virtual desktop in a completely modular way. Using a combination of virtual applications and Virtual Profiles, the desktop is built on demand. We are thus able to build multiple desktop types from common use component blocks.

Write cache requirements for normal Microsoft Office productivity type users are 300 to 500 MB. If the users use applications that make intensive use of temporary files, like some graphical application, then the requirements can be larger. Additionally if there are local logging requirements – Citrix EdgeSight for Endpoints, then that also should be taken into consideration. For the sake of simplicity, I have specified a 1 GB write cache, which should suffice for most scenarios.

If the vDisks are assumed to be 25 GB in size, and the write cache as 1 GB, then the storage requirements for 100 desktops are as follows:

$$25\,\text{GB} + 1\,\text{GB} \times 100 = 125\,\text{GB}$$

If we compare this to the Private mode vDisk example of 2.44 TB, we see that this is especially important for larger implementations.

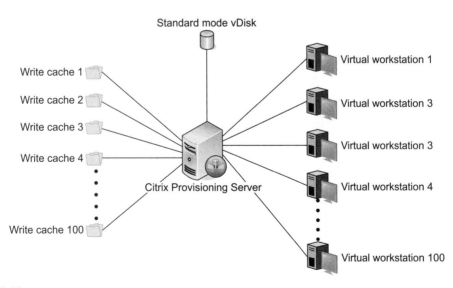

FIGURE 7.10

Utilizing a Standard mode vDisk.

In Chapter 11, "Integrating Virtual Applications into the Virtual Desktop," we discuss Virtual Profiles. Virtual Profiles are used to store user and application settings outside of the virtual desktop.

Recommendations

Standard mode vDisk has two very important advantages over Private vDisk mode. First it greatly reduces the storage requirements for your virtual desktop environment. The second advantage is not as immediately obvious, and that is the single-instance image management. Managing your virtual desktops based on one vDisk means that updates and fixes need only be made to one base image and these are applied across the board.

The task of maintaining a standard desktop build is much simpler when utilizing a Standard vDisk. In some larger environments, there may be requirements for both types of vDisks: Standard mode vDisks catering for most users and a smaller subset of users using Private mode vDisks. Wherever possible use Standard mode vDisks.

Create vDisk – Step by Step

1. Open the Provisioning Services Console – **Start | Programs | Citrix | Provisioning Services | Provisioning Services Console**.
2. The console can be run locally on the provisioning server, or on a remote host. In order to run the console on the provisioning server, leave the default at "localhost." To connect remotely, enter the hostname of the provisioning server. Click **Connect** (see Figure 7.11).

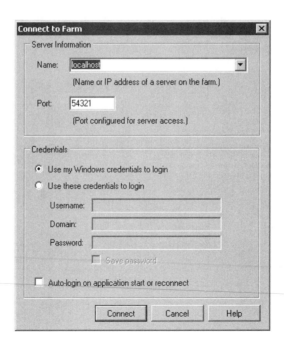

FIGURE 7.11

Connect to farm.

3. Select **Sites | <YOURSITENAME> | vDisk Pool | Create vDisk** (see Figure 7.12).

The VHD format allows you to create either a fixed format or a dynamic format. Fixed allocates the entire space required at creation, whereas a dynamic format disk will only allocate the disk space as required. In a VDI environment, a fixed VHD format is recommended (see Figure 7.13).

4. Enter your filename and a description. Edit the disk size, 15 GB is recommended for Windows XP and 25 GB for Windows 7. Click **Create Disk** (see Figure 7.13).

Your vDisk appears in the right-hand pane once it is created (see Figure 7.14).

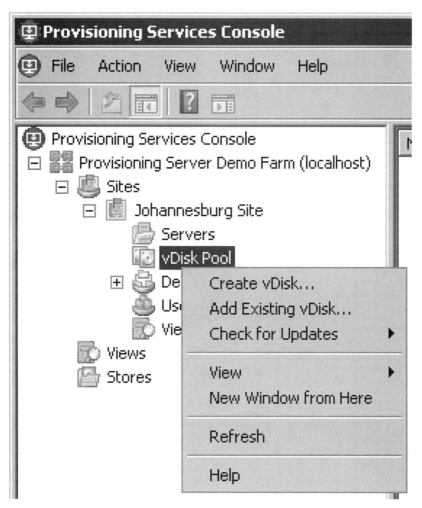

FIGURE 7.12

Create vDisk menu.

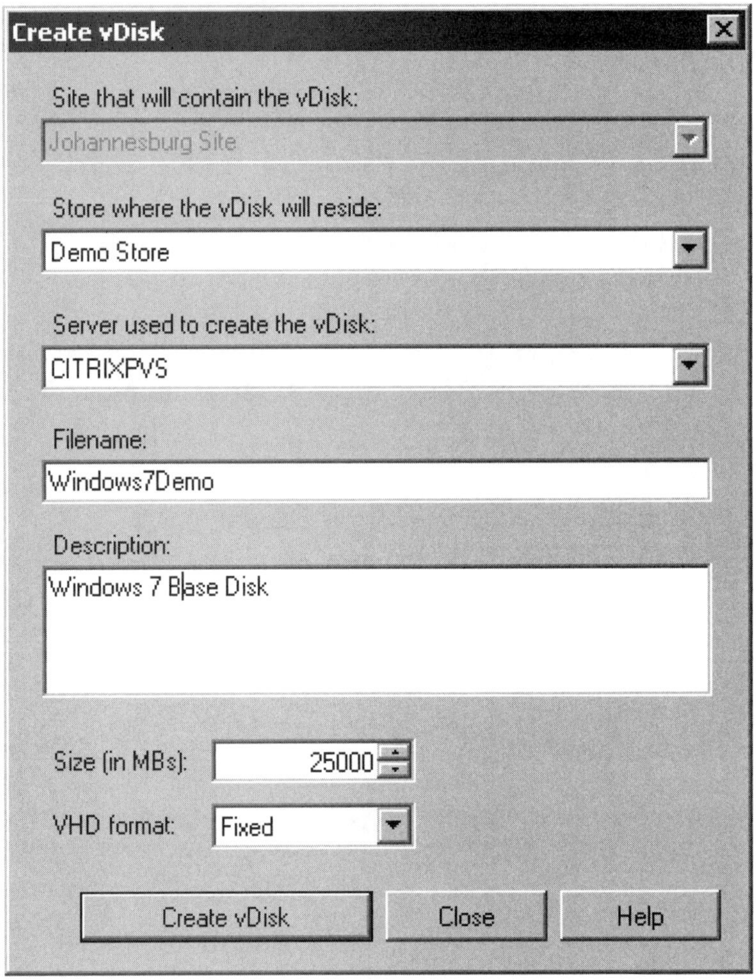

FIGURE 7.13

Create vDisk.

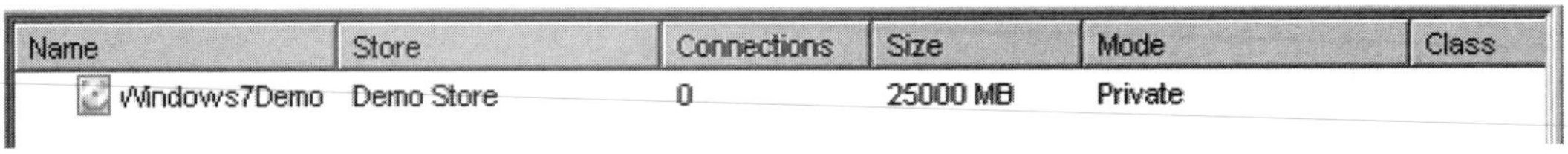

FIGURE 7.14

A vDisk created in the store.

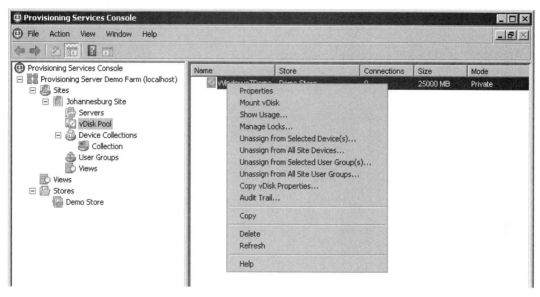

FIGURE 7.15

vDisk menu.

Configure vDisk Settings

Now that the vDisk has been created, how it functions can be configured from within the console.

1. Right-click on the vDisk, and select **Properties** (see Figure 7.15).
2. Load balancing settings can be configured from **General** tab. There are two options: **Use the load balancing algorithm** or **Use this server to provide the vDisk** (see Figure 7.16).

   In an environment with multiple provisioning servers, the load balancing option can be used to share connections to the vDisk between multiple servers. Specifying a server from the drop-down list makes that server the connection point for the vDisk.
3. Click on the **Edit File Properties**....

The **Mode** tab gives you the options to set the disk from Private Image to Standard Image. Whenever building an image, or making changes, the disk must be in Private Image mode, the disk is then switched back to Standard Image mode for regular use (see Figure 7.17).

The **Options** tab enables the high availability, Active Directory machine account password management, and print management features (see Figure 7.18).

High Availability

High availability is a very important setting to enable. If you configure multiple provisioning servers configured with your vDisk, it will automatically fail over to the alternative provisioning server, without any down time on the virtual desktop.

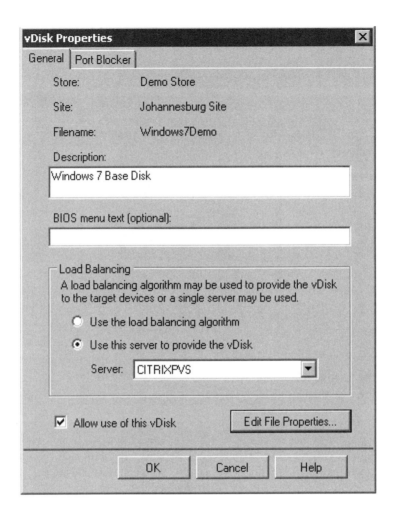

FIGURE 7.16

vDisk properties.

> **TIP**
>
> You can test your high availability by stopping the Streaming Service on one of your provisioning servers. The vDisk should automatically fail over.

Active Directory Integration

Active Directory machine account password management is another important setting for a VDI environment. Simply select the check box and the provisioning server will dynamically associate an Active Directory computer name with the vDisk at boot time. Active Directory integration needs to be configured in two places here, and under the server settings.

FIGURE 7.17

Configure the vDisk mode.

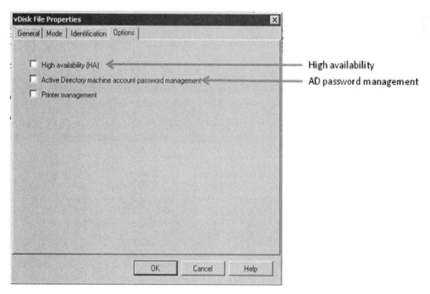

FIGURE 7.18

Configuring high availability and computer account management.

CREATE A BASE TARGET DEVICE

The vDisk needs to be associated with Target Device. In a VDI scenario, this is most commonly a virtual MAC address, which we are associating with a vDisk.

In this section, the base Target Device will be the virtual desktop that you created in Chapter 4, "Installing the Virtual Desktop." What we are now doing is taking that virtual machines disk, and cloning it such that multiple virtual desktops can boot off the disk we have created.

Provisioning Services automatically creates a default Device Collection called "Collection." You as the administrator could create additional Device Collections (see Figure 7.19).

A Device Collection is a group of Target Devices. A Device Collection can contain one or more Target Devices. This is essentially a management unit for multiple Target Devices. I can, for example, assign a vDisk to a Device Collection, and it will assign the vDisk to all the Target Devices in the Device Collection. Clearly being able to manage disk associations as a group rather than individually is important in a XenDesktop environment. One would typically create a Device Collection for a department or group of users to which you assign the same vDisk.

1. The above diagram shows how to create a new Device Collection. Right-click on the **Device Collections** node, and select **Create Device Collection** (see Figure 7.19).
2. Enter a name for your Device Collection.

In the following example, a Target Device will be added to the default Device Collection – "Collection."

1. Right-click on the collection, click **Create Device** (see Figure 7.20).
2. Enter a name and the MAC address of the virtual network card (see Figure 7.21).

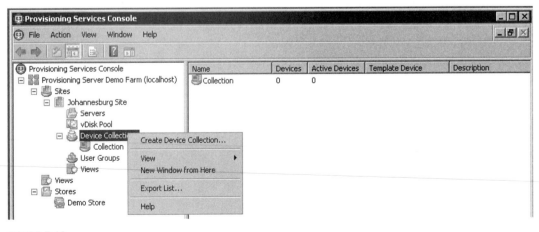

FIGURE 7.19

Device Collection menu.

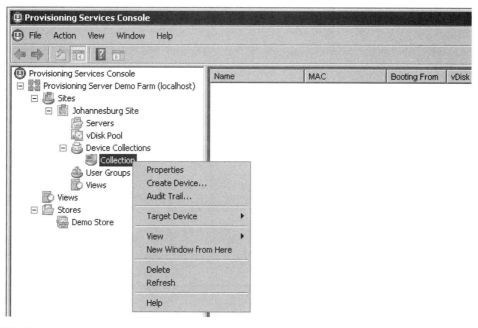

FIGURE 7.20

Collection menu.

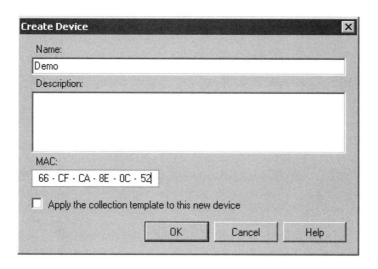

FIGURE 7.21

Create device.

Finding Your Virtual MAC Address

XenServer

1. Select the virtual machine and click on the **Network** tab – the MAC address is listed in the MAC column (see Figure 7.22).

SCVMM

1. Right-click on your virtual machine and **Properties** (see Figure 7.23).
2. Select the **Hardware Configuration** tab, and select **Network Adapter** – The MAC address is in the right-hand pane, under **Ethernet [MAC] address** (see Figure 7.24).

VMware vSphere

1. Open the vSphere Client, select your virtual machine, right-click, and select **Edit Settings…** (see Figure 7.25).
2. Select the **Network adapter** in the left-hand pane. The MAC address of the virtual machine appears in the right-hand pane (see Figure 7.26).

TIP

If the virtual machine is shut down, you can select the MAC address and copy it to the clipboard.

All Hypervisors

Once you have entered the MAC address, click **OK**.

The Target Device is now created (see Figure 7.27).

The "Booting From" is by default set to the vDisk. In the next section, we will change this to "Hard Disk."

FIGURE 7.22

XenCenter.

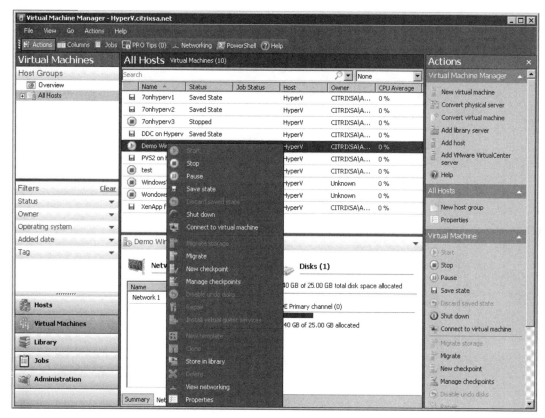

FIGURE 7.23

System Center Virtual Machine Manager.

Active Directory

Right-click on the **Target Device | select Active Directory | Create Machine Account** (see Figure 7.28). This will create a machine account in Active Directory based on the name on the device(s) you have created. You can select multiple devices and create multiple machine accounts (see Figure 7.29).

For the purpose of this initial Target Device creation, you will only need to create one machine account for this initial build machine.

Just for the purpose of example, Figure 7.29 shows the creation of machine accounts for W7demo1 to W7demo5, in the Demo Organizational Unit. The organizational unit can be chosen from the "Organizational unit" drop-down list.

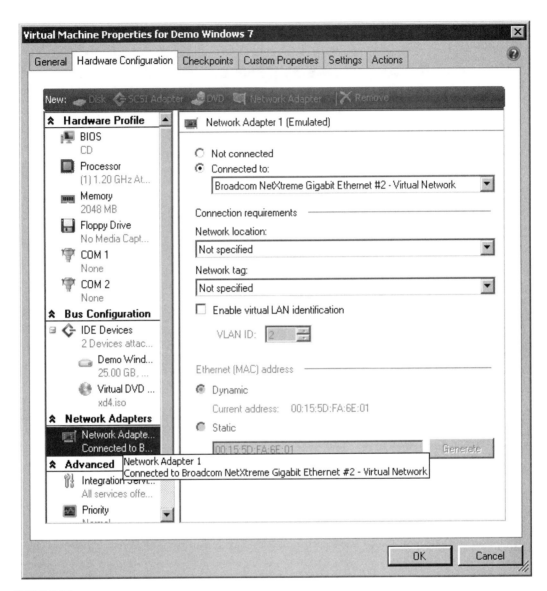

FIGURE 7.24

Virtual machine properties.

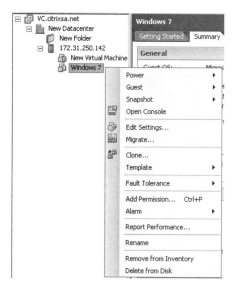

FIGURE 7.25

vCenter – Virtual machine menu.

FIGURE 7.26

Virtual machine properties.

FIGURE 7.27

A Target Device created in a collection.

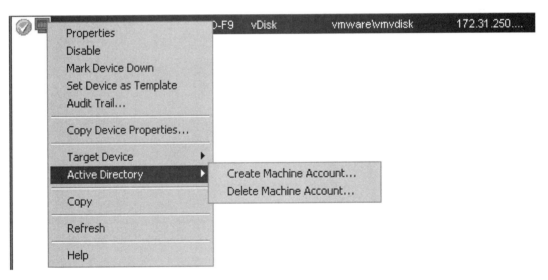

FIGURE 7.28

Computer account creation for a Target Device.

> **TIP**
>
> The **Reset Machine Account Password**... option (see Figure 7.30) can be used on powered off Target Devices if you are experiencing issues with the computer accounts. Multiple accounts can be selected and reset simultaneously.

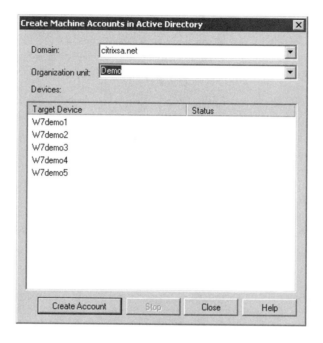

FIGURE 7.29

Creating multiple computer accounts.

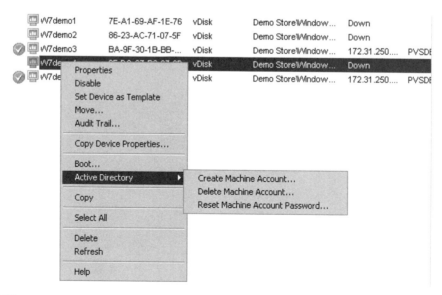

FIGURE 7.30

Target Device Active Directory actions.

Assign a vDisk to the Base Target Device

The vDisk is at present blank, and as such we need to boot the virtual machine from the existing hard drive, such that we can copy the existing hard drive contents to the vDisk.

1. Right-click on the vDisk, and select **Properties**.
2. Change the Boot from option to "Hard Disk" – as shown in Figure 7.31.

In order to attach the vDisk to the existing virtual machine running on the hypervisor, the boot order of the virtual machine needs to be changed to boot from the network.

XenServer

1. From the XenCenter Console, right-click and select **Properties** (see Figure 7.32).
2. Select **Startup Options** (see Figure 7.33).
3. Select **Network** in the right-hand pane, and "Move Up" to the top of the list, and then click **OK**.
4. Reboot the virtual machine.

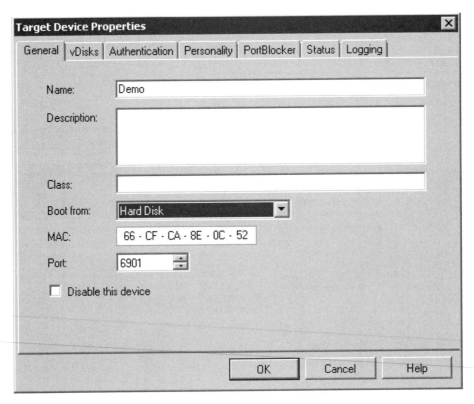

FIGURE 7.31

Target Device properties.

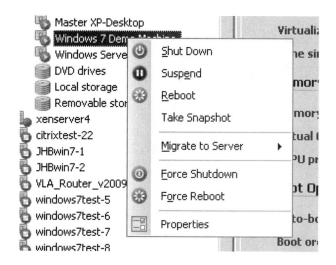

FIGURE 7.32

Virtual machine menu.

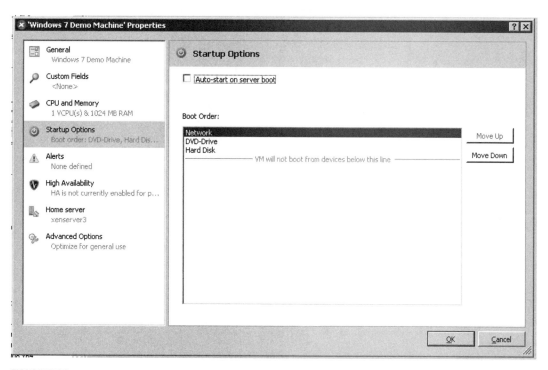

FIGURE 7.33

Startup options.

SCVMM
1. Right-click on your virtual machine, select **Properties** (see Figure 7.34).
2. Select the **Hardware Configuration** tab in the left-hand pane, select **BIOS**, and use the **UP** button to move PXE Boot to the top (see Figure 7.35).
3. Reboot the virtual machine.

VMware
1. Open the vSphere Client, select the virtual machine in the left-hand pane, and click **Edit virtual machine settings** in the right-hand pane (see Figure 7.36).
2. Select the **Options** tab, select **Boot Options**, and then select the **Force BIOS Setup** check box (see Figure 7.37).
3. Boot the virtual machine.

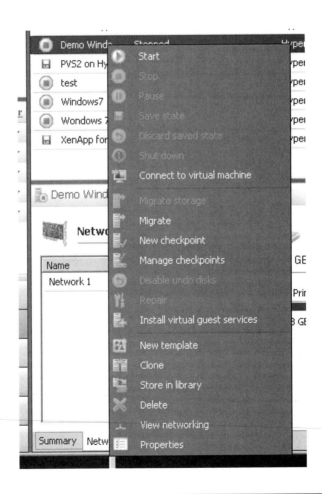

FIGURE 7.34

Virtual machine menu.

FIGURE 7.35

Hardware configuration – BIOS.

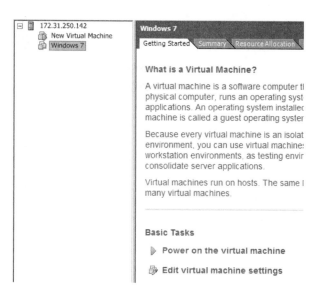

FIGURE 7.36

Virtual machine settings.

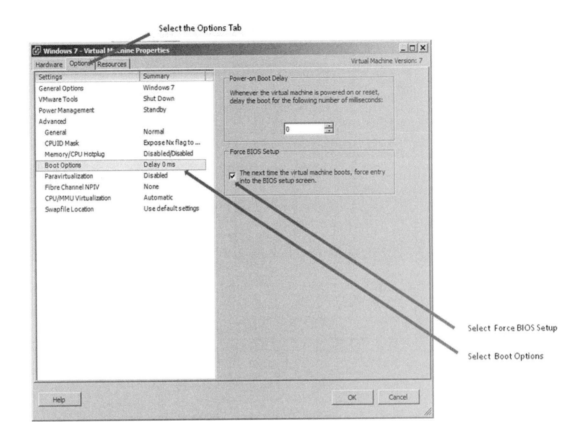

FIGURE 7.37

Virtual machine properties.

4. Use the arrow keys to tab to the Boot menu. Use the arrow keys to select the network card, and use the **+** key to move the network card to the top of the list. Use **F10** to Save and Exit (see Figure 7.38).
5. Hit **Enter** or move to highlight **Yes** to confirm (see Figure 7.39).

All Hypervisors

The boot screen of your virtual machine should show the network card attaching to the PXE boot server and downloading the ardbp32.bin file (see Figure 7.40).

Common Errors

No Entry found in database for device	The MAC address entry on the provisioning server doesn't match the virtual machine
Invalid Boot Sector	The virtual machine is trying to boot from a blank vDisk, change the boot selection on the provisioning server to "Hard Disk"

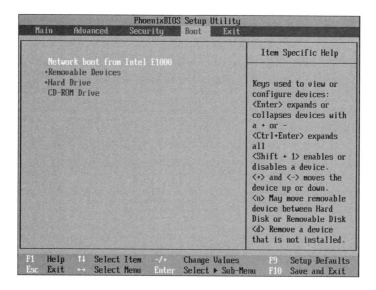

FIGURE 7.38

BIOS menu.

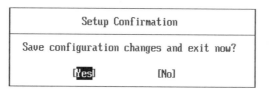

FIGURE 7.39

Setup confirmation.

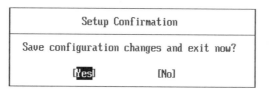

FIGURE 7.40

Downloading the boot file through TFTP.

Install the Target Device Software – Step by Step

In order to copy the hard disk of your virtual machine to the provisioning server vDisk, the provisioning server Target Device client must be installed on the virtual desktop.

1. Mount the provisioning server DVD (or ISO) to your virtual desktop. If it doesn't autorun, launch the autorun from the DVD.
2. Click **Target Device Installation** (see Figure 7.41).
3. Select **Target Device Installation** (see Figure 7.42).
4. Click **Install** (see Figure 7.43).
5. Click **Next** (see Figure 7.44).
6. Toggle the radio button to accept the license agreement, and click **Next** (see Figure 7.45).
7. Enter a user name and organization details, click **Next** (see Figure 7.46).
8. Click **Next** (see Figure 7.47).

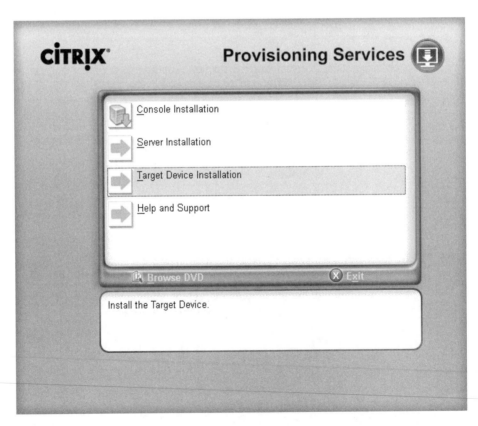

FIGURE 7.41

Provisioning services installation.

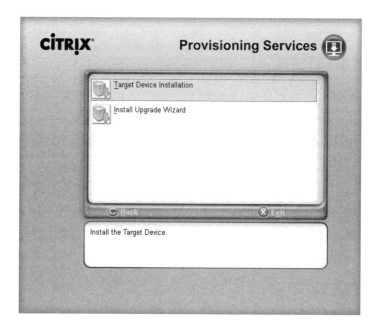

FIGURE 7.42

Target Device installation.

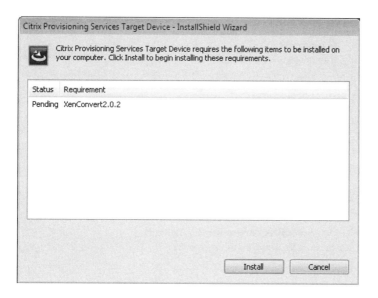

FIGURE 7.43

Target Device installation requirement.

FIGURE 7.44

Installation welcome.

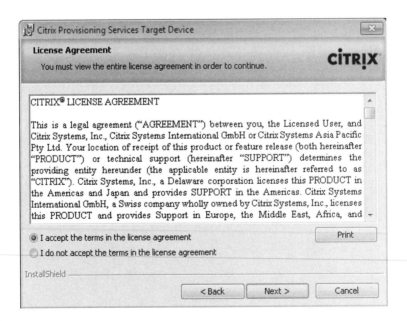

FIGURE 7.45

License agreement.

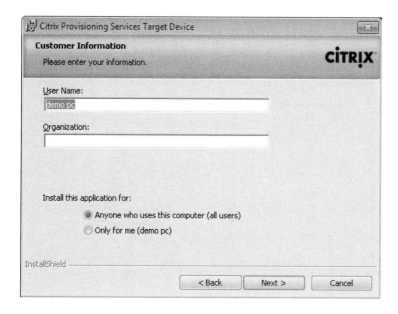

FIGURE 7.46

Customer information.

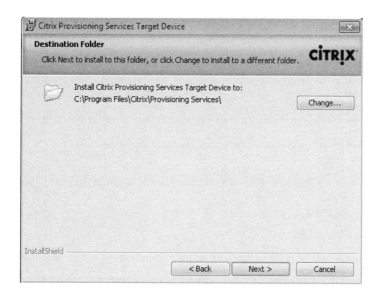

FIGURE 7.47

Destination folder.

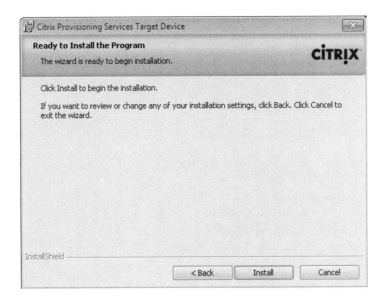

FIGURE 7.48

Ready to install.

9. Click **Install** (see Figure 7.48).
10. Click **Finish** (see Figure 7.49).

If the virtual desktop is being presented with more than one Network Interface by the hypervisor, you will need to deselect the adapter marked inactive, and then click **OK** (see Figure 7.50).

HYPER-V

If you created two network adaptors, one synthetic and one legacy, select the adaptor marked as (Emulated) for the provisioning server to bind to. If you want to execute this utility manually, it can be found on the virtual desktop under C:\Program Files\Citrix\Provisioning Services\BindCfg.exe.

---

11. Click **Format disk** (see Figure 7.51).
12. Click **Start** (see Figure 7.52).

The disk you are now formatting is the vDisk that has been mounted to your virtual desktop through the network card.

13. Click **OK** (see Figure 7.53).
14. Click **OK** (see Figure 7.54).

Your vDisk should now appear in the bottom right-hand corner in the task bar (see Figure 7.55).

TIP

Windows 7 hides these icons by default, change the Notification Area to "Show icon and notifications" for vDisk status.

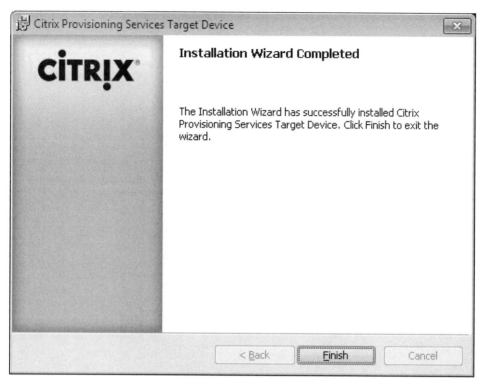

FIGURE 7.49

Installation wizard completed.

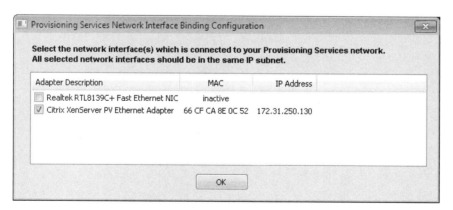

FIGURE 7.50

Selecting the Network Interface for use by provisioning server.

FIGURE 7.51

Format disk.

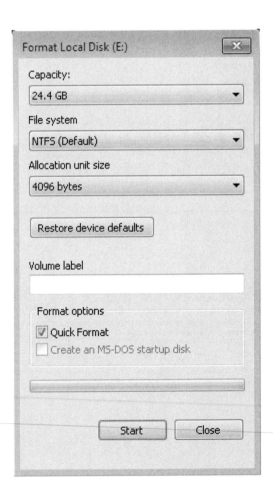

FIGURE 7.52

Format local disk.

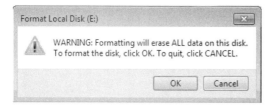

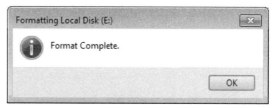

FIGURE 7.53

Format local disk – warning.

FIGURE 7.54

Format local disk – completed.

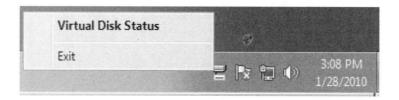

FIGURE 7.55

vDisk taskbar icon.

The vDisk status shows the provisioning server that the virtual desktop is connecting to and the mode the disk is currently in. The **Statistics** tab shows information about the read/write to the vDisk (see Figure 7.56).

Copy the Target Device Hard Drive to the vDisk – Step by Step

1. Click **Start | All Programs | Citrix**.
2. Select **XenConvert | XenConvert 2.0** (see Figure 7.57).
3. Click **Next** (see Figure 7.58).
4. Click **Optimize** (see Figure 7.59).

This will clean up and tweak the build before we copy it to the vDisk. The optimizations shown in Figure 7.60 are the best practice settings for a virtual desktop.

> **TIP**
>
> Some organizations use two logical drives as part of their standard build – OS and Applications, for example. You can choose to include or exclude the extra volumes.

5. Click **OK**.
6. Then click **Next**.
7. Click **Convert** (see Figure 7.61).
8. Click **Yes** (see Figure 7.62).
9. Click **Finish** (see Figure 7.63).

The **Log** button is a shortcut to the installation log file. This is useful when troubleshooting.

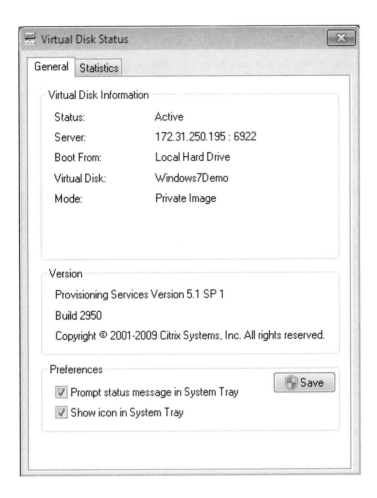

FIGURE 7.56

vDisk status dialog box.

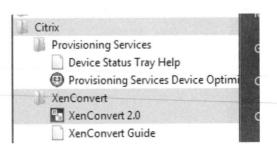

FIGURE 7.57

XenConvert menu item.

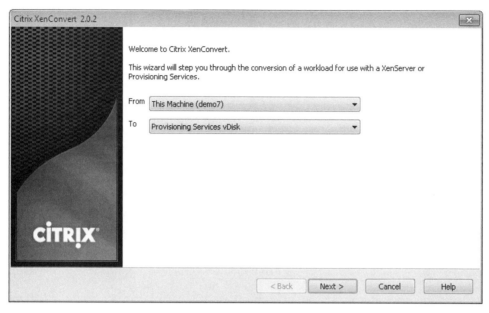

FIGURE 7.58

XenConvert workload type.

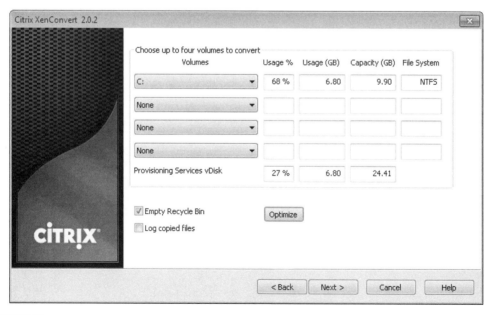

FIGURE 7.59

XenConvert – choose volumes.

FIGURE 7.60

Provisioning services device optimization tool.

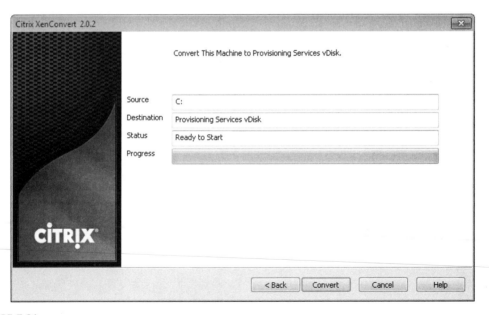

FIGURE 7.61

XenConvert – convert.

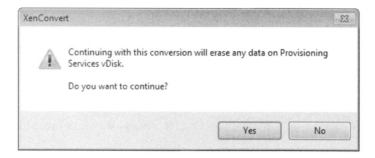

FIGURE 7.62

XenConvert – erase warning.

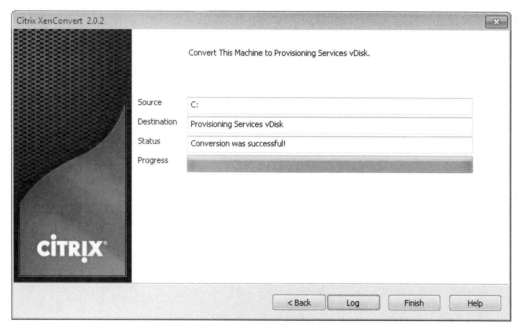

FIGURE 7.63

Conversion was successful.

10. Now that the disk has been duplicated to the vDisk, shutdown the Base Target Virtual Desktop. The Base machine currently has exclusive access to the vDisk as it is in "Private Mode."

> **TIP**
> Remember to set the "Idle Pool" to zero, or the Desktop Delivery Controller will keep restarting the virtual desktop.

Remove Locks on the vDisk

The mode of a vDisk can only be changed when there are no locks on the vDisk. A lock is registered by the provisioning server to indicate that the vDisk is in use. A clean shutdown of a virtual desktop mapped to a private mode vDisk will automatically remove the locks.

If a vDisk is in use, a padlock icon is displayed next to the vDisk (see Figure 7.64).

Removing Locks

If a virtual machine hasn't shut down gracefully, or is showing locks erroneously, they can be manually removed.

1. Right-click on the vDisk and select **Manage Locks...** (see Figure 7.65).
2. Click **Yes** (see Figure 7.66).
3. Click **Remove Locks** (see Figure 7.67).
4. Click **Close**.

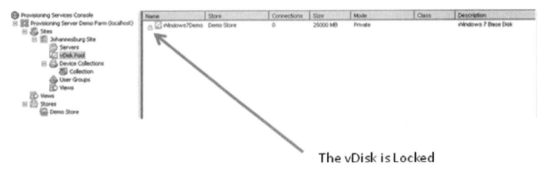

FIGURE 7.64

Locked vDisk.

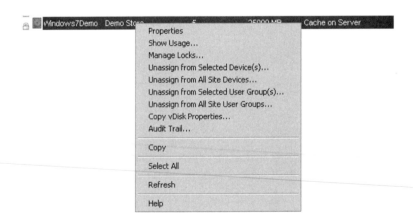

FIGURE 7.65

vDisk options menu.

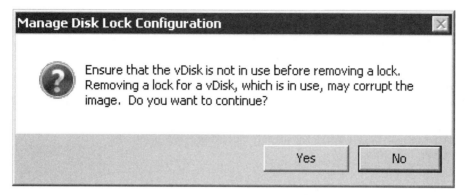

FIGURE 7.66

Manage disk lock configuration.

FIGURE 7.67

vDisk locks.

Mount the vDisk to a Test Virtual Desktop

In this section, we will mount the vDisk to new diskless virtual machines.

Open the Management Console for your hypervisor:

XenServer

The easiest way to create a second machine with the same settings as your base Target Device is to clone the base Target Device.

1. Right-click on the base Target Device and select **Copy VM** (see Figure 7.68).
2. Click **Copy** (see Figure 7.69).

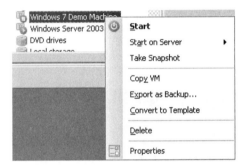

FIGURE 7.68

Virtual machine menu options.

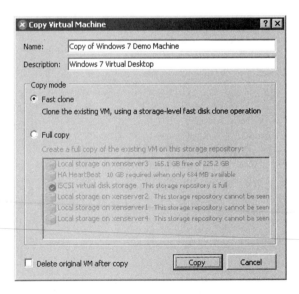

FIGURE 7.69

Copy virtual machine.

FIGURE 7.70

Virtual machine – Storage.

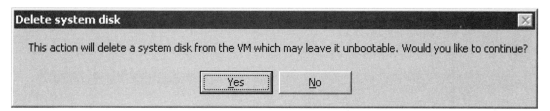

FIGURE 7.71

Delete system disk.

Fast clone is the best option – this is just a pointer to the original hard disk. The **Fast clone** is almost instant.

3. Select the **Storage** tab of the new VM and click **Delete** to delete the disk (see Figure 7.70).
4. Click **Yes** (see Figure 7.71).
5. Select the **Network** tab and copy the MAC address.

> **TIP**
>
> Clicking **Properties** on the **Network** tab, and changing the radio button to Manual, gives you the ability to "cut and paste" the MAC address for later use.

6. Repeat the process to create a second diskless virtual desktop.

SCVMM
1. Open SCVMM.
2. On the right-hand pane – select **New virtual machine** (see Figure 7.72).
3. Change the radio button to **Create the new virtual machine with a blank virtual hard disk** and click **Next** (see Figure 7.73).

Give your VM a name in the virtual machine name field, and click **Next** (see Figure 7.74).

4. Select **BIOS** and move "PXE Boot" to the top (see Figure 7.75).
5. Check the **Network Adapter** – make sure it is "Emulated" and *not* "Synthetic."
6. Select the **Hard Disk** under Bus Configuration, and click **Remove** (see Figure 7.76).

FIGURE 7.72

Virtual machine manager.

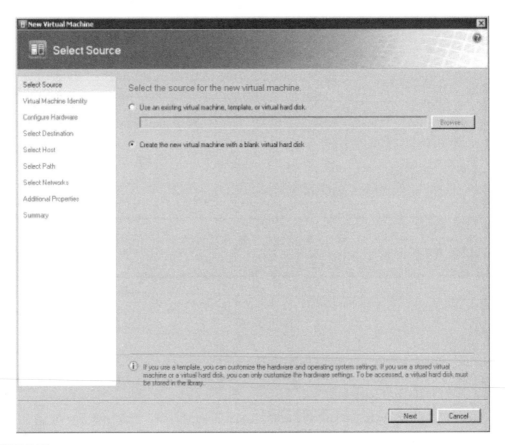

FIGURE 7.73

Select source.

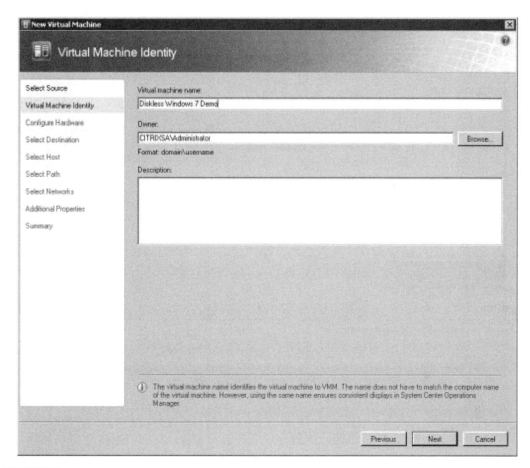

FIGURE 7.74

Virtual machine identity.

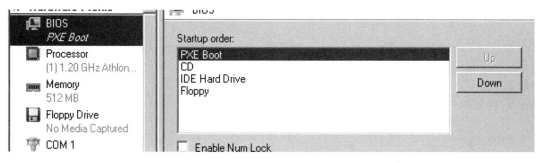

FIGURE 7.75

Configure hardware – BIOS.

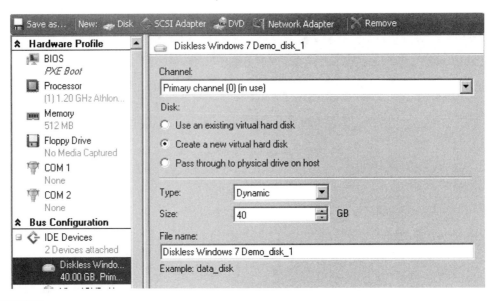

FIGURE 7.76

Configure hardware – bus configuration.

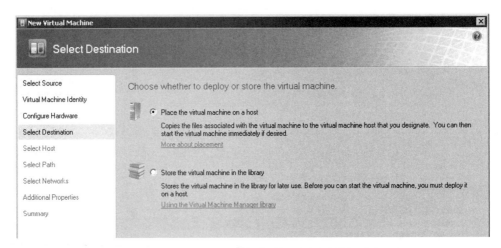

FIGURE 7.77

Select destination.

7. Click **Next**.
8. Click **Next** (see Figure 7.77).
9. Click **Next** (see Figure 7.78).
10. Click **Next** (see Figure 7.79).

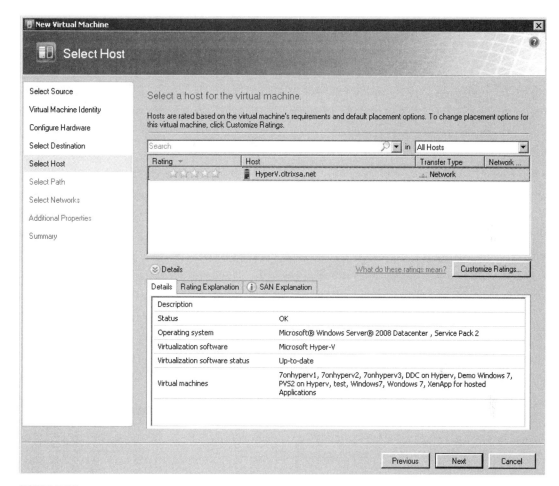

FIGURE 7.78

Select host.

11. Select the network adapter from the drop-down list and click **Next** (see Figure 7.80).

By default no adapter is connected, so this needs to be changed.

12. Click **Next** (see Figure 7.81).
13. Click **Create** (see Figure 7.82).

You will get a warning, which you can ignore (see Figure 7.83).

14. Right-click on your VM and select **Properties | Hardware Configuration | Network Adapter** (see Figure 7.84).
15. Change the **Ethernet (MAC) address** to **Static**, and click **Generate** to generate a MAC address.
16. Click **OK**.

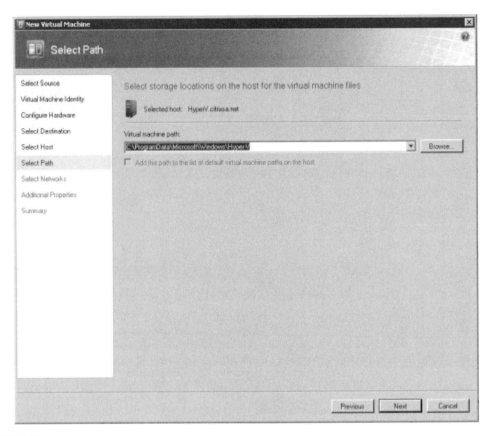

FIGURE 7.79

Select path.

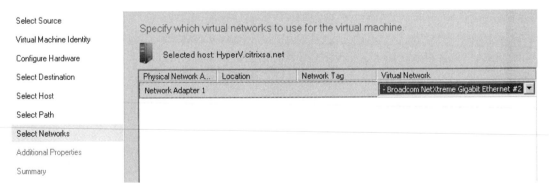

FIGURE 7.80

Select networks.

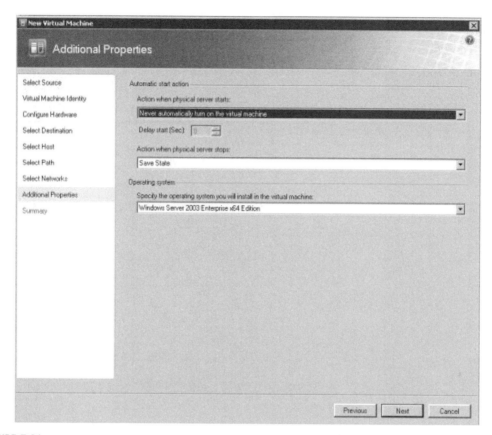

FIGURE 7.81

Additional properties.

TIP

Copy the MAC address to a text file so you can use it later on provisioning server.

---

17. Repeat the process to create a second diskless virtual desktop.

VMware

In order to create a diskless virtual machine on VMware vCenter, follow the same procedure as in Chapter 4, "Installing the Virtual Desktop." Alternatively, you could also right-click on your existing virtual machine, and select Clone to copy the virtual machine.

1. Right-click on the virtual machine, and click **Edit Settings**.
2. Select the **Hard disk**, and click **Remove** (see Figure 7.85).
3. Select **Remove from virtual machine and delete files from disk**, and click **OK** (see Figure 7.86).

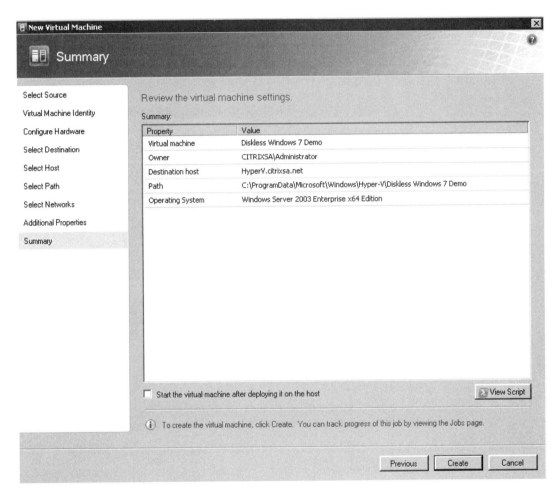

FIGURE 7.82

Summary.

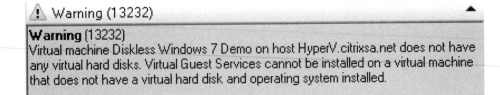

FIGURE 7.83

Warning – virtual hard disks.

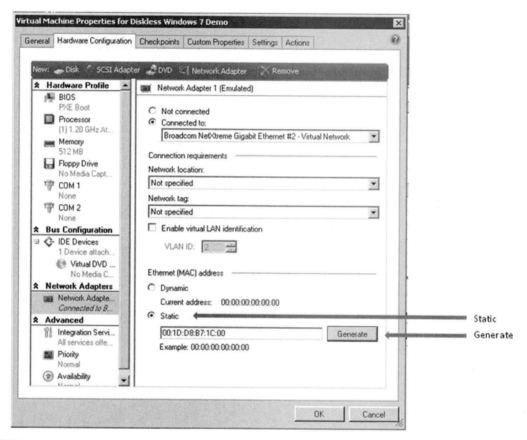

FIGURE 7.84

Network adapter.

Provisioning Server

1. Connect to the provisioning server, and open the Provisioning Services Console.
2. Right-click on **Device Collection** and select **Create Device Collection**… (see Figure 7.87).
3. Assign your collection a name, and click **OK** (see Figure 7.88).
4. Right-click on your new collection, and select **Create Device** (see Figure 7.89).
5. Enter a name in the Name field, and the MAC address in the MAC address field. Click **OK** (see Figure 7.90). Repeat this step for the second virtual desktop.

   Important: The name will be used as the computer account name in Active Directory.

TIP

To easily transpose the MAC address from the hypervisor, paste the MAC address you copied earlier into the Description field.

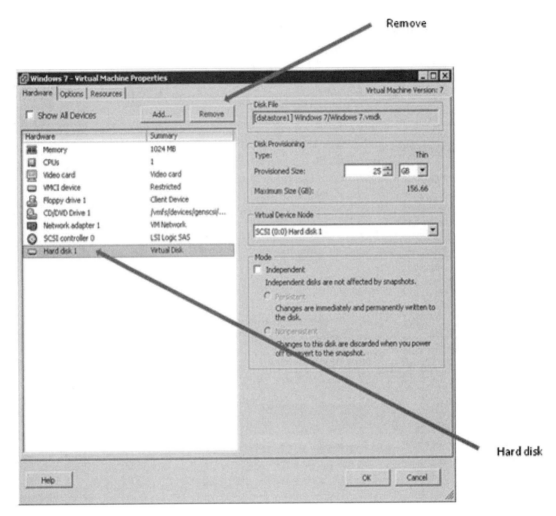

FIGURE 7.85

Virtual machine properties.

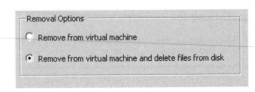

FIGURE 7.86

Removal options.

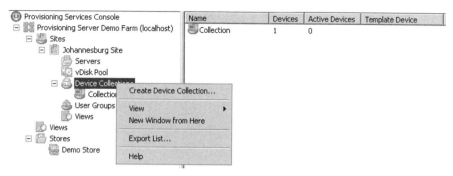

FIGURE 7.87

Device Collection options menu.

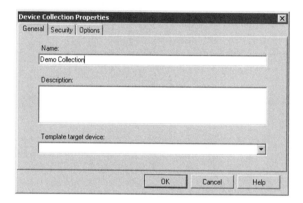

FIGURE 7.88

Device Collection properties.

FIGURE 7.89

Collection options menu.

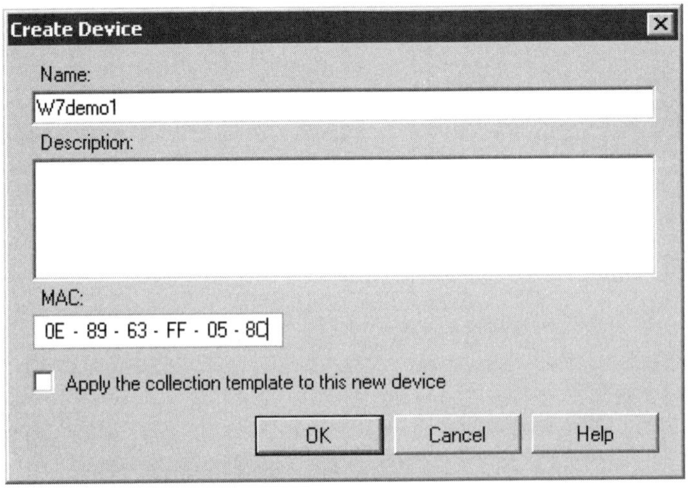

Create Device

Name:

W7demo1

Description:

MAC:

0E - 89 - 63 - FF - 05 - 8C

☐ Apply the collection template to this new device

OK   Cancel   Help

FIGURE 7.90

Create device.

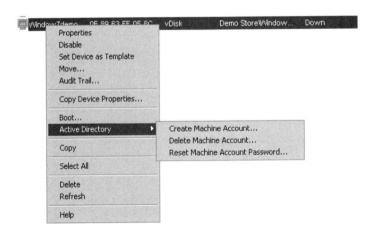

FIGURE 7.91

Target Device options menu.

6. Right-click on the device you have just added and select **Active Directory | Create Machine Account** (see Figure 7.91).

7. You can select a domain, and an organizational unit, and click **Create Account** (see Figure 7.92).

As you can see from the example above, you can also select more than one object to create an account for.

The dialog box should return a status of success. Click **Close**.

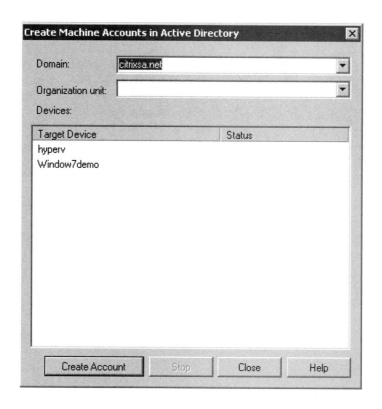

FIGURE 7.92

Create machine accounts in Active Directory.

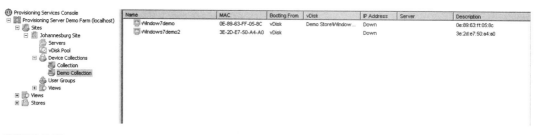

FIGURE 7.93

Device collection.

8. Your new virtual desktops should appear in the collection (see Figure 7.93).
9. Click **vDisk Pool**, select your vDisk, and drag it onto your collection.
10. Click **Yes** (see Figure 7.94).
11. Start the VMs on your hypervisor.

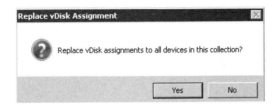

FIGURE 7.94

Replace vDisk assignment.

FIGURE 7.95

Desktop Group options menu.

> **NOTE**
> Only one will boot as the vDisk is in Private mode.

Add the Virtual Desktop to the Desktop Group

You may choose to create a new Desktop Group, or you can add the virtual desktop to an existing Desktop Group.

1. Right-click on the Desktop Group and select **Properties** (see Figure 7.95).
2. In the left-hand pane, select **Virtual Desktops**, then click the **Add...** button (see Figure 7.96).

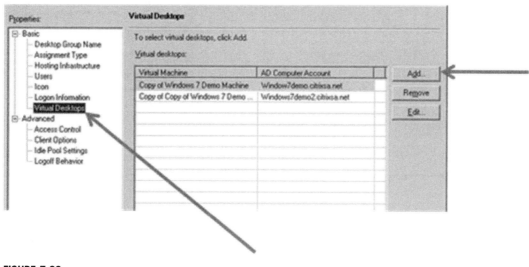

FIGURE 7.96

Virtual desktop properties.

Window7demo.citrixsa.net	Idle	-	No
Windows7demo2.citrixsa.net	Not Registered	-	No

FIGURE 7.97

Virtual desktop state.

One of the virtual desktops should appear in the Delivery Services Console, with a Desktop State of *Idle*. The second will still be in a *Not Registered State* (see Figure 7.97) – in the next section, we will change the vDisk to "Standard Mode."

> **TIP**
>
> If the new devices state is not Idle, refresh the view, if it remains in another state, check the event logs on the virtual desktop. Active Directory issues, computer account creation, and DNS issues, the virtual desktop resolving the address of the Desktop Delivery Controller, are the most common issues.

Mount the vDisk to Two Virtual Desktops Simultaneously

In the previous section, you mounted a vDisk to a single virtual desktop. We will now take the second diskless virtual desktop you created and mount the same vDisk to that virtual desktop.

FIGURE 7.98

vDisk pool.

1. Shut down both virtual desktops.

> **TIP**
>
> Make sure the Idle Pool Setting is set to zero – otherwise the Desktop Delivery Controller will just keep starting the virtual desktops.

2. Open the Provisioning Services Console – select **vDisk Pool**, right-click on your vDisk, and select **Properties** (see Figure 7.98).

> **TIP**
>
> If there is a padlock next to the vDisk, see earlier in this chapter to remove the locks.

3. Click **Edit File Properties**... (see Figure 7.99).
4. Select the **Mode** tab, select **Access mode** and change it to **Standard Image**, click **OK**, and click **OK** again – to close the vDisk properties (see Figure 7.100).

Cache type can be left at "Cache on server disk" – see the "Design Decisions" section for placement.

> **TIP**
>
> Hit **F5** in the console to refresh the display.

Open a connection to the Desktop Delivery Controller; modify the Idle Desktop Count to two virtual desktops. For the procedure, see Chapter 5, "Desktop Delivery Controller – Advanced Configuration Settings."

You may need to restart the virtual desktops to acquire their new vDisk assignment if they are hung at the PXE boot screen.

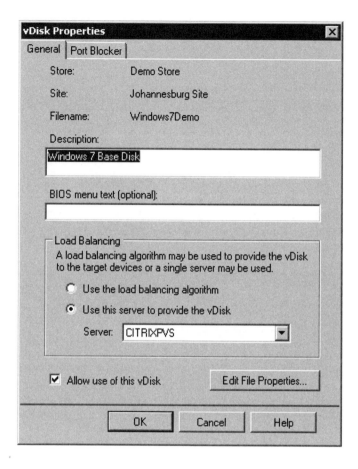

FIGURE 7.99

vDisk Properties.

Checkpoint 3 – Booting Two VMs from a vDisk

In this demonstration, you can demonstrate the connection to two virtual desktops, which are booting from a single vDisk over the network.

This demonstration is applicable to a technical and management audience.

1. Open the Hypervisor Console, and navigate to view the disk attached to the virtual desktop:

XenServer

Open the **Storage** tab of both virtual desktops and show how there is no disk attached (see Figure 7.101).

SCVMM

Open the **Properties** of the virtual machine, select **Hardware Configuration**, indicate under Bus Configuration that there is no hard drive attached (see Figure 7.102).

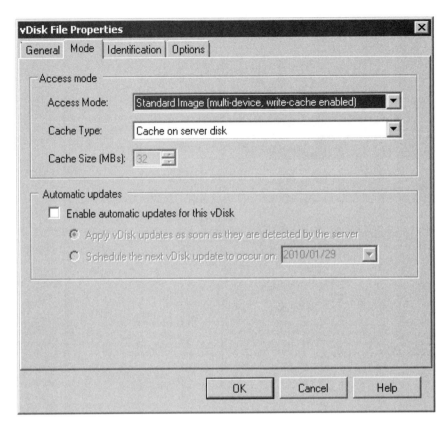

FIGURE 7.100

vDisk file properties.

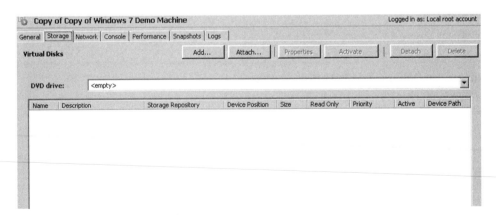

FIGURE 7.101

Virtual desktop **Storage** tab on XenServer.

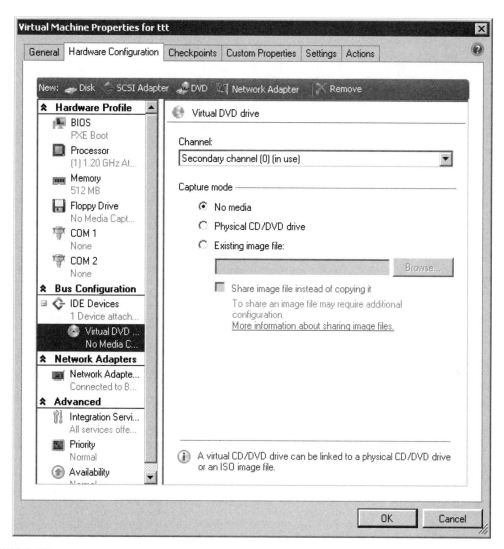

FIGURE 7.102

Virtual desktop bus configurations on Hyper-V.

VMware

Edit the virtual machine properties of the virtual desktop. On the **Hardware** tab indicate how no disk is attached (see Figure 7.103).

All Hypervisors

2. Open the Provisioning Services Console – <YOUR> **Farm** I **Sites** I <YOUR> **Site** I **vDisk Pool** and right-click on your vDisk (see Figure 7.104).
3. Click **Show Usage**....

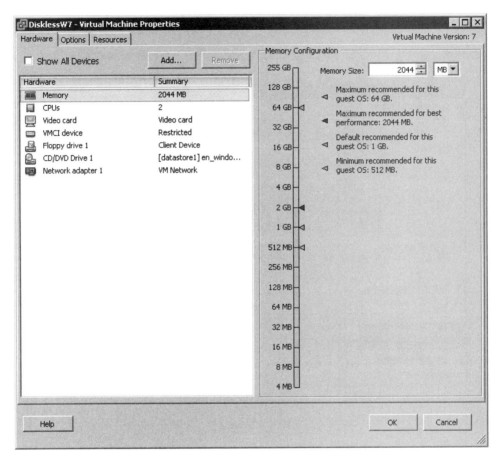

FIGURE 7.103

Virtual desktop **Hardware** tab.

FIGURE 7.104

vDisk options menu.

4. The dialog box shows how two Target Devices are using the vDisk (see Figure 7.105).

5. Open Windows Explorer on the provisioning server and show the folder where the WriteCache is stored (see Figure 7.106).

This shows how the "uniqueness" is saved outside of the vDisk.

6. Connect to the Desktop Delivery Controller – Open the Delivery Services Console, and display the Virtual Desktop Group that you have created (see Figure 7.107).

7. Open the Web Interface – HTTP://<IP Address or hostname of the Desktop Delivery Controller>.

The connect will follow the same process you followed in the Milestone 1 Demonstration.

Show how the desktop state changes to *In Use* when a desktop is connected (see Figure 7.108).

I have noticed that a lot people only really "get it" when they see that the virtual desktop has no disk assigned.

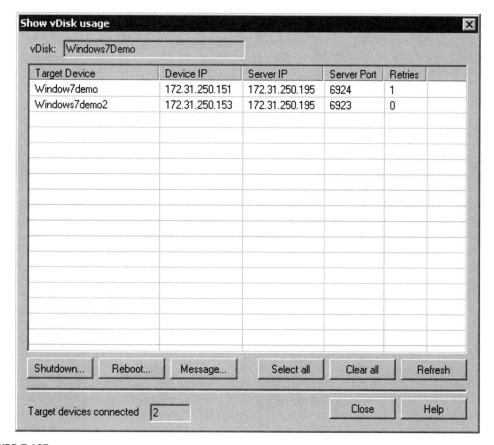

FIGURE 7.105

Show vDisk usage.

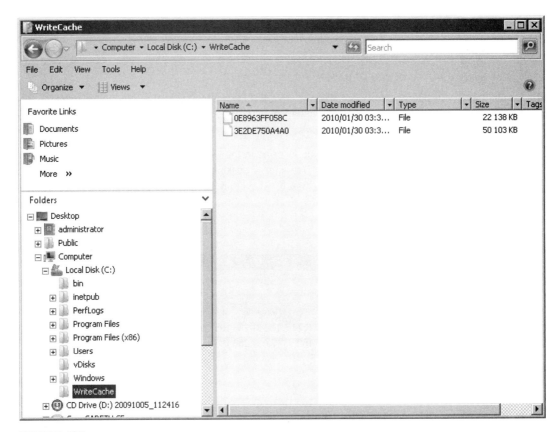

FIGURE 7.106

WriteCache files.

FIGURE 7.107

Virtual desktops – desktop state.

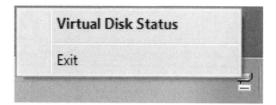

FIGURE 7.108

vDisk taskbar icon.

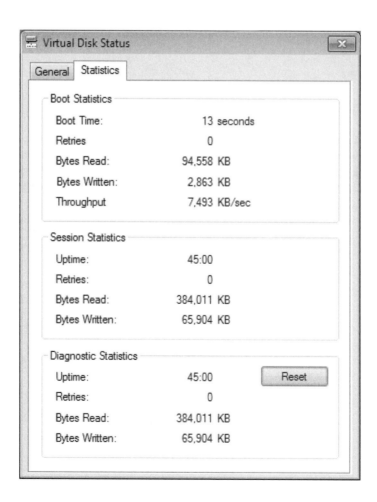

FIGURE 7.109

vDisk **Statistics** tab.

> **TIP**
>
> As an extra little demo, show live migration of the virtual desktop on the hypervisor, while you are logged on to it. The provisioning server is in effect acting as shared storage, so this can be done even if you have no SAN or iSCSI!

Network Traffic

If the question about network traffic arises – which it most certainly will if the network administrator is present – then right-click on the vDisk in the Notification Area on you virtual desktop.

Select **Virtual Disk Status** (see Figure 7.108).

Select the **Statistics** tab (see Figure 7.109).

You can show how much traffic has traversed the network due to the vDisk. In the case above, roughly 380 MB have been read, and 65 MB have been written in 45 min.

It takes roughly 70 to 80 MB to load the kernel of a Windows operating system over the network, thereafter the vDisk activity will be on demand.

SUMMARY

The previous chapter dealt with the installation of Citrix Provisioning Server, this chapter dealt with the creation of a vDisk and collections of Target Devices using Citrix Provisioning Server. We defined the "vDisk Store" to host the vDisk. We then created the "blank" vDisk. The vDisk was then mounted to an existing virtual desktop. The virtual desktop's drive contents were then copied to the vDisk. The vDisk was then mounted to other Target Devices, and they were booted from the vDisk. Lastly we covered the details of how to perform a demonstration of booting virtual desktops from the vDisk.

Additional Provisioning Server Configuration Settings

INFORMATION IN THIS CHAPTER

- Provisioning Server Configuration Programs
- Configure Server Settings
- Active Directory
- Configure Site Settings
- Using the Provisioning Services Boot Device Manager – Step by Step
- Adding a Disk for Write Cache

The Citrix Provisioning Server is a large topic that probably deserves a book in its own right. In this book, we only look at those aspects that are commonly required when using it in conjunction with XenDesktop.

This chapter covers some additional useful settings. Particular note should be taken of the Active Directory settings, without which XenDesktop may not correctly function.

PROVISIONING SERVER CONFIGURATION PROGRAMS

The configuration programs are under **Start Menu | Programs | Citrix | Provisioning Services** (see Figure 8.1).

The Provisioning Services Boot Device Manager is used in situations where PXE (Preboot Execution Environment) and/or Dynamic Host Configuration Protocol (DHCP) are not available to be used. This can be particularly useful in a proof of concept environment where DHCP is not available to be used in the datacenter. The use of DHCP is often restricted on networks. Care should also be taken with PXE that there are no clashes with other PXE services running. Microsoft SMS and Altiris Deployment Server are two examples of other programs that use PXE. The .ISO files can be used to provide the network location of the provisioning server, as well as to assign an IP address to the virtual desktop.

The Provisioning Services BOOTPTAB Editor can be used to manually edit the PXE boot file. It is not the recommended method of editing the boot file. The recommended mechanism to edit the boot file is to rerun the Provisioning Services Configuration Wizard, which will automatically make the changes to the file.

FIGURE 8.1

Provisioning server configuration programs.

The Provisioning Services Configuration Wizard runs automatically as part of the provisioning server installation. It can also be run manually post-installation to correct or change any of the configuration settings.

The Provisioning Services Console is the primary management tool for Citrix Provisioning Server.

CONFIGURE SERVER SETTINGS

The server settings are configured from the **Servers** node. Open the Provisioning Services Console, and select the **Farm | Sites | <Your Site> | Servers** (see Figure 8.2).

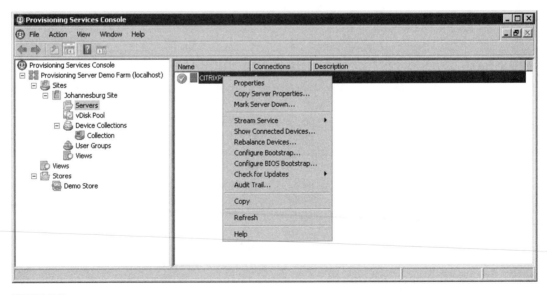

FIGURE 8.2

Configure server properties.

Right-click on the server to amend the server settings. Select the **Properties** option.

The Stream Service can also be configured from the option list. Select **Stream Service** to stop or restart the **Stream Service**.

Rebalance devices will manually perform load balancing across multiple provisioning servers. This can be useful if you shut down a provisioning server, and if you have multiple provisioning servers, they will take over the vDisk loads from the one that is shut down. Provisioning server won't automatically rebalance the load back to the server if it restarts. The manual rebalance can be used in this instance.

ACTIVE DIRECTORY

The Active Directory integration is set on the vDisk as described in Chapter 7, "Fundamental Configuration of the Citrix Provisioning Server." The server settings must also be configured to allow this to correctly function.

Select **Properties** to configure the server (see Figure 8.2).

Select **Enable automatic password support** (see Figure 8.3). As per Chapter 4, "Installing the Virtual Desktop," the password change will be initiated by provisioning server. The Active

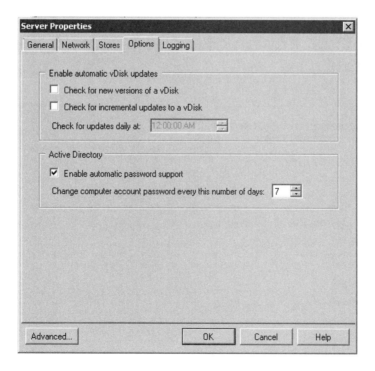

FIGURE 8.3

Enabling automatic password support.

Directory initiated changes are disabled through **Policy: Domain member: Disable machine account password** changes.

CONFIGURE SITE SETTINGS

Right-click on the farm node, select **Properties** (see Figure 8.4).

The **General** tab is purely informational. The **Security** tab enables security to be delegated to specific groups (see Figure 8.5). In order to add these groups, they must first be added on the **Groups** tab. Security can be configured at the farm, site, and collection levels, but the groups available to be assigned can only be configured at a farm level.

The **Licensing** tab (see Figure 8.6) enables you to amend the license server settings. There are two types of licenses: Desktop and Datacenter licenses. Datacenter licenses are used by server operating systems, and desktop licenses are used for Windows XP and Windows 7 desktops.

Select the **Options** tab (see Figure 8.7). The **Auto-add** feature allows a user booting a device through PXE to select a vDisk without the MAC address being prepopulated. This is useful and can be particularly useful in non-VDI environments, but is disabled by default for security reasons.

Auditing is disabled by default. This allows tracking of actions performed in the Provisioning Server Console.

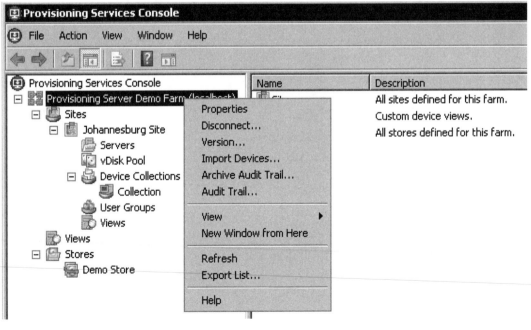

FIGURE 8.4

Configure farm properties.

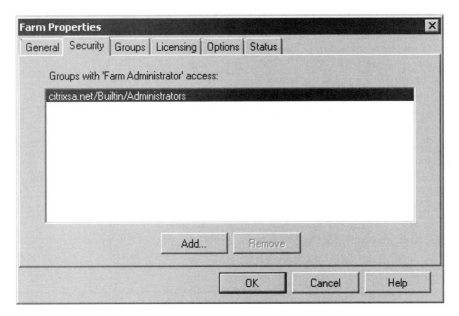

FIGURE 8.5

Farm security settings.

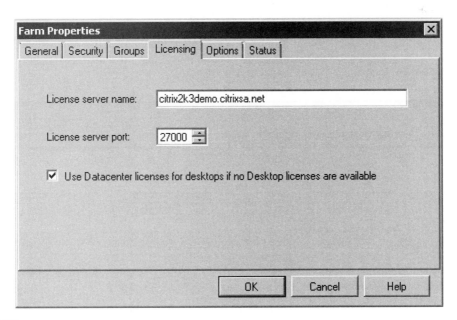

FIGURE 8.6

Farm license settings.

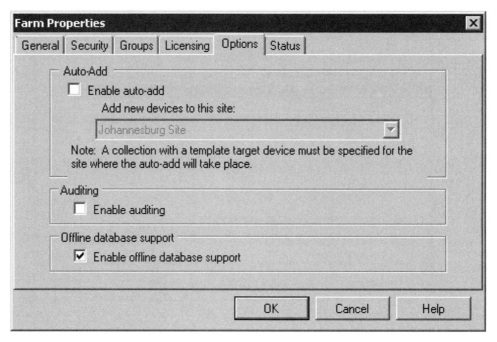

FIGURE 8.7

Provisioning server farm options.

Offline database support – is an important new feature, this allows the provisioning server to continue to be accessible even if the SQL database is unavailable. It does this by using a cached copy of the database.

TIP

Enable offline database support when designing for disaster recovery and business continuity.

USING THE PROVISIONING SERVICES BOOT DEVICE MANAGER – STEP BY STEP

Design Decisions

Using PXE is a simple and elegant solution in most scenarios. There are, however, situations where it would be best to use a boot ISO file.

1. There may be other PXE services running on the network – for example, Altiris or Microsoft SMS.
2. There may be a restriction based on a network policy.

The Provisioning Services Boot Device Manager can be used to create a boot file for a virtual machine. The boot file is loaded manually from an .ISO file rather than being copied over the network.

1. Launch Provisioning Services Boot Device Manager (see Figure 8.8).
2. Click **Add** to add an IP address. Click **Next** (see Figure 8.8).
3. Add the IP address of the Citrix Provisioning Server and click **OK** (see Figure 8.9).
4. Click **Next** (see Figure 8.10).
5. Click **Next** (see Figure 8.11).

Verbose Mode can be enabled for troubleshooting purposes.

DHCP

6. Configure the IP address mechanism (see Figure 8.12).

Using DHCP is much simpler as one .ISO file could be used to boot all the virtual desktops.

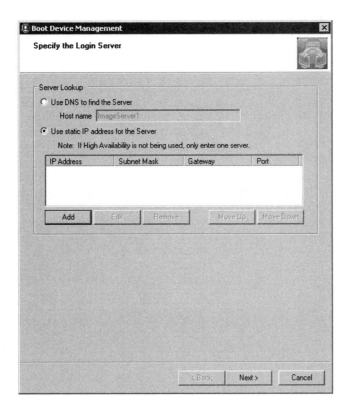

FIGURE 8.8

Boot device management.

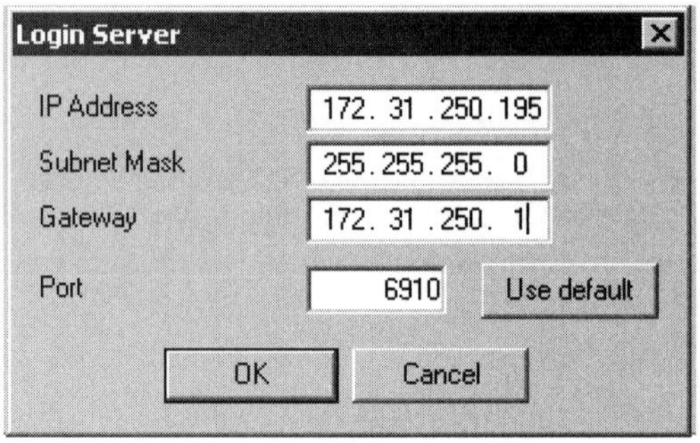

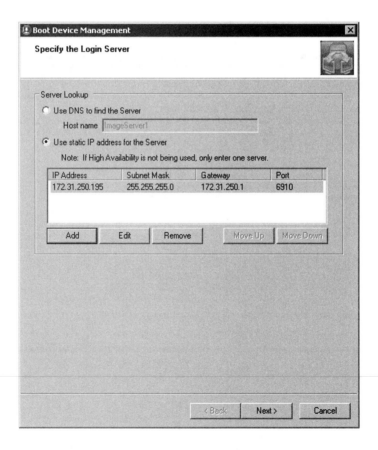

FIGURE 8.9

Login server.

FIGURE 8.10

Boot device management – specify the login server.

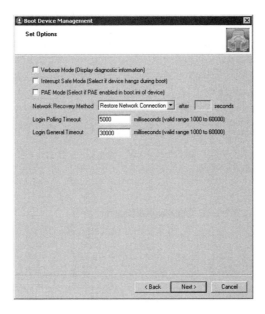

FIGURE 8.11

Boot device management – set options.

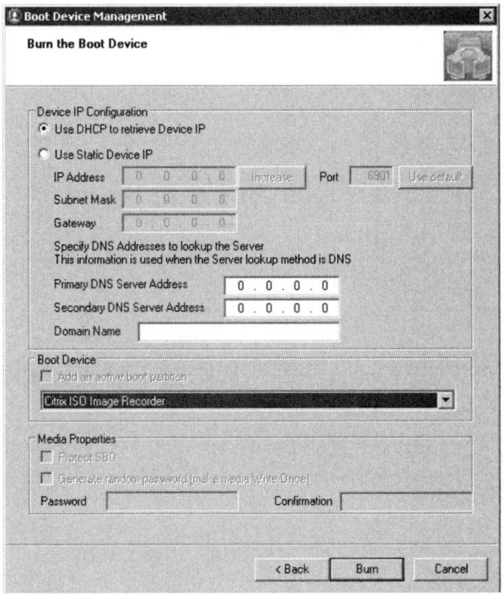

FIGURE 8.12

Boot device management – DHCP.

NO DHCP

If DHCP is not an option, then each virtual desktop needs an individual boot .ISO; each boot file contains the same server information but will use a unique assigned IP address (see Figure 8.13). The **Increase** button allows you to increment the IP address and the **Burn** button can then be used to create multiple boot .ISO files.

7. Click **Burn**.
8. Enter a descriptive file name, and then click **Save** (see Figure 8.14).

For the No DHCP Scenario, click **Increase** and then click **Burn** again. In this situation, naming the files is best tied to a virtual desktop name.

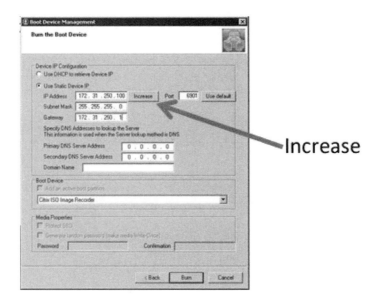

FIGURE 8.13

Boot device management – use static device IP.

FIGURE 8.14

Save as.

ADDING A DISK FOR WRITE CACHE

In the Design Decisions in Chapter 7, "Fundamental Configuration of the Citrix Provisioning Server," on write cache placement, it was stated that for best performance write cache be held on a location other than the provisioning server. Recommended location is on shared storage attached to the hypervisor. When creating your Base Target Device, attach 1 GB (or 2 GB if you are using EdgeSight monitoring) disk to your Template VM, this will be specified as write cache.

Shut down all the Target Devices using the vDisk. Change your Idle Pool to zero using the Delivery Services Console on the Desktop Delivery Controller.

Place the vDisk in Private mode (see Figure 8.15); although we will be formatting the physical drive, and not the vDisk, we do need the settings, like the drive letter, to be saved to the vDisk.

Change the Idle Pool to 1 in the Delivery Services Console, and this will automatically start the virtual desktop. Login to the desktop.

As we will be amending the hardware allocations at a hypervisor level, it is simplest to login through the hypervisor console.

Attaching a Disk

XenServer

1. Select the virtual machine, and in the right-hand pane select the **Storage** tab (see Figure 8.16).
2. Change the **Name** to something sensible like write cache. Change the size to 1 GB, and click **Add** (see Figure 8.17).

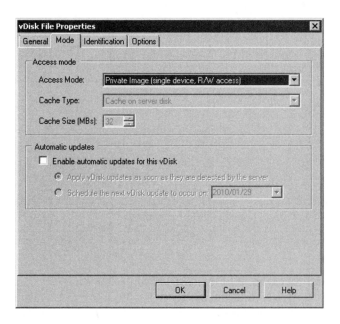

FIGURE 8.15

Changing the vDisk mode.

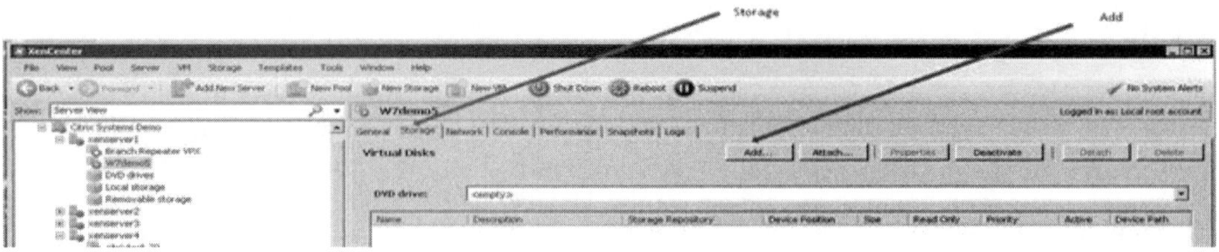

FIGURE 8.16

XenCenter – storage.

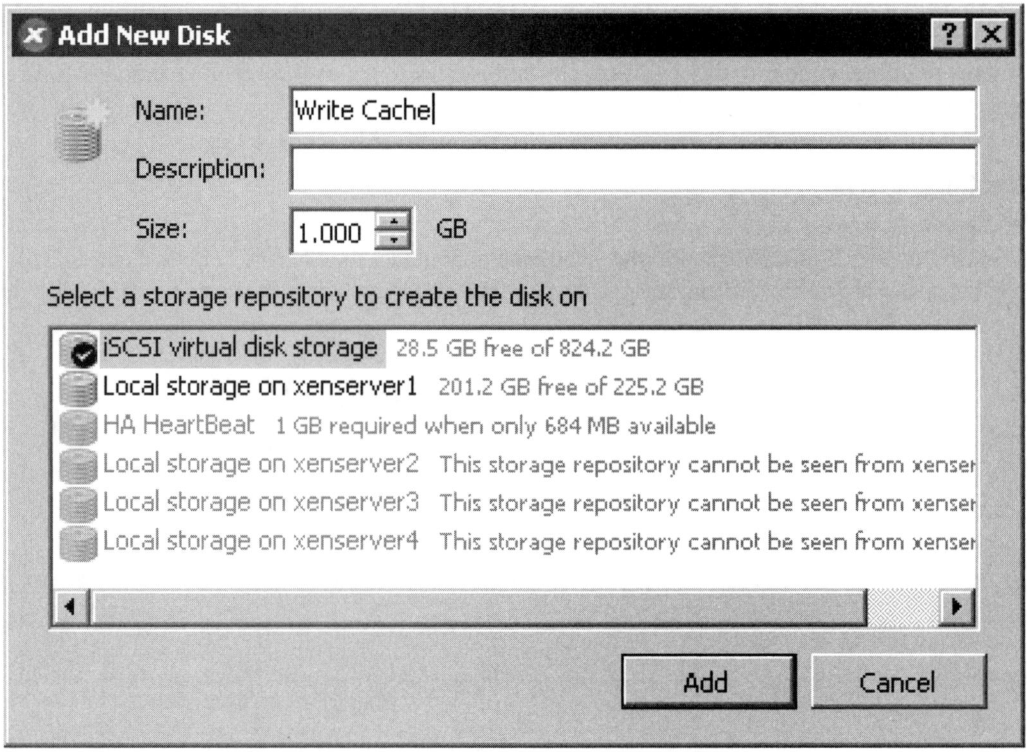

FIGURE 8.17

Add new disk.

System Center Virtual Machine Manager (SCVMM)

1. Right-click on you diskless virtual desktop and select **Properties** (see Figure 8.18).
2. Select the **Hardware Configuration** tab, select the **IDE Devices** in the left-hand pane, then click **Disk** (see Figure 8.19).
3. Change the type to **Fixed**, and disk size to 1GB, then click **OK** (see Figure 8.20).

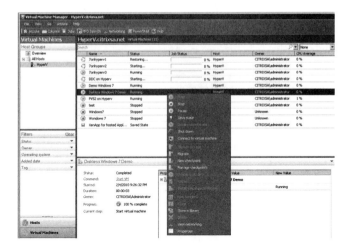

FIGURE 8.18

SCVMM – virtual machine options menu.

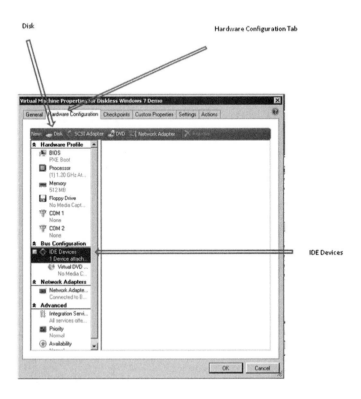

FIGURE 8.19

Hardware configuration – bus configuration.

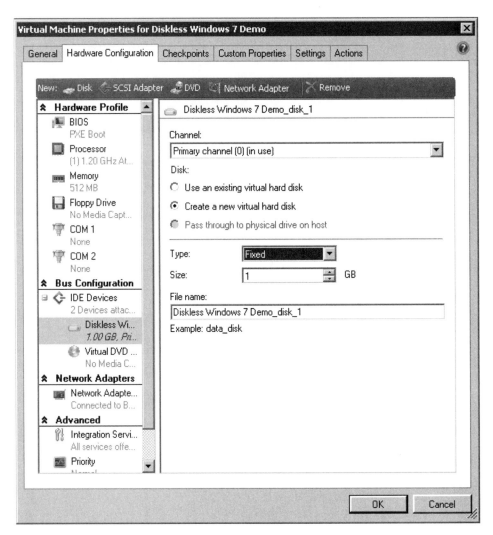

FIGURE 8.20

Hardware configuration – disk type.

VMware

1. Open the vCenter, right-click on the diskless virtual machine you previously created. Select **Edit Settings**….
2. Click **Add**… (see Figure 8.21).
3. Select **Hard Disk**, and click **Next** (see Figure 8.22).
4. Select **Create a new virtual disk**, and click **Next** (see Figure 8.23).
5. Change the disk size to 1 GB (or however large you require the write cache disk), click **Next** (see Figure 8.24).

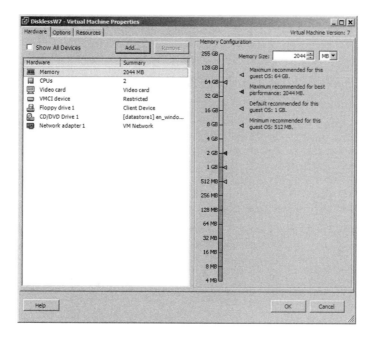

FIGURE 8.21

Virtual machine properties – hardware.

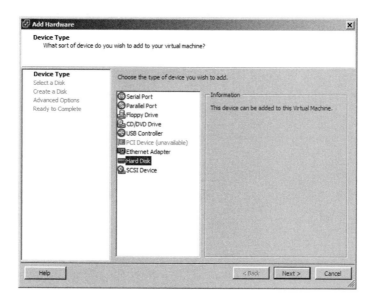

FIGURE 8.22

Add hardware – device type.

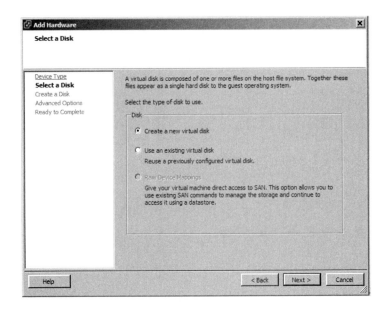

FIGURE 8.23

Add hardware – select a disk.

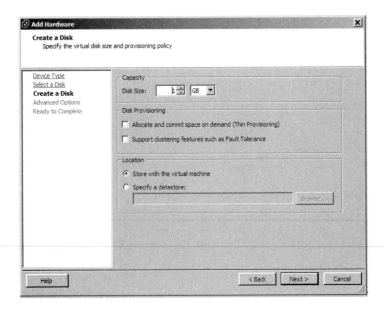

FIGURE 8.24

Add hardware – create a disk.

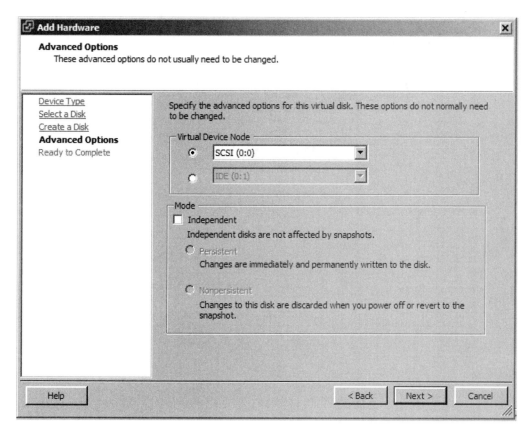

FIGURE 8.25

Add hardware – advanced options.

6. Click **Next** (see Figure 8.25).

The mode settings aren't relevant to a XenDesktop VDI implementation and can be left at defaults.

7. Click **Finish** (see Figure 8.26).

All Hypervisors
1. Open Computer Management on the virtual desktop.
2. On the Start Menu, right-click on **Computer** and Select **Manage** (see Figure 8.27).
3. Select **Disk Management**, the Initialize Disk dialog box will automatically pop up. Click **OK** (see Figure 8.28).
4. Select the new disk, right-click and select **New Simple Volume** (see Figure 8.29).

Follow the prompts to create a new volume called write cache, and format it with the New Technology File System (NTFS).

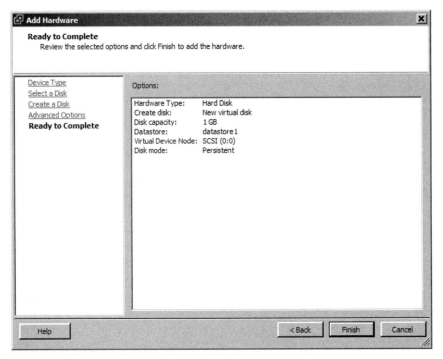

FIGURE 8.26

Add hardware – ready to complete.

FIGURE 8.27

Computer manager.

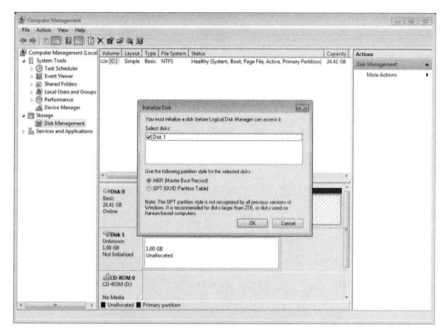

FIGURE 8.28

Initialize disk.

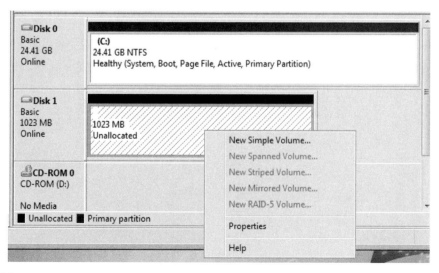

FIGURE 8.29

Disk options.

SUMMARY

In Chapter 6, "Installation of the Citrix Provisioning Server," we dealt with installation and in Chapter 7, "Fundamental Configuration of the Citrix Provisioning Server," we dealt with implementation of vDisks to Target Devices. Chapter 8 delved into operational settings, and some more detailed configuration settings. We discussed the components of the Provisioning Services Console looking into server and site settings. We then looked at using the Boot Device Manager to create a boot file as an alternative to using PXE boot. Lastly, we covered adding a physical write cache disk for enhanced performance.

Using the Setup Wizard to Create Multiple Desktops

INFORMATION IN THIS CHAPTER

- Prerequisites
- Create a Template Virtual Machine
- Xendesktop Setup Tool Installation

The XenDesktop Setup Wizard is a very important implementation tool, without which, the creation of virtual desktops would be an arduous time-consuming task.

The XenDesktop Setup Wizard is used to perform bulk virtual desktop creation. The wizard ties together all the various XenDesktop components to create the virtual desktops.

PREREQUISITES

1. If required, a unique organizational unit for the Desktop Group in the Active Directory.
2. Create a Template VM on your hypervisor on which the hardware settings will be based.
3. A Desktop Group can be precreated in the Desktop Delivery Services Console on the Desktop Delivery Controller.
4. A vDisk in Standard image mode.

CREATE A TEMPLATE VIRTUAL MACHINE

The XenDesktop Setup Wizard requires a Template Virtual Machine to base the hardware configuration on. Depending on where you want write cache, you will either have a diskless virtual machine, or it may have a small write cache disk attached.

XenServer

1. Open the XenCenter; in the left-hand pane, select one of the virtual machines you created in the earlier chapters.
2. Click **VM | Convert to Template** (see Figure 9.1).
3. Click **OK** (see Figure 9.2).
4. The virtual machine has now been converted to a template (see Figure 9.3).

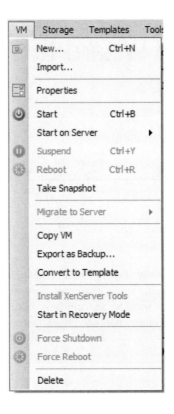

FIGURE 9.1

XenCenter VM menu.

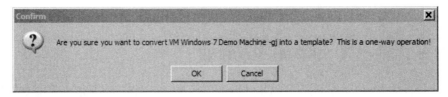

FIGURE 9.2

Template convert warning.

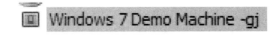

FIGURE 9.3

Template icon.

SCVMM

1. Open the System Center Virtual Machine Manager; select the virtual desktop created in the previous chapter (see Figure 9.4).
2. Right-click and select **New template**.
3. Click **Yes** (see Figure 9.5).
4. Create a name for your template, and click **Next** (see Figure 9.6).

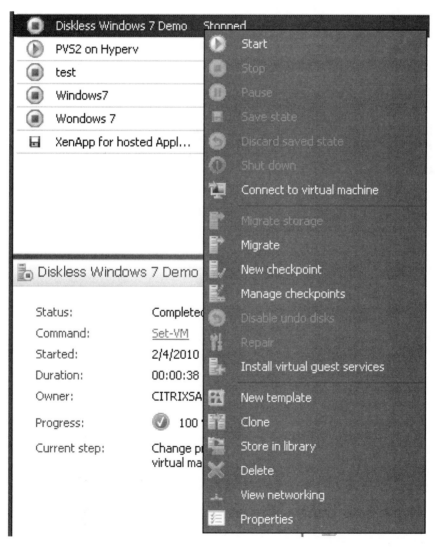

FIGURE 9.4

Virtual machine menu options.

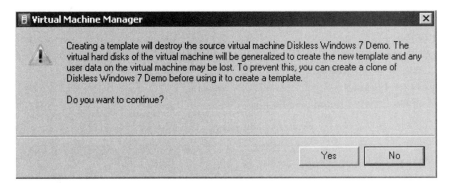

FIGURE 9.5

Template create warning.

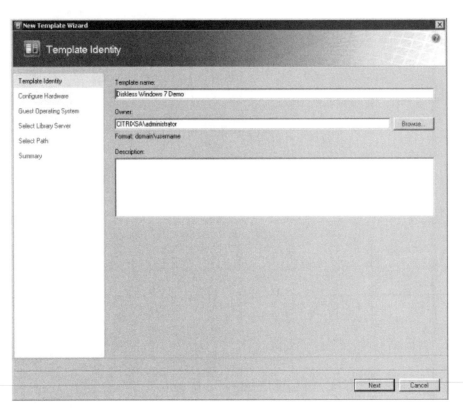

FIGURE 9.6

Template identity.

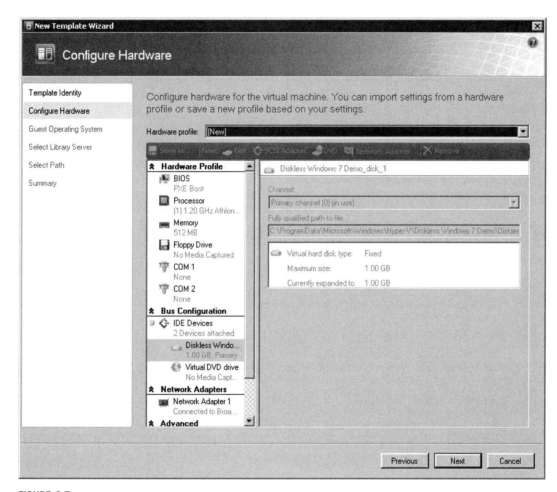

FIGURE 9.7

Configure hardware.

5. Leave the hardware configuration as it is and click **Next** (see Figure 9.7).
6. Change the "Guest operating system profile" to **Customization not required** (see Figure 9.8). Provisioning server will perform the customization tasks.
7. Select a library server for placement (the default should be fine in most cases), click **Next** (see Figure 9.9).
8. Browse to the MSSSCVMMLibrary to define the virtual machine path for the template, and click **Next** (see Figure 9.10).
9. Click **Create** to create the template (see Figure 9.11).

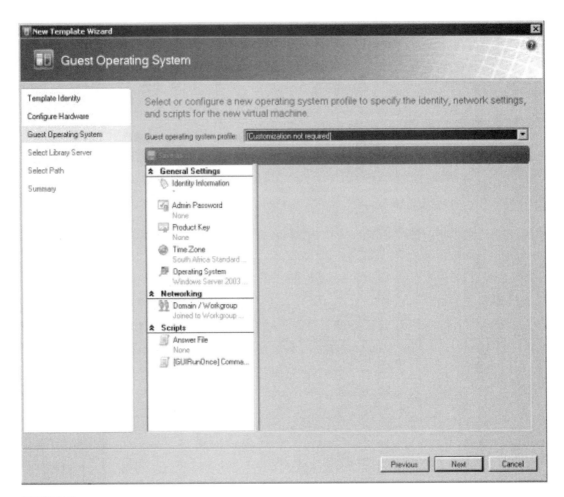

FIGURE 9.8

Guest operating system.

There is currently an issue with write cache disks attached to a template created on SCVMM. This is not an issue with XenServer or VMware. The XenDesktop Setup Wizard doesn't attach the write cache disk defined in the template. This results in the virtual desktops being created, but without the write cache disk. You should manually attach a write cache disk in small environment. There is a workaround for this issue in the Citrix Document: *CTX124687 – XenDesktop Design Guide For Microsoft Windows 2008 R2 Hyper-V Version 1.1.* This document contains in its appendix a script to add write cache disks to VMs.

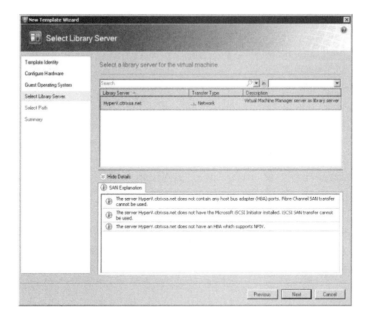

FIGURE 9.9

Select library server.

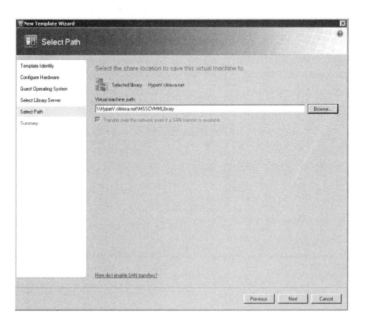

FIGURE 9.10

Select path.

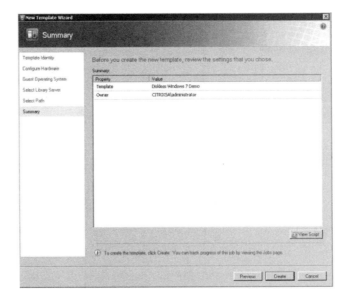

FIGURE 9.11

Summary.

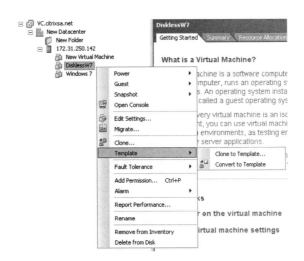

FIGURE 9.12

vCenter – Template options menu.

VMware

1. Open the vCenter; select the virtual desktop, right-click and select **Template | Clone to Template**… (see Figure 9.12).

XENDESKTOP SETUP TOOL INSTALLATION

1. Mount the XenDesktop 4 DVD on the **Provisioning Server**. The tool is not on the Provisioning Server Installation DVD as the provisioning server installation is generic, but the tool is specific to XenDesktop.
2. Browse to <DVD Drive>:\w2k3\en\XenDesktop Setup Tool, or <DVD Drive>:\x64\en\ XenDesktop Setup Tool (which contains the same files!).
3. Double-click **Setup** and it will launch the .msi (either the 32-bit or 64-bit version depending on your provisioning server) (see Figure 9.13).
4. Click **Next** (see Figure 9.14).
5. Accept the license agreement, and click **Next** (see Figure 9.15).
6. To accept the default install path, click **Next** (click **Browse**... to install the files elsewhere) (see Figure 9.16).
7. Click **Install** (see Figure 9.17).
8. Click **Finish** (see Figure 9.18).

FIGURE 9.13

XenDesktop Setup Tool folder.

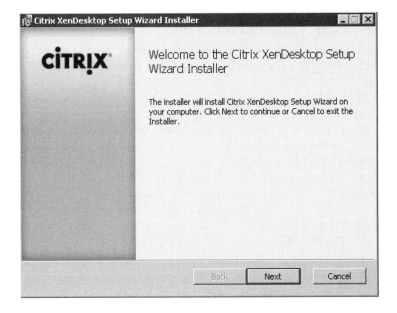

FIGURE 9.14

Citrix XenDesktop Setup Wizard Installer – welcome.

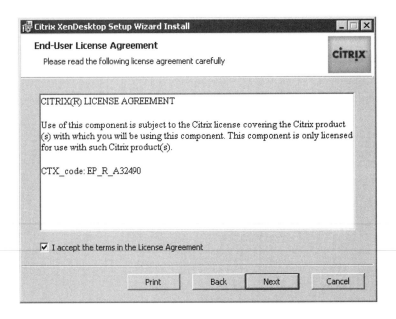

FIGURE 9.15

End-user license agreement.

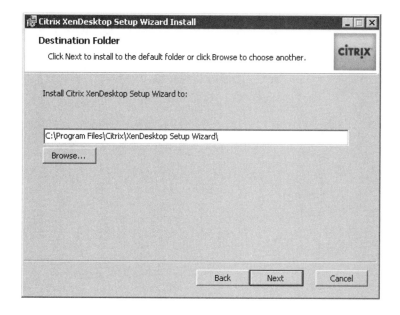

FIGURE 9.16

Destination folder.

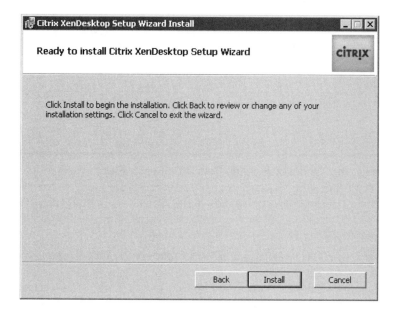

FIGURE 9.17

Ready to install.

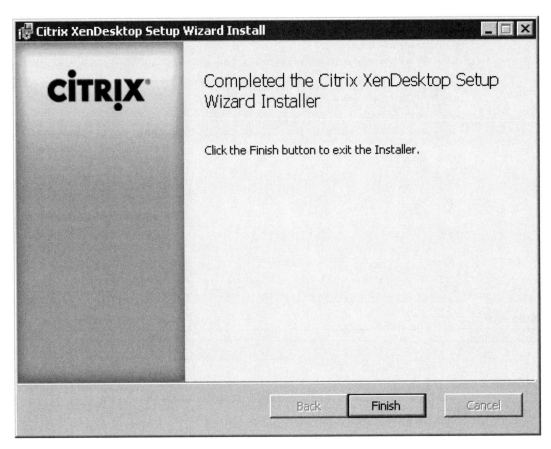

FIGURE 9.18

Completed the Citrix XenDesktop Setup Installer.

Checkpoint 4 Using The Xendesktop Setup Tool – Demonstration

Using the XenDesktop Setup Wizard is certainly an important checkpoint for you as an implementer. The demonstration of this set of capabilities would most likely be combined with the previous checkpoint. As with the previous checkpoint, this functionality will be best appreciated by a technical audience, and those involved in the implementation phase.

1. Click **Start I Programs I Citrix I Administrative Tools I XenDesktop Setup Wizard** (see Figure 9.19).
2. Click **Next** (see Figure 9.20).
3. The wizard interrogates Active Directory for a list of XenDesktop farms. If there is more than one Xen-Desktop farm in your environment, it will appear in the drop-down list. Select your XenDesktop farm, and click **Next** (see Figure 9.21).
4. Select your hypervisor from the Hosting Infrastructure drop-down (see Figure 9.22).

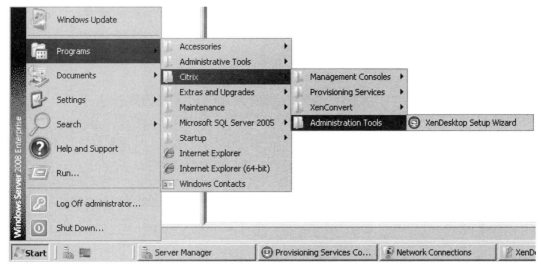

FIGURE 9.19

XenDesktop Setup Wizard start menu item.

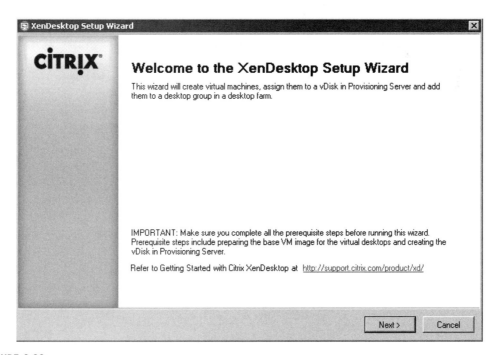

FIGURE 9.20

XenDesktop Setup Wizard – welcome.

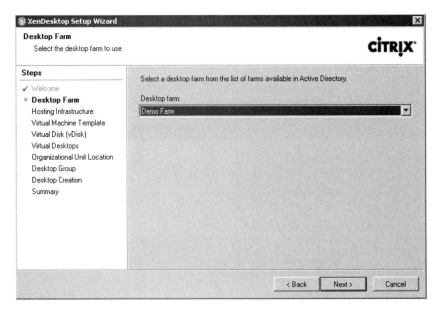

FIGURE 9.21

Desktop farm.

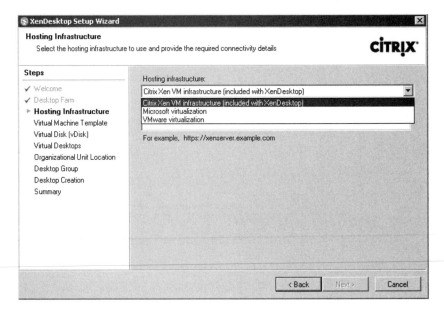

FIGURE 9.22

Hosting infrastructure – virtualization.

XenServer

1. Enter the IP address or computer name of the XenServer acting as the pool master (see Figure 9.23).

To find your pool master, log onto one of your XenServers. You can use putty to connect direct to the command line, or you can access the command line through the XenCenter Console (see Figure 9.24).

xe host-list	Lists the hosts in the pool and their UUIDs
xe pool-list	Lists the pool information – the tag master (RO) has the UUID (Universally Unique Identifier) of the host currently acting as the master

For example:

```
[root@xenserver1 ~]# xe host-list
uuid ( RO)                  : a9aab50d-83e7-4fc7-94c2-2b5e0cec0da9
        name-label ( RW): xenserver2
   name-description ( RO): Default install of XenServer


uuid ( RO)                  : 93749c21-bfe6-4cfb-beac-b33f76e2b09c
        name-label ( RW): xenserver1
   name-description ( RO): Default install of XenServer


uuid ( RO)                  : ba18891c-32bf-45b9-83d8-ae780e1d507e
        name-label ( RW): xenserver3
   name-description ( RO): Default install of XenServer


uuid ( RO)                  : d537ad21-fd24-45cc-b1c1-3360a6767592
        name-label ( RW): xenserver4
   name-description ( RO): Default install of XenServer


[root@xenserver1 ~]# xe pool-list
uuid ( RO)                  : cb6067c9-04ac-6436-5b29-d6cbb91da066
        name-label ( RW): Citrix Systems Demo
   name-description ( RW):
            master ( RO): 93749c21-bfe6-4cfb-beac-b33f76e2b09c
       default-SR ( RW): ceb3c00d-d887-38bb-743b-822733b1b3e8
```

We can see in this example that xenserver1 is the master (bold text for illustrative purposes).

2. Click **Next** to connect to the XenServer.
3. Enter the root username and password of the XenServer (see Figure 9.25).
4. The wizard retrieves the template list (see Figure 9.26).

Note the check box – if you are using an ISO to boot your virtual desktops, you may need to change this.

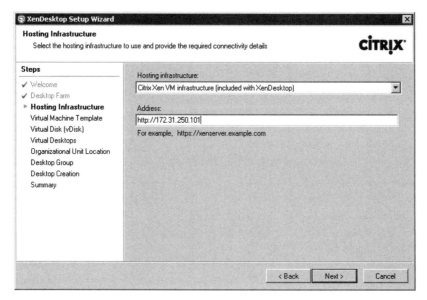

FIGURE 9.23

Hosting infrastructure – address.

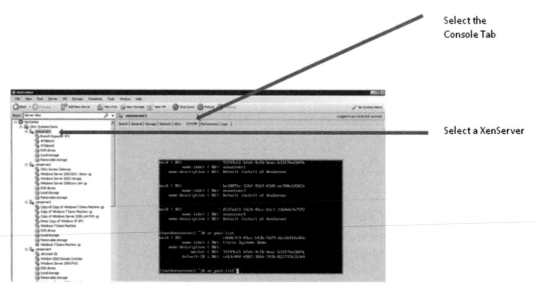

FIGURE 9.24

Accessing the XenServer Console.

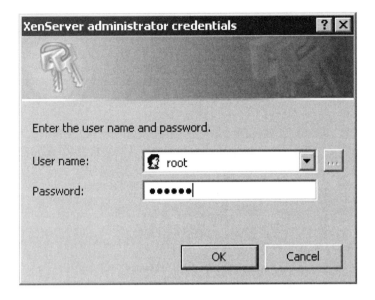

FIGURE 9.25

XenServer administrator credentials.

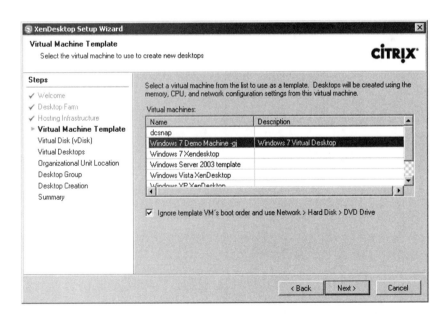

FIGURE 9.26

Virtual machine template.

SCVMM

1. Enter the computer name of your System Center Virtual Machine Manager server. Click **Next** (see Figure 9.27).
2. Enter domain credentials for the SCVMM server, and click **OK** (see Figure 9.28).
3. The wizard retrieves the available templates. Select a template from the System Center Virtual Machine Manager. Click **Next** (see Figure 9.29).

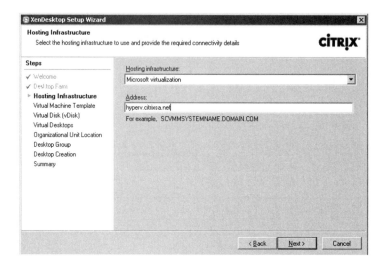

FIGURE 9.27

Hosting infrastructure.

FIGURE 9.28

System Center Virtual Machine Manager administrator credentials.

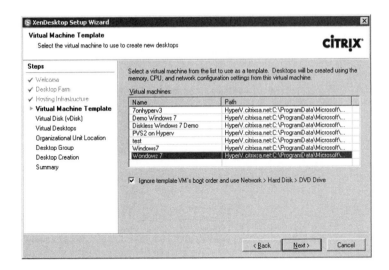

FIGURE 9.29

Virtual machine template.

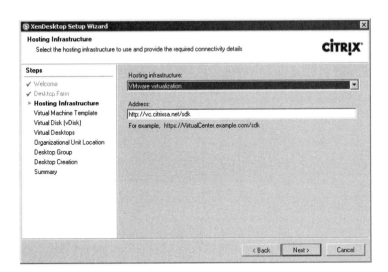

FIGURE 9.30

Hosting infrastructure.

VMware

1. Enter the name of your vCenter Server and the path to the SDK (see Figure 9.30) for example: HTTP (s)://<vCenterServer>/sdk.

2. When prompted, enter the vCenter credential that has permissions to access the template and relevant resource group (see Figure 9.31).

3. Select the template you created earlier (see Figure 9.32).

FIGURE 9.31

Virtual Center administrator credentials.

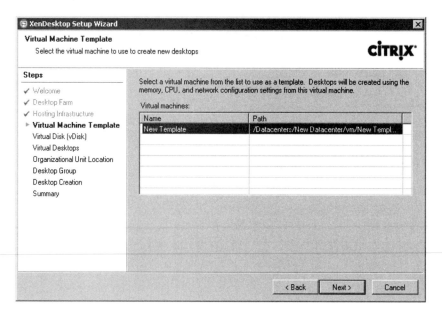

FIGURE 9.32

Virtual machine template.

All Hypervisors

4. Select a vDisk from your list of vDisks. Select **Specify target device collection** (see Figure 9.33).

> **NOTE**
>
> By default the **Specify target device collection** is unchecked, and the Target Devices are created in the default collection. For management purposes, I recommend a separate Device Collection.

5. Specify a name for the Device Collection, and click **Next** (see Figure 9.34).

6. Specify the computer names that you want created for your desktops (see Figure 9.35).

> **NOTE**
>
> These names are not labels, but the actual Active Directory Computer Accounts that will be created.

> **TIP**
>
> This example will create W7demo1 to W7demo5, if you wanted to create W7demo6 to W7demo10 later, simply change the Start from to 6 and leave the number of desktops at 5.

7. Change the OU selection to **Custom OU**, browse to the OU you have been allocated, or have created for this project (see Figure 9.36).

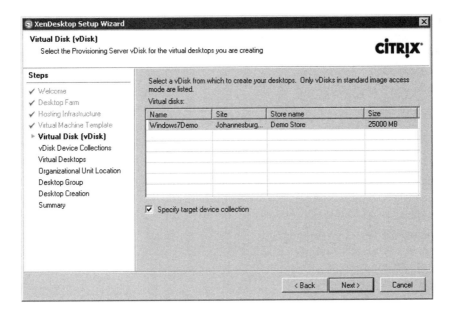

FIGURE 9.33

Virtual Disk (vDisk).

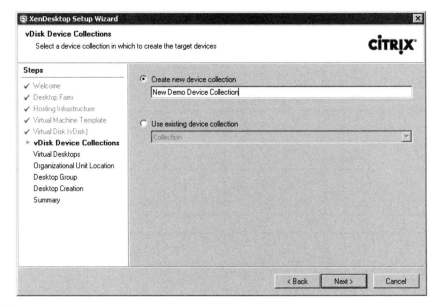

FIGURE 9.34

vDisk Device Collections.

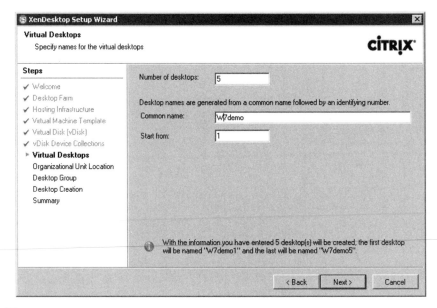

FIGURE 9.35

Virtual desktops.

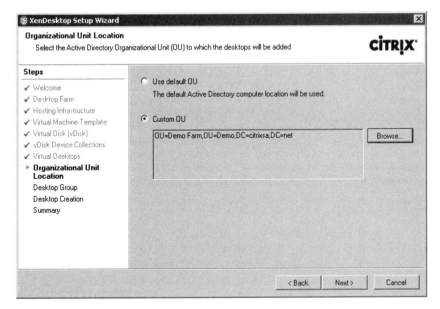

FIGURE 9.36

Organizational unit location.

8. Enter the name you wish to create for your Desktop Group in the **Create new desktop group** field, and click **Next** (see Figure 9.37).
9. Check whether the details are correct, and click **Next** (see Figure 9.38).
10. Click **Finish** (see Figure 9.39).

The Result

To illustrate what the wizard has performed, open **Active Directory Users and Computers**.

1. Navigate to the OU that you specified the wizard has created the computer accounts in the domain (see Figure 9.40).
2. Opening the XenCenter you will notice that two of the new virtual desktops have started (see Figure 9.41).
3. On the **Network Properties** tab, you can see that each virtual desktop has a unique MAC address and IP address.
4. Open the Provisioning Services Console.
5. Navigate to the Device Collection you specified, the computer names in the provisioning server are those created in Active Directory, and the MAC addresses are those created at the hypervisor level (see Figure 9.42).
6. Open the Desktop Delivery Services Console.
7. Open the **Desktop Groups** nodes, the virtual desktops are shown in the right-hand pane. Due to the fact that the default Idle Pool is set to two, only two are currently powered up. The Desktop Delivery Controller can dynamically communicate with the hypervisor to power on or power off desktops (see Figure 9.43).

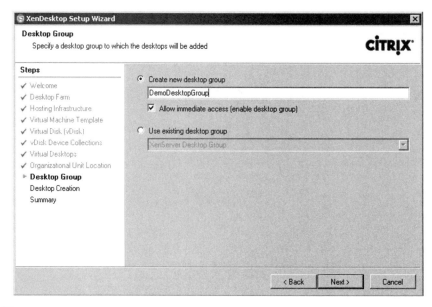

FIGURE 9.37

Desktop Group.

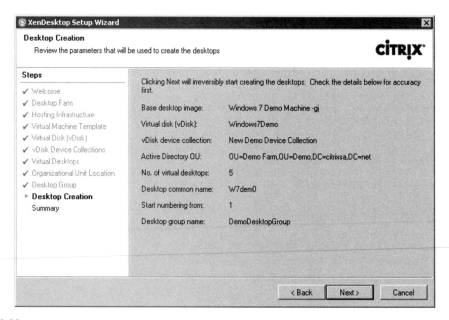

FIGURE 9.38

Desktop creation.

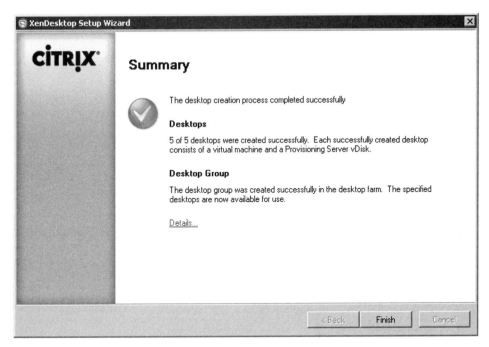

FIGURE 9.39

Summary.

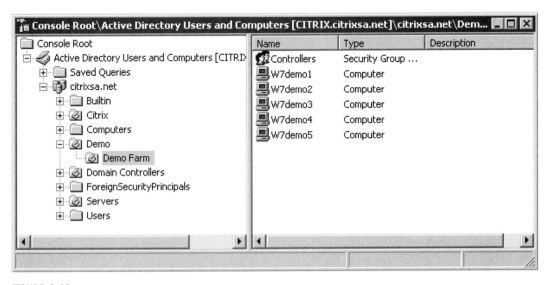

FIGURE 9.40

Active Directory Users and Computers.

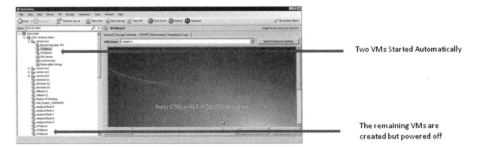

Two VMs Started Automatically

The remaining VMs are created but powered off

FIGURE 9.41

XenCenter – virtual machines.

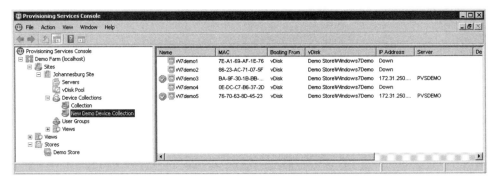

FIGURE 9.42

Provisioning Services Console – Device Collection.

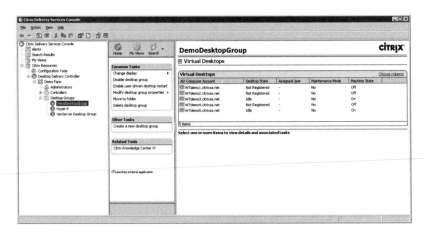

FIGURE 9.43

Citrix Delivery Service Console – Desktop Groups.

So to recap, the XenDesktop Setup Wizard

- Creates the Active Directory Computer Accounts.
- Creates the virtual machines on the hypervisor.
- Uses the MAC addresses on the hypervisor, and the computer accounts in Active Directory, to create the Target Devices on the provisioning server.
- Creates a Desktop Group containing the virtual machines created on the hypervisor.

SUMMARY

The XenDesktop Setup Wizard is a small but significant subject; operationally, it enables rapid bulk creation of virtual desktops. In this chapter, we looked at what is required for the wizard, the templates on the various hypervisors, and then the installation of the wizard. We then put the pieces together with instructions of how to use the wizard.

Configure Citrix XenApp
for Application Provisioning

XenApp provides us with the mechanism required to keep the application layer separate from the operating system. Based on a user's Active Directory group membership, we can configure that users will receive different applications to suit their roles.

There are three different types of application provisioning we can use, and each has a particular use case.

1. XenApp-hosted application is the application provisioning that most people traditionally associate with Citrix – the application is installed on a server operating system running Remote Desktop Services (formerly Terminal Services) and the application executes using CPU and memory on the server and only displays on the virtual desktop.
2. VM-hosted application is the newest type of application provisioning delivered by Citrix. VM-hosted applications work almost identically to XenApp-hosted applications, with the exception that they are delivered remotely from a desktop operating system, rather than a server operating system.
3. XenApp-streamed applications are packaged in and deployed into a virtual sandbox on the virtual desktop. XenApp-streamed applications execute on the virtual desktop using CPU and memory on the virtual desktop. Microsoft App-V performs the same function as XenApp-streamed applications – App-V can be utilized in environments where App-V is the application virtualization standard.

XenApp-hosted applications are very useful in terms of application compatibility. The primary use case is to provide the user access to Windows XP–compatible applications when running Windows 7 as the virtual desktop. The majority of applications that are compatible with Windows XP will run on

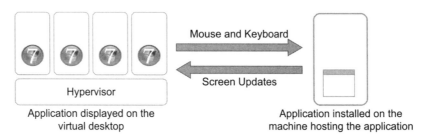

Mouse and Keyboard

Screen Updates

Hypervisor

Application displayed on the
virtual desktop

Application installed on the
machine hosting the application

FIGURE 10.1

Hosted applications are remotely presented to the virtual desktop.

Windows 2003 (Terminal Services), and for those that don't, there is VM-hosted Apps. XenApp-hosted applications have the additional benefit of offloading the application overhead off the virtual desktop onto the server as shown in Figure 10.1.

> **NOTE**
>
> The XenDesktop installation DVD for XenApp now refers to XenApp-hosted applications as – "Server-hosted Apps."

VM-hosted applications are a relatively new technology, which extends what XenApp does with Remote Desktop Services (formerly Terminal Services) from a server operating system to the desktop operating system. We can now take an application that is not compatible with Remote Desktop Services, and publish it as a single instance from one desktop operating system to another. The most common use case would be to install an application on a Windows XP operating system – running as a VM (virtual machine) – and to publish that application to a Windows 7 virtual desktop. The application actually executes in memory and CPU on the Windows XP machine and only displays on the Windows 7 desktop. The down side is that you require a Windows XP virtual instance for every single user needing to use the application that is only Windows XP compatible. The high resource requirements means that this tends to have a limited use case for a few "Power Users" with a specific requirement.

> **NOTE**
>
> It is worth noting that the Windows 7 feature – XP mode, isn't compatible with Windows 7 installed on a hypervisor. XP mode leverages Microsoft virtual PC, and virtual PC uses the virtualization assist processor features, which aren't available to a virtual CPU (vCPU).

XenApp-streamed applications fall into the category of what is generally regarded as application virtualization. Application virtualization does a great job of isolating applications from each other such that we can even run multiple versions of the same application on one machine. Various vendors have application virtualization offerings, they include Citrix XenApp-streamed applications, Microsoft App-V (formerly Softricity), VMware ThinApp, and Altiris SVS. The details vary, but the basics are the same; they present a virtual hard drive and a virtual registry to the application, the application thus runs in an isolated sandbox as shown in Figure 10.2. What application virtualization does not address is operating

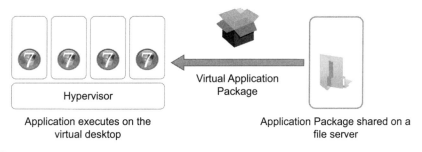

Application executes on the
virtual desktop

Application Package shared on a
file server

FIGURE 10.2

XenApp-streamed applications copy the package to the virtual desktop.

system compatibility, in instances where the application has a specific operating system dependency; the application should be installed on its intended target operating system and presented to the virtual desktop using XenApp-hosted applications, or VM-hosted Apps.

XenApp-streamed applications allow the desktop to be built out in a completely modular way. Each user can have a customized desktop built on the same base build. Because applications are isolated from each other, they don't conflict like traditional locally installed applications do.

INSTALL XENAPP FOR VIRTUAL APPLICATIONS
Design Decisions for Application Provisioning to Virtual Desktops

For a POC, you can use Access, SQL Express, or SQL Server. For live/production environments, use SQL Server only.

FAQ

Can I use the same Web Interface site for both XenApp and XenDesktop?

Yes, you can run the same Web Interface site for both desktops and applications.

The Web Interface server should be installed on a separate server (typically virtual due to low resource requirements) from XenApp. The exception to this would be in a proof of concept where functionality is just to be tested.

Prerequisites Windows 2003

Control Panel | Add/Remove Programs | Add/Remove Windows Components | Terminal Server

This adds Terminal Services – Application Mode as shown in Figure 10.3.

The Java Runtime Environment, Version 1.5.0_9, and .NET Framework Version 2.0 will automatically be installed if they aren't already present.

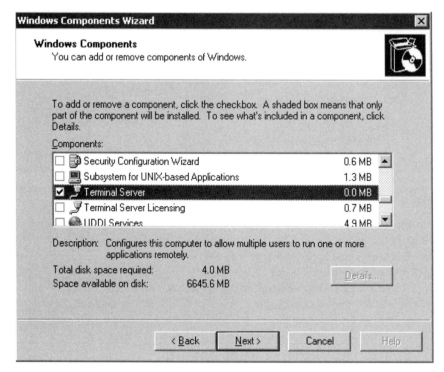

FIGURE 10.3

Terminal Server component.

Prerequisites Windows 2008

Add the following roles, using the Server Manager as shown in Figure 10.4:

- Terminal Services
- Application server

If sharing a port between the Citrix XML service and IIS, add the Web Server (IIS) role and these role services:

- Security
- Windows Authentication
- IIS 6 Management Compatibility and all its subcomponents
- ISAPI Extensions
- ISAPI Filters

NOTE

If possible, for performance reasons, do not install IIS on the same server as the XenApp server.

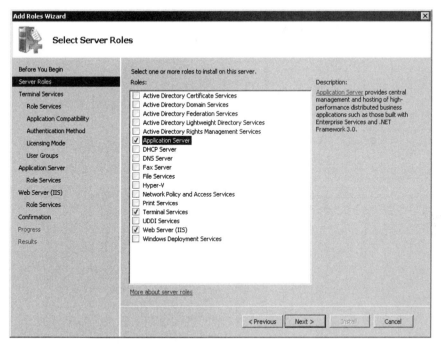

FIGURE 10.4

Configure application server role.

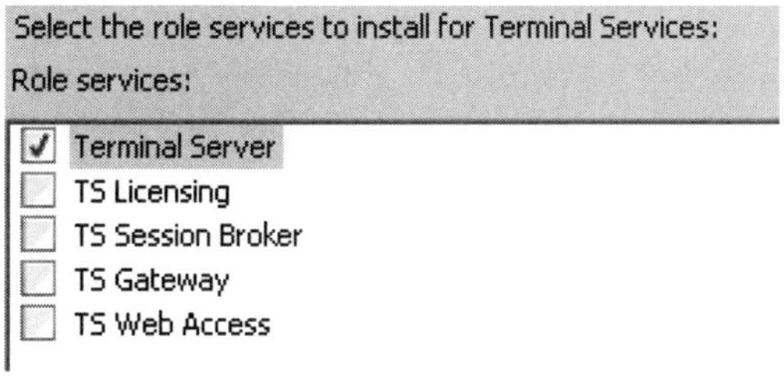

Select the role services to install for Terminal Services:

Role services:

- ☑ Terminal Server
- ☐ TS Licensing
- ☐ TS Session Broker
- ☐ TS Gateway
- ☐ TS Web Access

FIGURE 10.5

Add the Terminal Server Role services.

You will be prompted to configure the role.

You need only to select **Terminal Server** (see Figure 10.5).

Select **Do not require Network Level Authentication** (see Figure 10.6).

Select the type of Microsoft TSCAL (now called RDS CAL) your organization uses. If in doubt select **Per User** (see Figure 10.7).

XenApp for Windows 2008 requires .Net version 3.0, this is installed as an operating system feature through server manager.

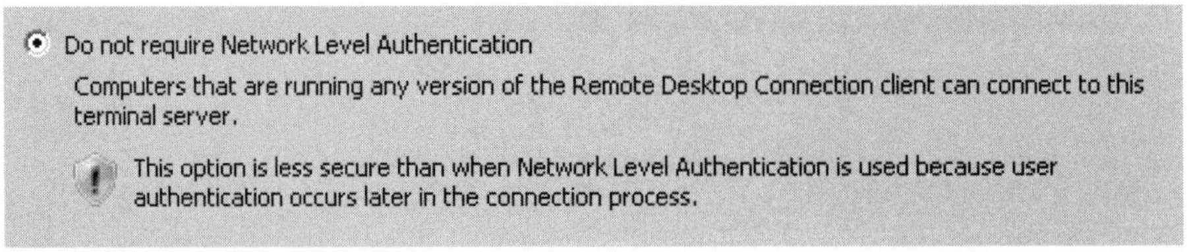

⊙ Do not require Network Level Authentication

Computers that are running any version of the Remote Desktop Connection client can connect to this terminal server.

⚠ This option is less secure than when Network Level Authentication is used because user authentication occurs later in the connection process.

FIGURE 10.6

Network level authentication is not required.

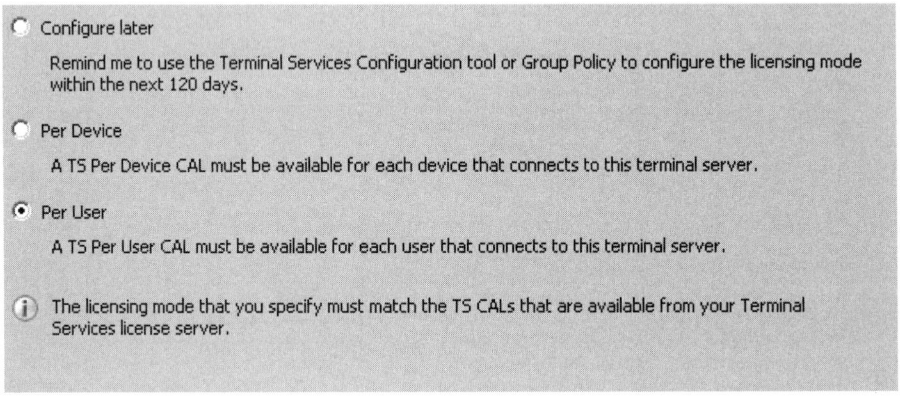

○ Configure later

Remind me to use the Terminal Services Configuration tool or Group Policy to configure the licensing mode within the next 120 days.

○ Per Device

A TS Per Device CAL must be available for each device that connects to this terminal server.

⊙ Per User

A TS Per User CAL must be available for each user that connects to this terminal server.

ⓘ The licensing mode that you specify must match the TS CALs that are available from your Terminal Services license server.

FIGURE 10.7

Configure TS CAL type.

Select the **.NET Framework 3.0 Features** tick box (see Figure 10.8).

Adding the .NET Framework 3.0 will automatically prompt you to additionally add some required Role Services (see Figure 10.9):

- Web Server (IIS)
- Windows Process Activation Service

Install JRE

The JRE is installed automatically as part of the XenApp installation on Windows 2003, however on Windows 2008 you are required to manually install the JRE.

Download JRE 1.6 Update 5 and install it. The software can be obtained from www.java.com.

> **TIP**
>
> The JRE on the XenDesktop 4 DVD will also suffice, mount XDS_4_0_0.ISO and navigate w2k3 or x64 depending on your operating system, then to the \en\ Support\JRE1.5 subfolders and execute jre-1_5_0_15-windows-i586-p.exe.

Click **Accept** to install the JRE using the standard recommended features (see Figure 10.10).

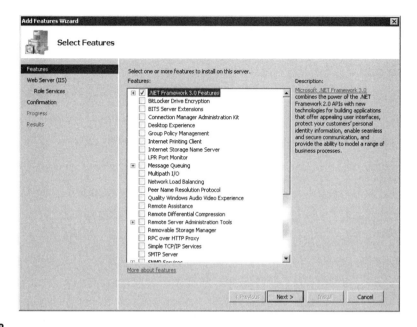

FIGURE 10.8

Adding the .NET Framework 3.0 features dialog box.

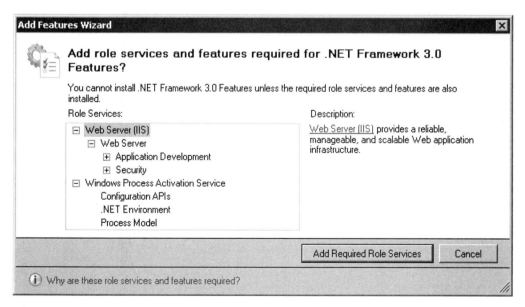

FIGURE 10.9

Required role services for .NET Framework 3.0.

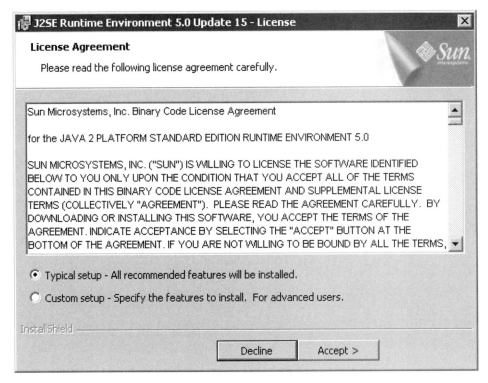

FIGURE 10.10

Sun JRE license agreement.

Web Interface

The options below only apply if you require IIS for Web Interface.

In the application server selection process, you will need to choose a number of options. Select application server foundation then scroll down (see Figure 10.11).

Select

- ASP.NET
- .NET Extensibility
- ISAPI Extensions
- ISAPI Filters

Under Health and Diagnostics, select (Web Interface):

- HTTP Logging
- Request Monitor

Under **Security** option, select **Windows Authentication** (Web Interface) (see Figure 10.12).

Scroll down and select everything under IIS 6 Management Compatibility (Web Interface) as shown in Figure 10.13.

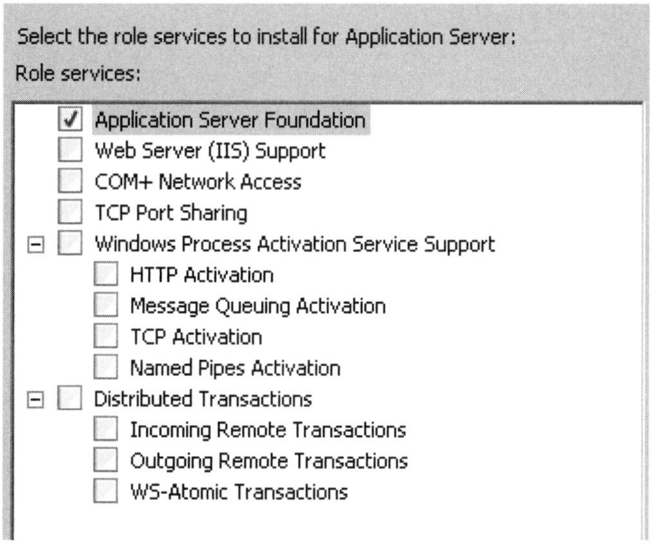

FIGURE 10.11

Application server foundation role service.

FIGURE 10.12

Application development role services.

☐ Management Service
☐ ☑ IIS 6 Management Compatibility
☑ IIS 6 Metabase Compatibility
☑ IIS 6 WMI Compatibility
☑ IIS 6 Scripting Tools
☑ IIS 6 Management Console
☐ ☐ FTP Publishing Service

FIGURE 10.13

IIS 6 Management Compatibility role services.

Install .NET35

Mount the XA50_WS08_EN.ISO, and run <CDROM>\Support\DotNet35\dotnetfx35.exe to install .NET35.

Click **Install** to proceed with the installation (see Figure 10.14).

Install XenApp Step by Step

In this section, we will go through the process of installing XenApp. For the sake of simplicity, I have chosen not to install the Password Manager or EdgeSight components at this stage.

1. Insert the XenApp DVD or mount the XenApp ISO image (the name will vary depending on the version). Launch the autorun on the root of the DVD if it doesn't launch automatically.
2. Select your edition, I have selected Platinum (see Figure 10.15).
3. Select application virtualization (see Figure 10.16).
4. Toggle the radio button to accept the license agreement and click **Next** (see Figure 10.17).
5. Click **Next** to get past the "Prerequisites" dialog box (see Figure 10.18).
6. Typically, you would deselect **Citrix Licensing** – if you have already installed a license server for XenDesktop, you will share the same license server. Deselect **Web Interface** if it is to be installed separately (see Design Decisions) – for a proof of concept typically you will place this component on the same server (see Figure 10.19).

I recommend adding the XenApp Client to the server for a POC – simply for testing a loopback connection to the server if necessary. For production servers, don't add the client as it adds extra overhead (see Figure 10.20).

7. Click **OK**.

You will receive a warning on Windows 2008 – which you can safely ignore.

8. Select **Yes** to pass your logon credential through to the XenApp Client. Click **Next** (see Figure 10.21).

NOTE

You would only select "No" if the client end point device were in a separate domain from the XenApp server. In this instance, the client end point device is the actual XenApp server.

FIGURE 10.14

.NET Framework 3.5 installation dialog box.

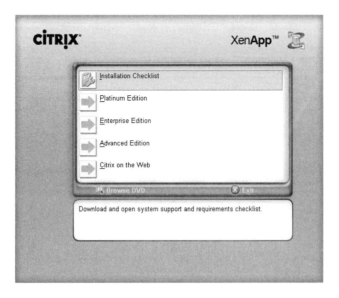

FIGURE 10.15

Citrix installation dialog box.

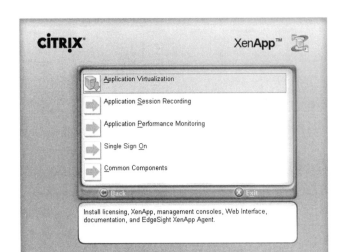

FIGURE 10.16

Installation component selection.

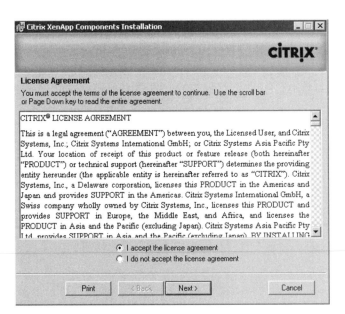

FIGURE 10.17

License agreement.

FIGURE 10.18

Prerequisites installation dialog box.

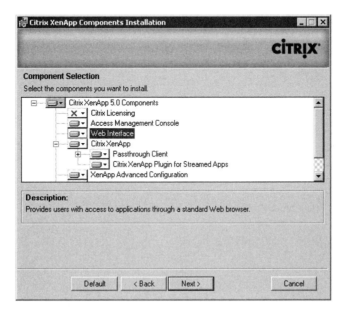

FIGURE 10.19

XenApp components dialog box.

FIGURE 10.20

Benign warning on Windows 2008.

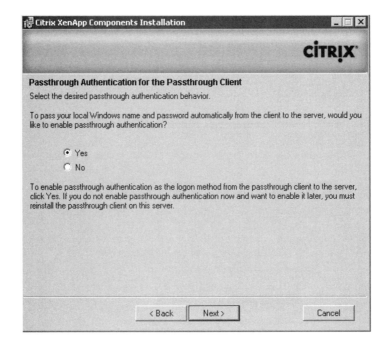

FIGURE 10.21

Domain passthrough authentication dialog box.

9. Enter the name of the Web Interface server. In this example, I have installed Web Interface on the XenApp server hence – http://localhost. This should read http://<Web Interface Name or IP Address> (see Figure 10.22).

10. Select **I already have a license server** – and click **Next** (see Figure 10.23).

11. Select **Yes** to allow the installation of the Microsoft Visual C++ Redistributable (see Figure 10.24).

12. Click **Next** to install the Management Console snap-ins (see Figure 10.25).

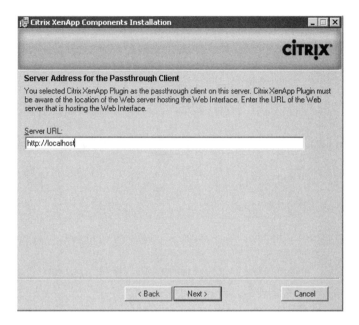

FIGURE 10.22

Web Interface server address dialog box.

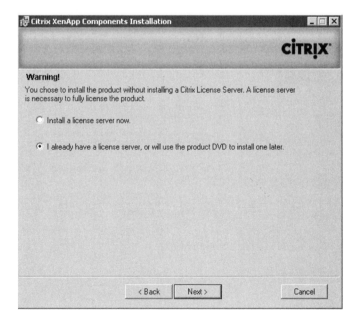

FIGURE 10.23

License server installation dialog box.

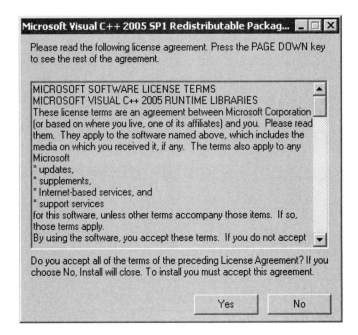

FIGURE 10.24

Microsoft Visual C ++ 2005 license agreement dialog box.

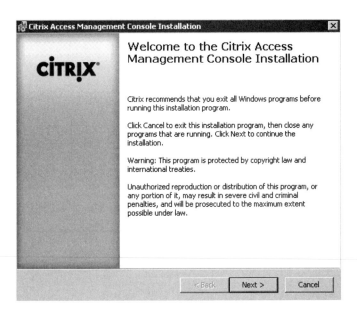

FIGURE 10.25

Access Management Console installation dialog box.

13. Verify everything installed without errors and click **Next** (see Figure 10.26).

14. Click **Finish** to complete the console installations (see Figure 10.27).

If you have selected to Install Web Interface with XenApp Server, the Web Interface installation will occur now as part of your XenApp install – see the following section "Install Web Interface" for details.

15. Click **Next** to start the installation of the core components (see Figure 10.28).

16. Click **Next** (see Figure 10.29).

17. Select **Create a new farm** for the first XenApp server – subsequent servers will **Join an existing farm** (see Figure 10.30).

See the "Design Decisions" section on page 309 for the selection of the database components.

If selecting an SQL server, you can follow the same steps as when using SQL for the DDC 2.2.1 Steps 8 through 14. This leads you through the process of creating a file DSN for your database connection.

18. Enter the name of your farm and click **Next** (see Figure 10.31a, b).

19. Click **Next** to confirm the credentials that will be used as the farm administrator (see Figure 10.32).

TIP

Use your credentials at this stage, and change them later if necessary – only the credentials entered here will be the initial farm administrator.

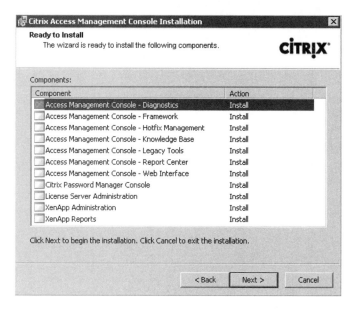

FIGURE 10.26

Access Management Console installation list.

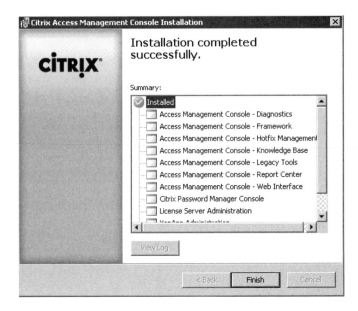

FIGURE 10.27

Installation results dialog box.

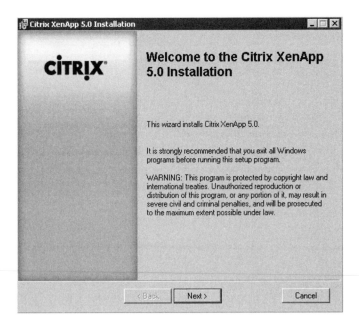

FIGURE 10.28

XenApp 5.0 installation.

FIGURE 10.29

XenApp 5.0 components dialog box.

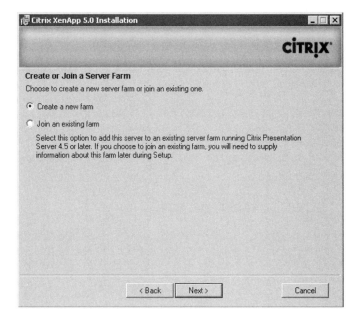

FIGURE 10.30

Create or join a server farm dialog box.

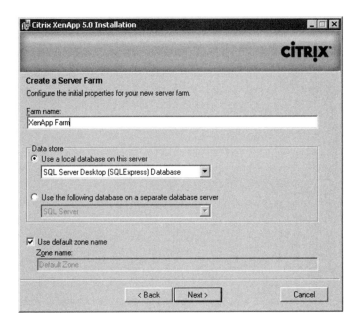

FIGURE 10.31a

Datastore configuration dialog box.

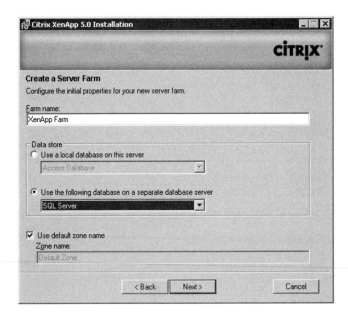

FIGURE 10.31b

Datastore configuration dialog box.

FIGURE 10.32

Assign farm administrator dialog box.

20. Click **Next** (see Figure 10.33).

IMA encryption is only required by some military and financial organizations; generally speaking I would recommend leaving it off.

21. Enter the same license server as for XenDesktop – bear in mind that XenDesktop Enterprise and XenDesktop Platinum both include XenApp licenses, which you are able to use (see Figure 10.34).
22. Tab to **Continue the product without installing licenses**, and click **Next** (see Figure 10.35).

You may receive a license server warning, which you can ignore (see Figure 10.36).

23. Click **Next**.

NOTE

Shadowing security settings can only be changed at installation, so be careful to select the level of security required by your organization. These settings have been tied to the installation to prevent administrators from surreptitiously shadowing users. Previously, the acceptance popup could be enabled or disabled by the administrator.

If you have installed IIS on the XenApp server, you will receive the dialog box shown in Figure 10.37.

24. Accept the default to share port between IIS and the XML service, click **Next**.

IIS is not the only application that uses port 80 – some hardware vendor tools use a Tomcat service, which may also clash with the XML service – see the Tip on page 330. The Citrix XML Service is normally listed under Services, unless it is sharing with IIS, in which case it is not listed.

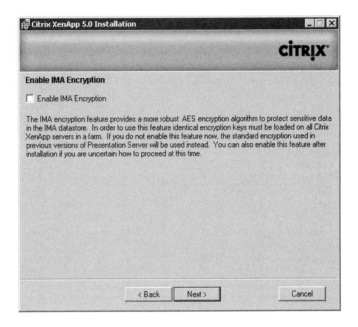

FIGURE 10.33

IMA encryption option.

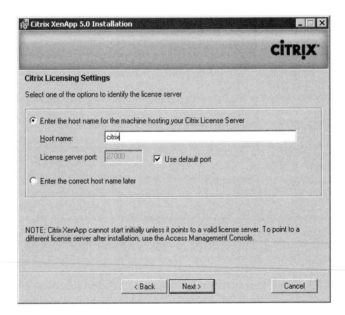

FIGURE 10.34

Citrix License Server settings.

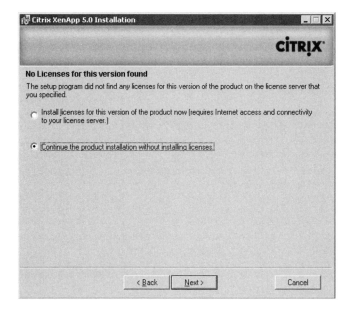

FIGURE 10.35

No licenses warning dialog box.

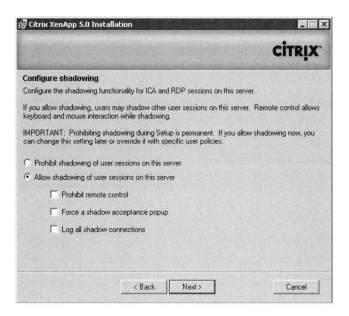

FIGURE 10.36

Configure shadowing dialog box.

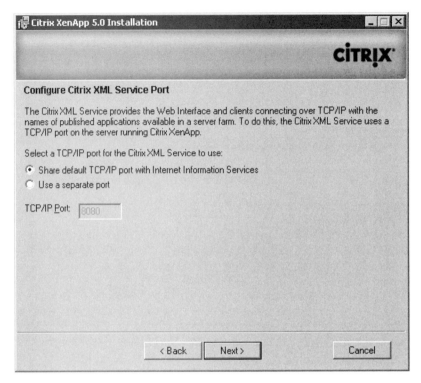

FIGURE 10.37

Configure Citrix XML service port.

> **TIP**
>
> The XML Port is the one area that is prone to clashing with other services. Scan through you list of services, if Citrix XML Service isn't listed (and it isn't sharing with IIS), then you will need to reregister the service. From the command line type: **ctxxmlss /R8080**. This will register the XML service on port 8080. Take care to change this port in Web Interface and in the server settings in the Delivery Services Console.

25. Select **Add the list from the Users Group now** option, and deselect **Add Anonymous users also**, then click **Next** (see Figure 10.38).

The anonymous users will add local user accounts to the XenApp server, which will more often than not be a security issue.

26. Click **Finish** to confirm the installation summary (see Figure 10.39).

If Web Interface is being installed on Windows 2008, you will be prompted to confirm the changing of the security settings (see Figure 10.40).

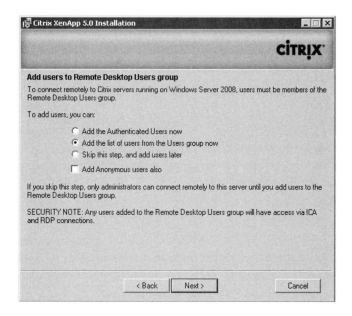

FIGURE 10.38

Add users to the Remote Desktop Users group.

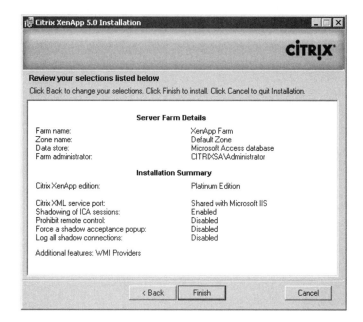

FIGURE 10.39

Review selections dialog box.

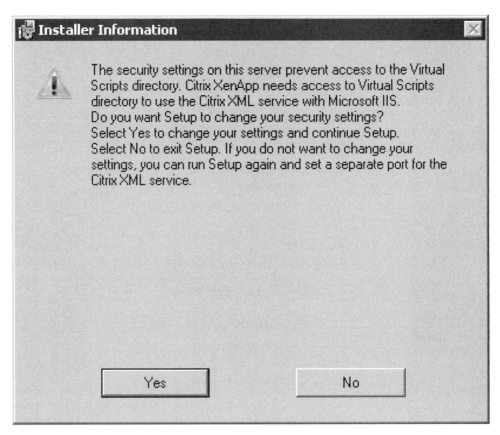

FIGURE 10.40

Virtual Scripts Security changes dialog box.

27. Click **Yes**.
28. Click **Close** to finish this part of the installation (see Figure 10.41).

   This section installs the Java-based Console for Citrix Policies (see Figure 10.42).

29. Click **Next**.
30. Confirm the path, and click **Next** (see Figure 10.43).
31. Click **Next** to install (see Figure 10.44).
32. Click **Finish** to confirm successful installation (see Figure 10.45).
33. Click **Next** to install the documentation (see Figure 10.46).
34. Confirm the path and click **Next** (see Figure 10.47).
35. Click **Finish** (see Figure 10.48).
36. The summary displays all the components installed. Click **Finish** (see Figure 10.49).
37. Click **Yes** to restart immediately (see Figure 10.50).

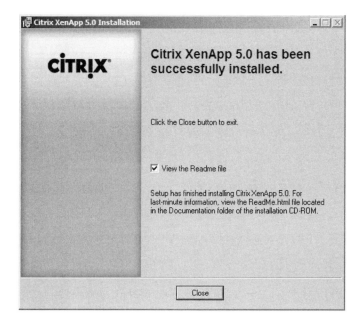

FIGURE 10.41

Successful installation dialog box.

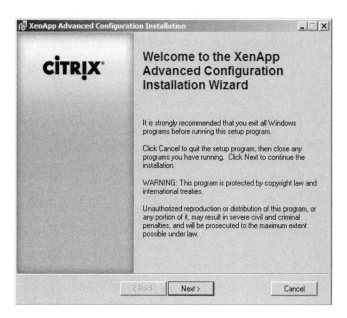

FIGURE 10.42

Advanced configuration installation dialog box.

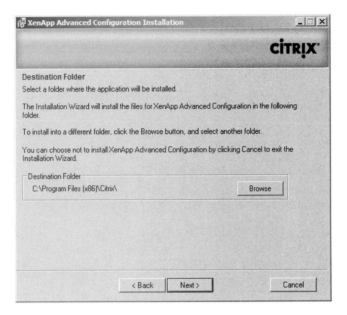

FIGURE 10.43

Destination folder selection dialog box.

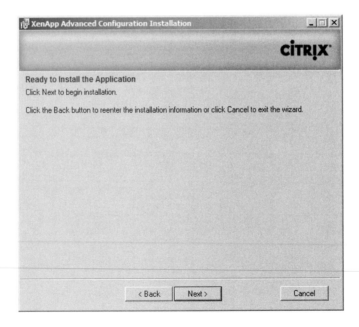

FIGURE 10.44

Install advanced configuration.

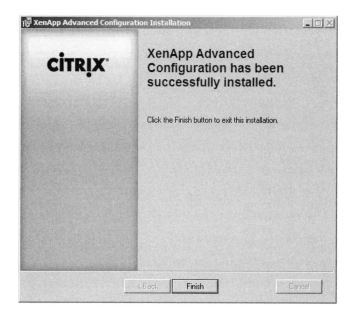

FIGURE 10.45

Successful installation dialog box.

FIGURE 10.46

Document library installation dialog box.

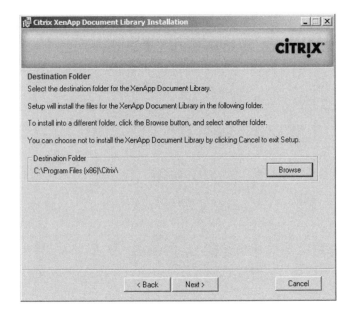

FIGURE 10.47

Document library destination folder.

FIGURE 10.48

Document library successful installation.

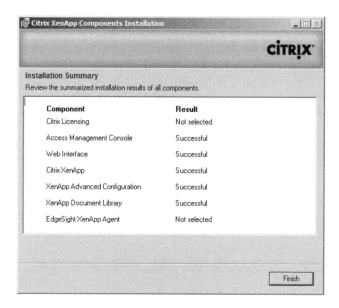

FIGURE 10.49

XenApp components installation summary.

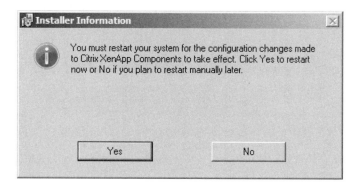

FIGURE 10.50

XenApp post install restart.

INSTALL WEB INTERFACE

In a POC environment, you may choose to install this component on the XenApp server, and in production/live environments, this should be installed separately on a dedicated Web server.

1. Insert the XenApp DVD or mount the XenApp ISO image. Navigate to <DVD>:\Web Interface \WebInterface.exe.

2. Select **OK** for English (see Figure 10.51).

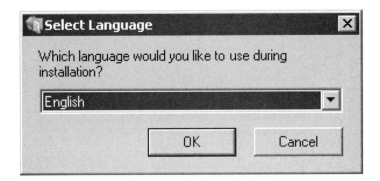

FIGURE 10.51

Select language dialog box.

FIGURE 10.52

Web Interface installation informational dialog box.

3. Click **Next** to install Web Interface (see Figure 10.52).
4. Toggle the radio button to accept the license agreement, and click **Next** (see Figure 10.53).
5. Confirm the path and click **Next** (see Figure 10.54).
6. Select – **Copy the clients to this computer** – this was previously on a separate DVD, but is now included on the same media (see Figure 10.55).

FIGURE 10.53

License agreement dialog box.

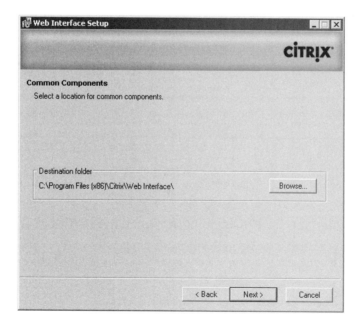

FIGURE 10.54

Common components destination folder.

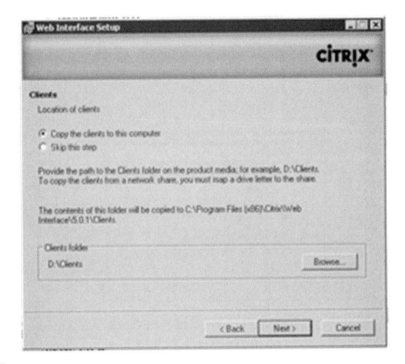

FIGURE 10.55

Citrix client option dialog box.

TIP

I recommend copying the clients – even if it is more time consuming – it will save you the complexity of having to configure the XenApp clients on the Web Interface later. If the clients aren't installed as part of the initial installation, Web Interface redirects users to download the client from the Internet.

---

7. Click **Next** to install (see Figure 10.56).
8. Click **Finish** to complete (see Figure 10.57).

Configure Web Interface for Provisioning Applications to Virtual Desktops

Web Interface for virtual desktops requires that the applications be seamlessly integrated into the desktop. The best approach is to use a XenApp services site with pass-thru authentication from the virtual desktop.

1. Open the Access Suite Console on the Web Interface server.
2. Select **Citrix Resources | Configuration Tools | Web Interface | right-click** on the Web Interface, select **Create site** (see Figure 10.58).
3. Change the radio button to **XenApp Services**, and click **Next** (see Figure 10.59).

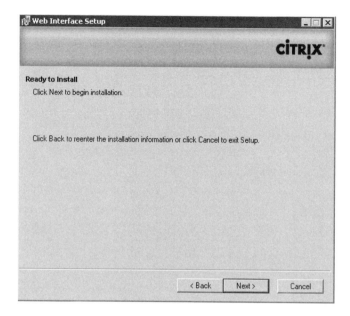

FIGURE 10.56

Installation initiation dialog box.

FIGURE 10.57

Successful installation dialog box.

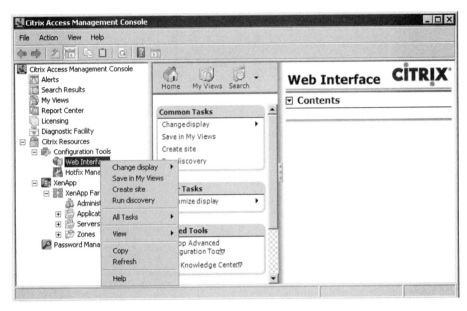

FIGURE 10.58

Citrix Access Management Console.

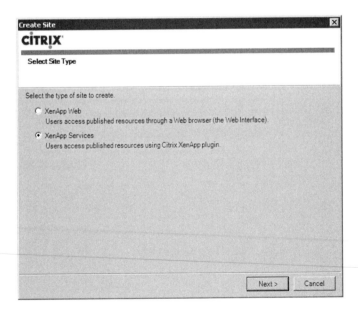

FIGURE 10.59

Select site type dialog box.

> **NOTE**
>
> XenApp services was previously known as Program Neighborhood Agent, hence some of the legacy references to PNAgent.

4. Accept the default settings, and click **Next** (see Figure 10.60).

5. Confirm your settings, and click **Next** (see Figure 10.61).

6. Click **Next** (see Figure 10.62).

7. Enter a description for the XenApp farm. This doesn't have to match the actual farm name. Click **Add...** to add XenApp servers, enter the names of your XenApp servers. Move the primary XML server to the top of the list and click **Next** (see Figure 10.63).

> **NOTE**
>
> If there are multiple servers in the farm, it is a good practice to add a number of XenApp servers for resiliency. Larger XenApp farms may use a dedicated server to provide XML services, the servers are accessed in order. For best performance, the data collector should not be top of the list. The Web Interface site will by default use port 80 to communicate with the XML service of the XenApp servers. Remember to change the XML port to match that on the XenApp servers.

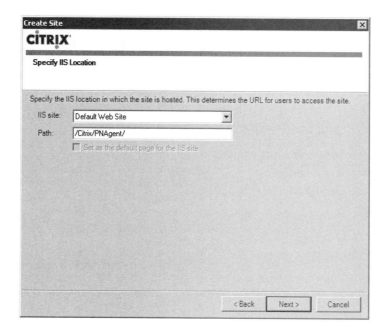

FIGURE 10.60

Specify IIS location dialog box.

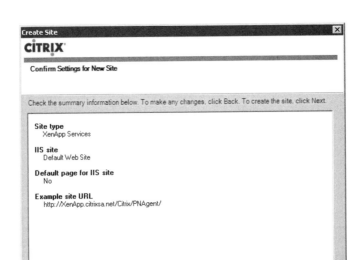

FIGURE 10.61

Confirm settings dialog box.

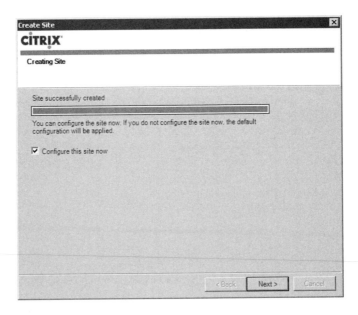

FIGURE 10.62

Site creation progress dialog box.

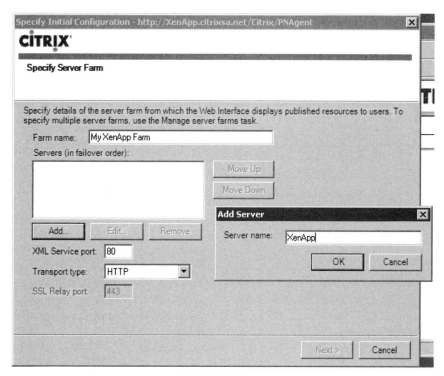

FIGURE 10.63

Specify server farm dialog box.

8. Change the Published Resource Type to **Dual mode streaming** (see Figure 10.64).

> **NOTE**
> The default is "Remote," which would only provision hosted applications (and VM-hosted applications). To provision both remote and streamed applications, this must be changed to **Dual mode streaming**.

9. Confirm your settings and click **Finish** (see Figure 10.65).
10. Select the Web Interface site you have just created and right-click on the **config.xml** node. Select **Configure authentication methods** (see Figure 10.66).
11. Select the **Pass-through (default)** check box. Click **OK** (see Figure 10.67).

> **NOTE**
> In the context of the virtual desktop, the XenApp client must seamlessly pass through the authentication XenApp server, and create the users' applications in the background.

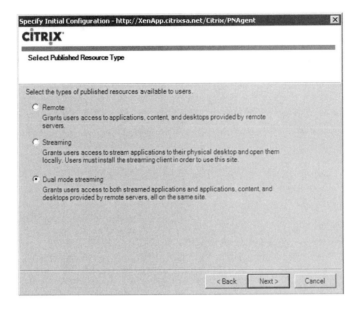

FIGURE 10.64

Select published resource type.

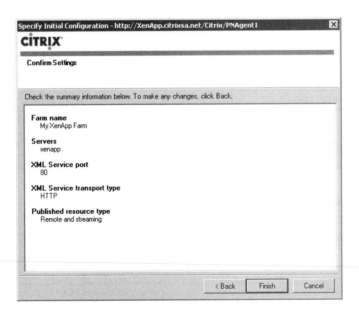

FIGURE 10.65

Confirm settings dialog box.

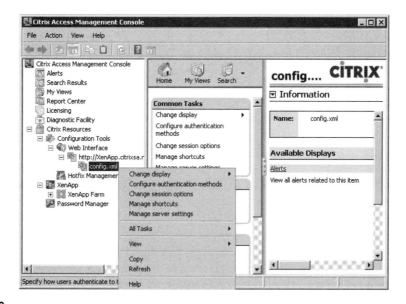

FIGURE 10.66

Access Management Console – configure authentication methods.

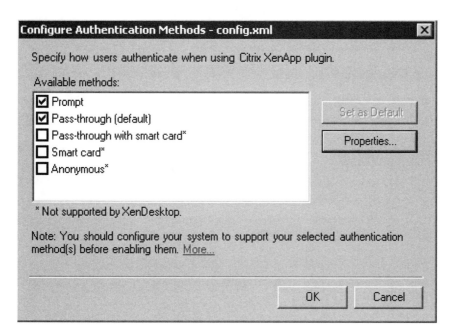

FIGURE 10.67

Configure authentication methods.

CONFIGURE XENAPP SERVER

This section illustrates the discovery process used by the Access Management Console for Citrix XenApp.

1. Select **Start | Programs | Citrix | Management Consoles | Access Management Console** (see Figure 10.68).

   By default, it will automatically launch the "Configure and run discovery" wizard.

NOTE

The discovery is run each time the console is opened. This requirement will be removed in the XenApp 6.0 version of the product.

---

2. Click **Next** (see Figure 10.69).
3. Click **Next** (see Figure 10.70).

TIP

To save time, deselect any products that you haven't installed.

---

4. Click **Next** to use the locally stored configuration files (see Figure 10.71).

   In some larger environments comprising multiple Web Interface servers, the configuration can be centralized.

5. Click **Add Local Computer** (see Figure 10.72).

   You could also click **Add**… to browse for additional XenApp servers. This is a good practice for resiliency.

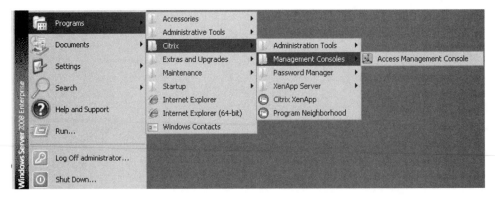

FIGURE 10.68

Access Management Console start menu item.

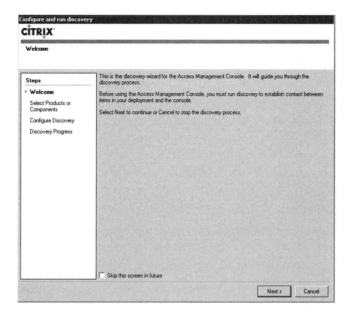

FIGURE 10.69

Discovery wizard welcome dialog box.

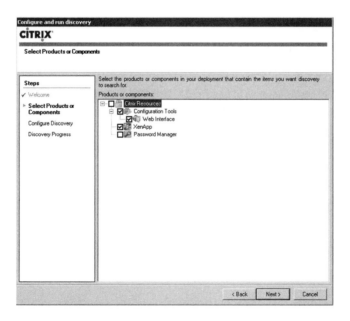

FIGURE 10.70

Discovery wizard product component selection.

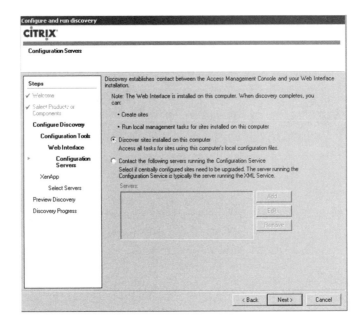

FIGURE 10.71

Configuration services location.

FIGURE 10.72

XenApp – Select Servers dialog box.

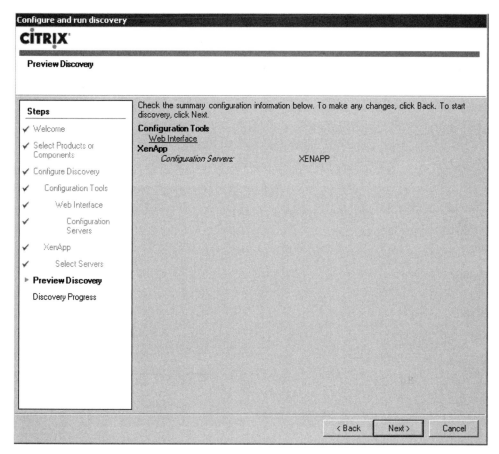

FIGURE 10.73

Preview discovery dialog box.

6. Click **Next** to confirm (see Figure 10.73).
7. Click **Finish** (see Figure 10.74).

The Access Management Console allows you to configure most aspects of your XenApp farm, including administration (security), applications, and servers (see Figure 10.75).

TIP

Add a secondary administrator or administrator group after installing XenApp – and grant the "Full Administration" privileges. If the user account that performed the applications is unavailable (locked out, deleted, and so on) you will be unable to administer the Citrix farm. The **Add local administrators** option is a good choice in many environments – if your security policies allow it.

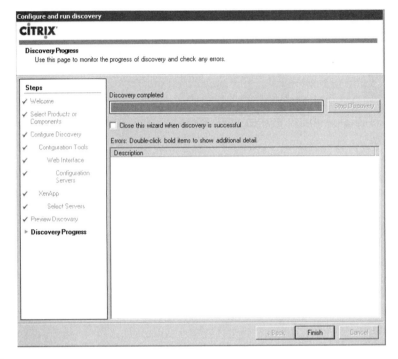

FIGURE 10.74

Discovery results dialog box.

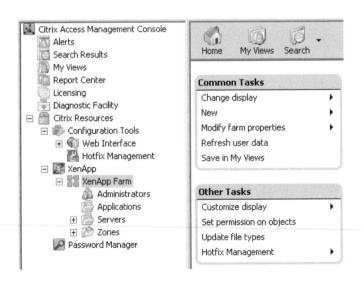

FIGURE 10.75

Access Management Console.

HOSTED APPLICATIONS – REGULAR INSTALLED

Hosted applications can be installed in the traditional manner directly onto all the XenApp servers in a farm. When applications are installed in the traditional manner care should be taken in more complex environments that applications do not clash. Using traditional methods, multiple versions of applications (e.g., Microsoft Office) cannot coexist on one server.

This method is, however, the simplest and quickest method to do basic testing. I would recommend using this method in a POC, especially if you are time constrained. In terms of your project plan, make sure that you have clear objectives – do you want to achieve desktop virtualization, application virtualization, or both? If you want to demonstrate the full features of both, then this impacts the project timeline.

Applications are installed on Windows 2003 or 2008 server. Terminal Services/Remote Desktop Services is used to allow the server to host multiple users, and the application is then presented over the network to the virtual desktop. The virtual desktop is in turn presented to the client device. The application is effectively tunneled from the XenApp server, inside the virtual desktop to the user (see Figure 10.76).

Publish a Hosted Application – Step by Step

1. Open the Delivery Services Console, under the **XenApp** node, select your farm, and right-click on the **Applications** folder, select **New | Publish application** (see Figure 10.77).
2. Click **Next** (see Figure 10.78).
3. Enter a display name for your application, and a description if desired then click **Next** (see Figure 10.79).

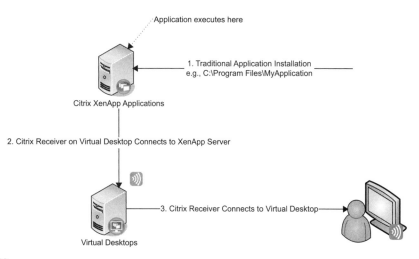

FIGURE 10.76

Hosted applications presented inside a virtual desktop.

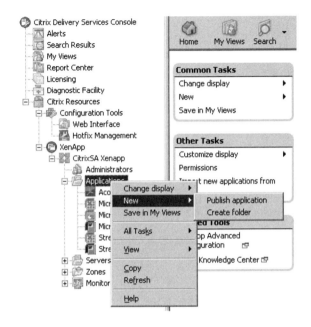

FIGURE 10.77

Publish application menu in the Delivery Service Console.

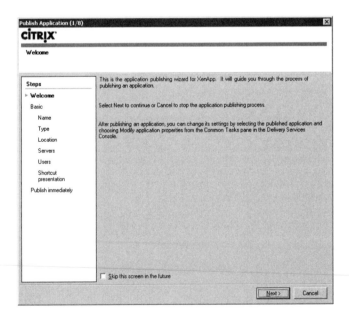

FIGURE 10.78

Publish application welcome dialog box.

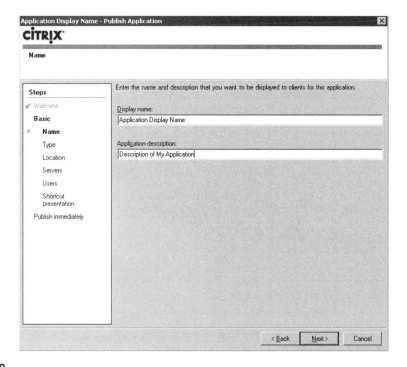

FIGURE 10.79

Published application display and description.

NOTE

The display name is what appears to the user, so make it intuitive. The description field is not required, but can be useful for tracking applications and for whom they are intended – for example, a description could be "Legacy application version 10 required by users in Cape Town."

---

4. Select **Application**, and under "Application type," select **Accessed from a server**. The server application type should be "Installed application" (see Figure 10.80).
5. Enter or browse for a command line and working directory for the executable and then click **Next** (see Figure 10.81).

NOTE

Citrix Streaming technologies overlap in some respects with the Application Isolation Environment (AIE) mechanism, including sharing some files. I would recommend using one of the two. Broadly speaking, the streaming supersedes AIE, and should be used instead.

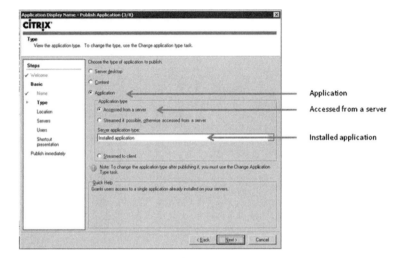

FIGURE 10.80

Application type to publish.

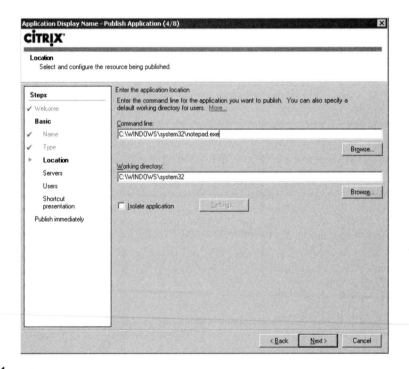

FIGURE 10.81

Application location dialog box.

6. To select the servers on which the application will be run, click **Add**…, from the Select Servers dialog box, click **Add** (or Add All to add all servers), click **OK** and then click **Next** (see Figure 10.82).

7. Click **Add**… to add users (see Figure 10.83).

NOTE

This mechanism works in exactly the same way as that of the Desktop Delivery Controller, when we added users to Desktop Groups.

---

8. Click **Next** (see Figure 10.84).
- Client application folder – can be used to organize how applications are presented to the user in Web Interface or through the online plug-in.
- Add to the client's **Start Menu** – creates an icon shortcut on the **Start Menu**, which can be useful in terms of usability – the **Start Menu** in this case would be that of the virtual desktop.
- Place under the Programs folder – configures the previous setting to present the icons under the Programs folder on the **Start Menu**.
- **Start Menu** folder – creates a custom folder on the client's **Start Menu**.
- Add shortcut to the client's desktop – Adds the application icon to the users' desktops.

9. Select **Configure advanced application settings now** check box (see Figure 10.85).

NOTE

You can configure these later, but for illustrative purposes, we will look briefly at all the options.

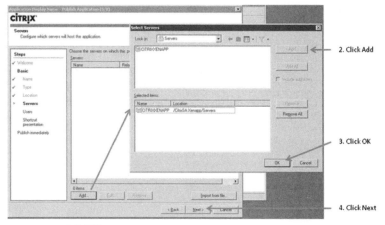

FIGURE 10.82

Select server to host the application.

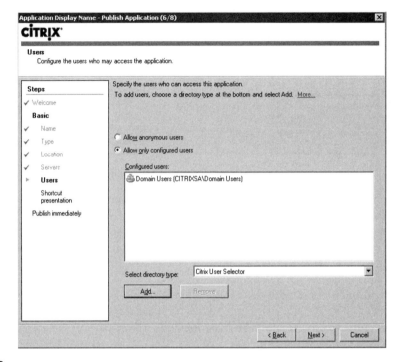

FIGURE 10.83

Configure users authorized to access the application.

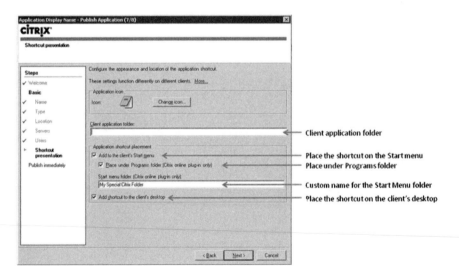

FIGURE 10.84

Configure application shortcut presentation.

FIGURE 10.85

Publish immediately – or configure settings.

10. Click **Next** (see Figure 10.86). (You can ignore these settings when publishing applications to virtual desktops.)

NOTE

These settings are only applicable if you are filtering your applications based on an Access Gateway access scenario. In this scenario, we are publishing applications to virtual desktops in the datacenter, and as such these settings would not be used in conjunction with VDI.

---

11. This is where you would set up FTA – file type associations. The FTA created here will create the FTA on the virtual desktop and automatically launch the application based on the file type. Select the relevant file types, and when finished, click **Next** (see Figure 10.87).

TIP

If you have multiple applications that share file types, tweak these here to associate the desired application with the file type. For example, you may want .pdf documents to associate with Adobe Reader, and not Adobe Acrobat, or you may want .xls files to associate with Excel 2003 rather than Excel 2007.

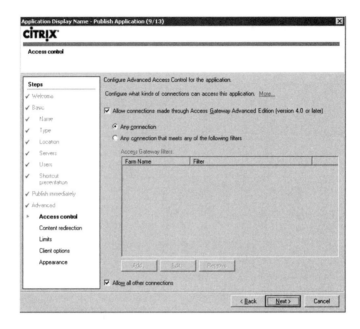

FIGURE 10.86

Configure Advanced Access Control.

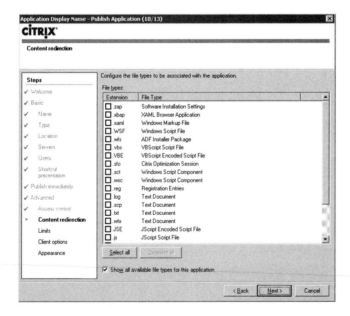

FIGURE 10.87

Configure file types to be associated.

12. Leave the default options, and click **Next** (see Figure 10.88).
- **Limit instances allowed to run in server farm** – This can be useful if you have a limited number of licensed copies of an application.
- **Allow only one instance of the application for each user** – This can be used for license management, and also for those applications that only allow a user one session to a back end database.
- You can additionally change the CPU priority of an application. I would not recommend tampering with this setting unless absolutely necessary.

13. Leave the default settings, and click **Next** (see Figure 10.89).

There are three client options that could be configured here: **Client audio**, **Client encryption**, and **Printing**. The audio and encryption settings are normally not applicable when used with Xen-Desktop VDI, but the **Printing** option may still be applicable.

- Client audio
  - Enable legacy audio – This option enables the redirection of audio from the XenApp server to the client.
  - Minimum requirement – This option disallows clients that don't have audio support.

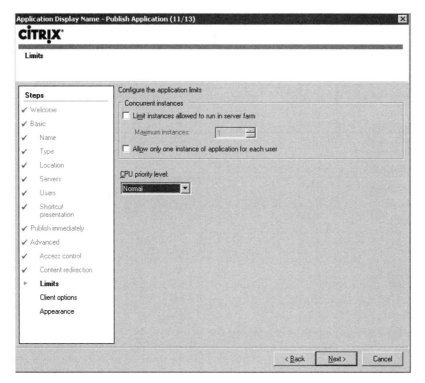

FIGURE 10.88

Configure application limits.

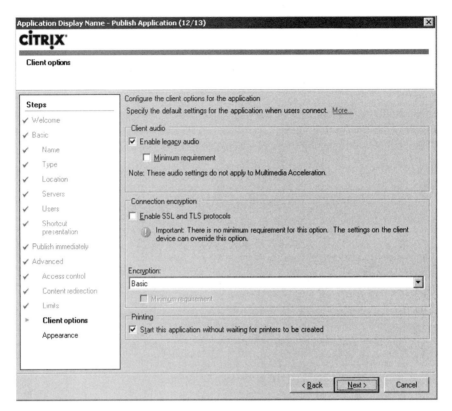

Configure client options.

- Client encryption
  - Enable SSL and TLS protocols – This option enables the use of SSL/TLS for connection to the application.
  - Encryption – Basic, 128-bit login only, 40-bit, 56-bit, and 128-bit RC-5 encryption. These options enable the encryption of the ICA protocol. This is normally only necessary on an unsecured network.
  - Minimum requirement – This option only allows access to client connecting using the encryption level defined above.
- Printing
  - **Start this application without waiting for printer to be created** – This is the default, and that is to create printers asynchronously – otherwise your logon is delayed until all your printers are created.

14. These settings only affect sessions that aren't running in seamless mode and can thus largely be ignored. Click **Finish** (see Figure 10.90).

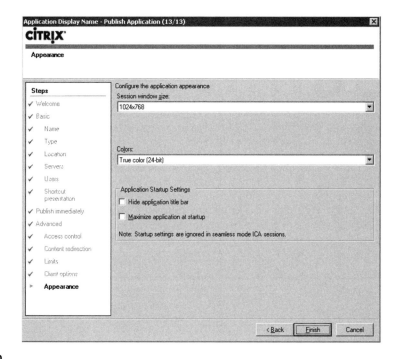

FIGURE 10.90

Configure application appearance.

HOSTED APPLICATIONS – STREAMED TO SERVER

Streamed to server applications are applications that have been profiled on the Server OS of the XenApp server. These applications aren't installed in the traditional manner, but rely on the streaming client on the XenApp server to execute in a virtual container on the XenApp server. This has benefits in more complex environments – applications are isolated from each other and they are simple to install and update across the XenApp farm. Using streaming, multiple versions of Microsoft Office can coexist on a single server.

This method requires the profiling of all the required applications. It is best practice to stream your applications in a XenApp environment.

I would recommend streaming only a single application in a POC especially if you are time constrained, and in that way you can demonstrate the concept without having to profile all the applications (install the rest of the applications in the traditional manner).

Applications are streamed to the XenApp server, where the virtual application is placed in the radecache folder. The application is not installed per se; however, it does execute in an isolation environment on the XenApp server. The streamed application is presented to the virtual desktop over the network using the ICA/HDX protocol in exactly the same way as a traditionally installed application. From there, the application is tunneled from the XenApp server to the virtual desktop and on to the client device (see Figure 10.91).

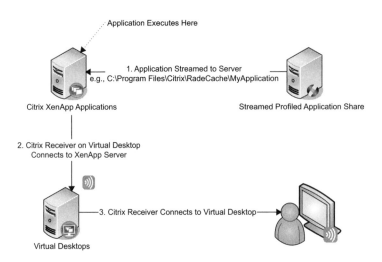

FIGURE 10.91

Application streamed to XenApp and presented to virtual desktop.

Publish a Streamed to Server Application

Publishing a streamed to server application follows much the same procedure as publishing a traditionally installed application. Follow the steps laid out in the previous section up to Step 3. The process of creating a profiled application will be discussed in the next section. In this section, we will assume that one has already been created.

1. Select **Application**, **Access from a server**, and **Streamed to server** from the drop-down list (see Figure 10.92).
2. Enter the path to the profile application share, or browse to the share. Select the application to launch from the drop-down list (see Figure 10.93).

TIP

%* is the command-line parameter required to pass the content redirection to the client, such that a file type will automatically be associated with the published application.

You may need to choose the relevant application from a profiled suite – like MS Office for example (see Figure 10.94).

You can then follow the same steps as publishing regularly installed hosted applications.

There is only one other additional option that differs for publishing streamed applications, and that is to specify alternative profile paths based on the client's IP address. This is generally used if you are streaming to physical devices in multiple locations. It can be useful in this scenario if the XenApp servers are split across more than one physical site as it gives you the facility to stream the application from a local file server (see Figure 10.95).

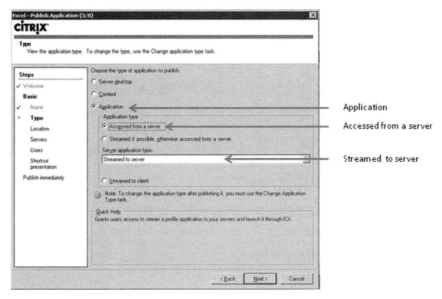

FIGURE 10.92

Application type dialog box.

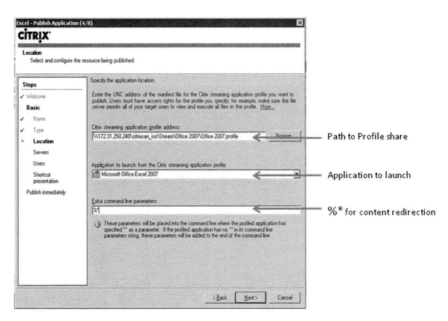

FIGURE 10.93

Application location dialog box.

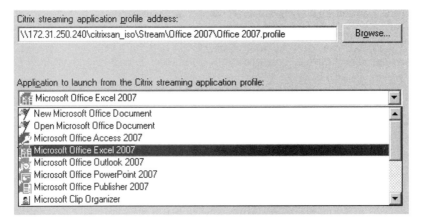

FIGURE 10.94

Multiple applications in a profiled application suite.

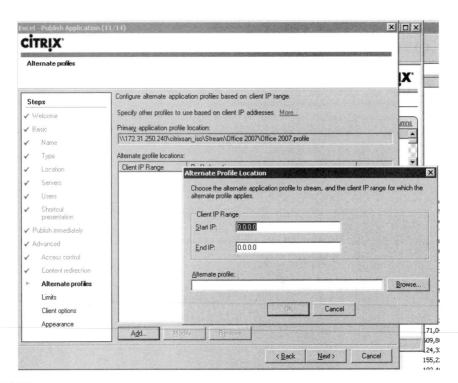

FIGURE 10.95

Specifying an alternative location for a profiled application.

STREAMED TO END POINT APPLICATIONS

In a VDI environment, the end point to which the application is streamed is the virtual desktop.

Streamed applications should be profiled on the target operating system. In other words, if your virtual desktop is Windows 7, then you should profile the application on a Windows 7 desktop. The application should be profiled on a clean build workstation (nothing other than the operating system).

When the application is streamed to the virtual desktop, the XenApp client is only used to authenticate the user, and authorize the use of their assigned applications. These packages are then streamed down to the virtual desktop (in practice, they are generally "prestreamed") and they execute in an isolated environment on the virtual desktop. The application thus executes on the virtual desktop, which is presented over the network to the user through ICA/HDX (see Figure 10.96).

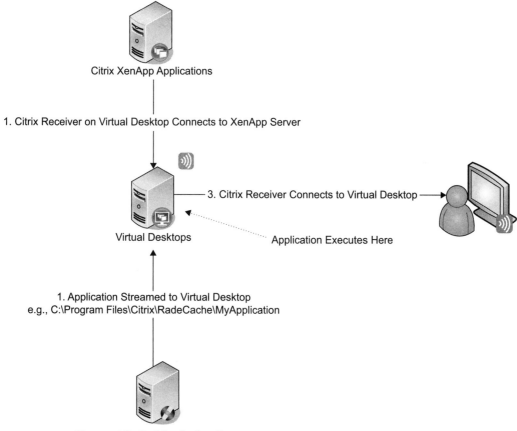

FIGURE 10.96

Applications streamed to end point.

Install the Application Streaming Profiler

1. Insert the XenApp DVD (or mount the iso) to your workstation, and browse to **Application Streaming Profiler**, CitrixStreamingProfiler.exe (see Figure 10.97).
2. Leave the default at English and click **Next** (see Figure 10.98).
3. Click **Next** (see Figure 10.99).
4. Toggle the radio button to accept the license agreement, and click **Next** (see Figure 10.100).
5. Leave the installation folder at defaults, and click **Next** (see Figure 10.101).
6. Click **Next** (see Figure 10.102).
7. Click **Finish** (see Figure 10.103).
8. Click **Yes** to restart the workstation (see Figure 10.104).

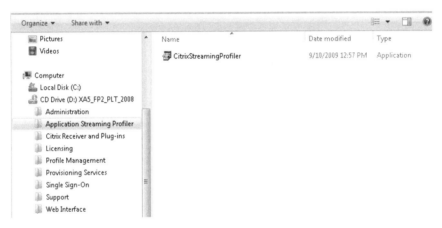

FIGURE 10.97

Citrix Streaming Profiler installation executable.

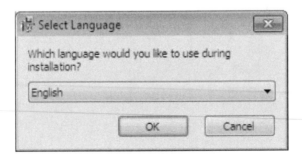

FIGURE 10.98

Select language dialog box.

FIGURE 10.99

Citrix Streaming Profiler welcome dialog box.

FIGURE 10.100

Citrix license agreement.

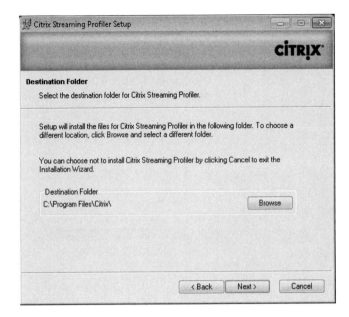

FIGURE 10.101

Destination folder dialog box.

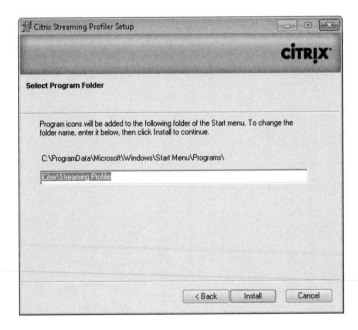

FIGURE 10.102

Select program folder dialog box.

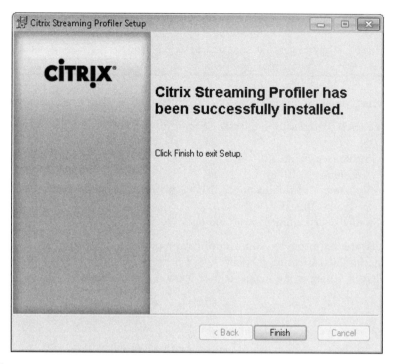

FIGURE 10.103

Successful installation dialog box.

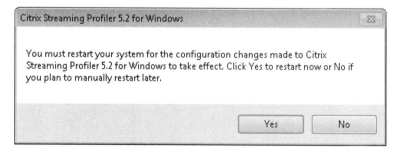

FIGURE 10.104

Restart Windows dialog box.

Profile a Streamed Application – Step by Step

In this example, I will profile a simple application, in this case "Microsoft Word Viewer." Some more complex applications, for example Office 2007, require specific procedures in order to stream the application.

> **TIP**
>
> Do a quick search for your application on the support.citrix.com support site, to find if there are any specific requirements for the application you want to profile.

In general terms, simple applications will not require any "tweaking" for you to profile them.

1. Click **Start | All Programs | Citrix | Streaming Profiler | Streaming Profiler** (see Figure 10.105).
2. Click **New Profile** (see Figure 10.106).
3. Click **Next** (see Figure 10.107).
4. Enter a profile name – in this example, I have given it the name "Word Viewer," and then click **Next** (see Figure 10.108).
5. Leave the **Enable User Updates** clear, and click **Next** (see Figure 10.109).

User updates are required by some applications, where the application may download updates from the Internet. Clearing this check box prevents most applications from automatically updating. The default setting is not to enable user updates – i.e., cleared.

FIGURE 10.105

Streaming Profiler start menu item.

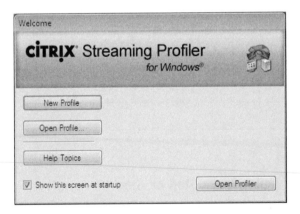

FIGURE 10.106

Streaming Profiler welcome dialog box.

FIGURE 10.107

New Profile Wizard informational dialog box.

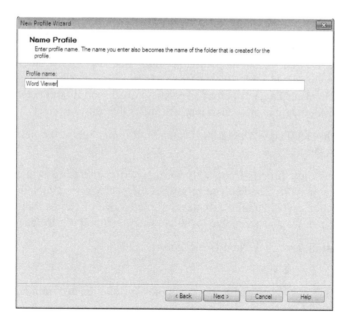

FIGURE 10.108

Configure profile name.

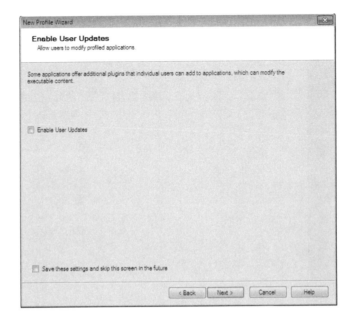

FIGURE 10.109

Enable User Update option.

6. "Set up Inter-Isolation Communication" is available for more complex virtual application interactions. Click **Next** (see Figure 10.110).

Where would you use Inter-Isolation Communication? Inter-Isolation Communication is required in instances where the virtualized applications need to communicate. For example, a third-party application makes a call to Microsoft Excel as part of a specific process, and if both the third-party application and Excel are virtualized, then this provides a mechanism for the two to interact.

7. You can leave the Set Target Operating System and Language at the defaults and click **Next** (see Figure 10.111).

Some applications only function correctly on a specific operating system and service pack combination. This functionality enables you to restrict the package to compatible operating system/ service pack combinations. The defaults will allow a broad range of compatibility. In this example, a package created on Windows 7 is accessible to Windows 7 32 bit, all service packs.

8. Select **Quick Install,** and click **Next** (see Figure 10.112).

Advanced Install

An advanced install may be required for more complex installation requirements, these include the following (see Figure 10.113):

- Run install program or command-line script
- Install IE plugins, Web applications, or online updates (Microsoft Internet Explorer only)

FIGURE 10.110

Set up Inter-isolation Communication.

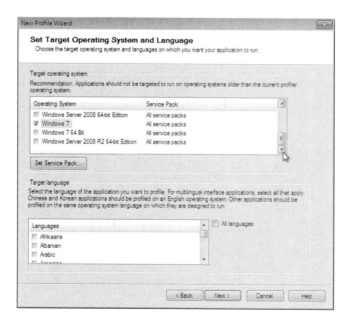

FIGURE 10.111

Set target operating system and language.

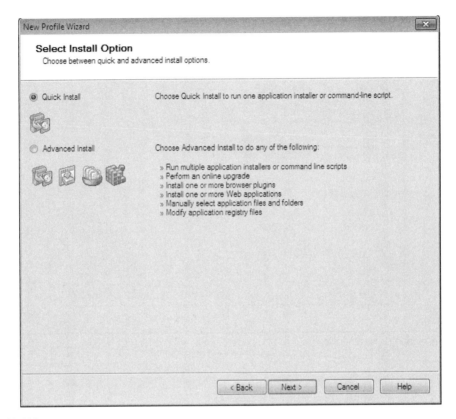

FIGURE 10.112

Select install option dialog box.

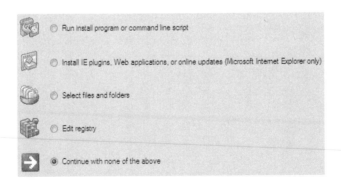

FIGURE 10.113

Advanced install options.

- Select files or folders
- Edit registry

You could, for example, package something as simple as registry changes as a package, and then deploy it.

9. Click **Browse**... and navigate the installation setup file executable, .msi or script and then click **Next** (see Figure 10.114).

Click **Launch Installer**. The installation will take place into a virtual container, as noted on the screen. It can also perform a virtual reboot of the container (see Figure 10.115).

10. Follow the regular installation process.

> **NOTE**
> If you look on the hard drive of the profiler, you will see that no files have actually been installed.

11. The **Next** button on the Run installer dialog box will become available when the install is complete. Click **Next**.

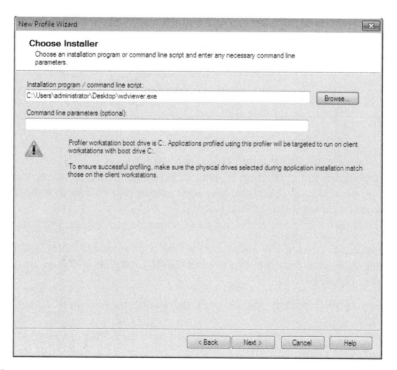

FIGURE 10.114

Choose installer dialog box.

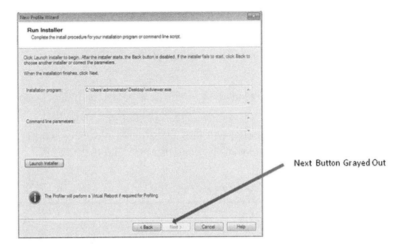

FIGURE 10.115

Run installer dialog box.

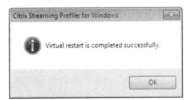

FIGURE 10.116

Virtual restart notification.

12. Click **OK** to confirm the virtual restart (see Figure 10.116).
13. Select the application and click **Run**. If there is more than one application, then run all of the applications in the window. This allows any processes or registrations that should take place on the first pass to be captured (see Figure 10.117).
14. Once you finish performing any additional tasks, close the application, and click **Next**.

The Select applications dialog box allows you to add or remove application executables that you want to publish to your users. You can also use the **Modify**... button to change the display name of the application (see Figure 10.118).

15. If required by security policy, you can sign the profile using a certificate. Click **Next** (see Figure 10.119).
16. Click **Finish** to complete the installation. You still have the option at this point to go back and change settings (see Figure 10.120).

The profiled application can now be saved. You can also manually edit the package if required (see Figure 10.121).

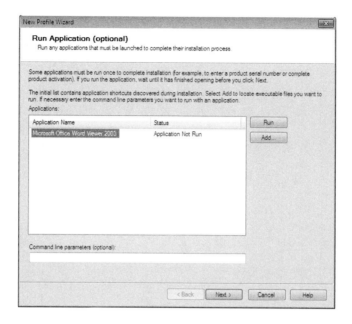

FIGURE 10.117

Run application dialog box.

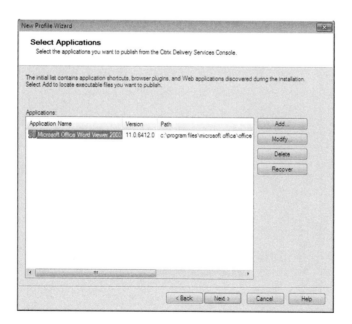

FIGURE 10.118

Select applications dialog box.

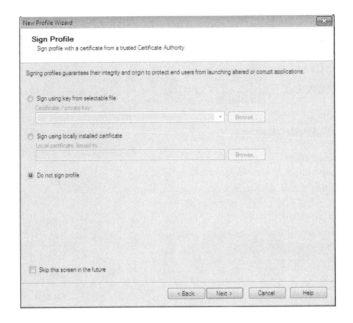

FIGURE 10.119

Sign profile dialog box.

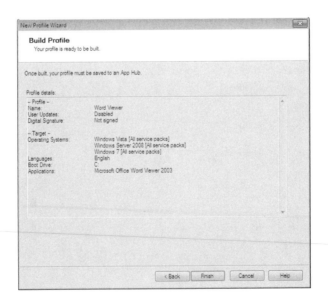

FIGURE 10.120

Build profile dialog box.

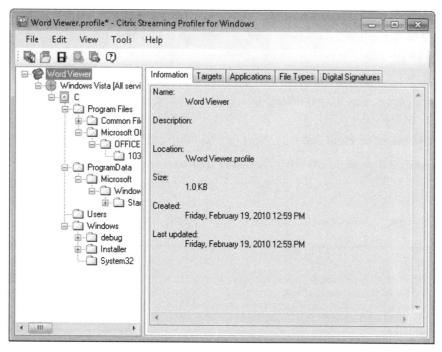

FIGURE 10.121

Citrix Streaming Profiler.

FIGURE 10.122

Saves As pop up box.

17. Click **File | Save**.

18. Browse to a network share, and save the profiled application (see Figure 10.122).

NOTE

The profile is best stored on a file server. For best performance, the package will be best delivered from a server that is optimized to be a file server. Do not use a XenApp server to act as a file server.

Publish a Streamed Application

In this section, we will look at how to take the package we just created, and to publish it to our users. The publishing mechanism is performed from the Citrix XenApp Access Management Console.

Precaching applications in the build will be discussed in this section.

Follow the same steps for publishing an application as per previous section, up to the point of selecting an application type.

1. Select **Streamed to client** and click **Next** (see Figure 10.123).

The **Streamed if possible, otherwise accessed from server** option is a mobility solution, which fails back to remotely accessing the application on the XenApp server. This is not really applicable to VDI type deployments.

2. Click **Browse…** to navigate to the <application>.profile file (see Figure 10.124).

> **NOTE**
>
> For application suites, where more than one executable is provided by the profiled package – use the **Application to launch from the Citrix streaming application profile** from the drop-down list to select the relevant application executable. The Microsoft Office Suite, for example, would provide a list of the Microsoft Office components – Excel Word, PowerPoint, and so on.

3. Leave the **Enable offline access** option deselected, and click **Next** (see Figure 10.125).

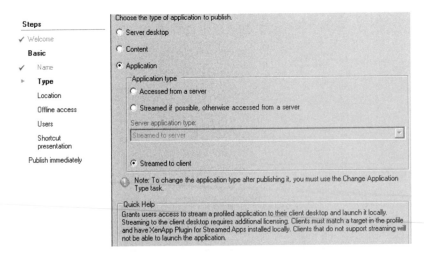

FIGURE 10.123

Application type options.

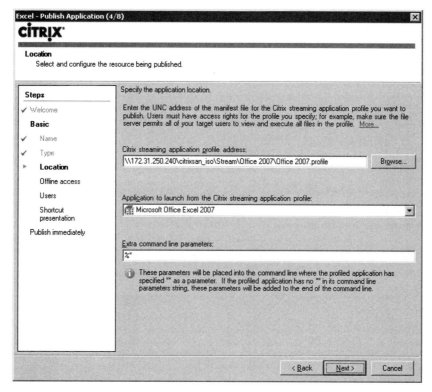

FIGURE 10.124

Application location selection.

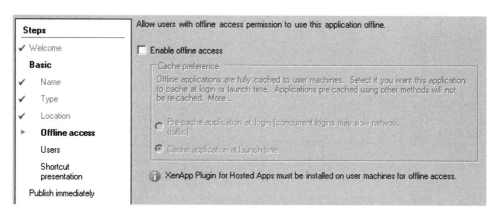

FIGURE 10.125

Offline access dialog box.

> **NOTE**
>
> Enabling offline access is unnecessary as the virtual desktop is always online. If you are using Private mode (Read/Write)\virtual desktops, my preference is to choose **Cache application at launch time**, as this prevents all the applications trying to load as you log on.

The following steps are very similar to those steps for publishing a regularly installed hosted application; however, there are enough differences that we will briefly step through the relevant steps to assist you in publishing a streamed application.

4. Click **Add**..., and browse the Active Directory for your desired User Group. Click **Next** (see Figure 10.126).
5. Select **Add to the client's Start menu** and **Add shortcut to client's desktop** (see Figure 10.127).
6. Select **Configure advanced application settings now** and click **Next** (see Figure 10.128).
7. Leave the defaults – allowing all connection types, and click **Next** (see Figure 10.129).
8. Select the file type associations; this will cause the associated application to automatically launch if the user clicks on a file of that type. Click **Next** (see Figure 10.130).

> **NOTE**
>
> File type associations are an important aspect of virtual applications due to the fact that they aren't static on the virtual desktop. File type associations are established at logon, the XenApp streaming client establishes file type associations, and passes the information to the virtual desktop. If, based on the users group memberships', both Microsoft Word Viewer and Microsoft Word are streamed to the desktop, then the application that streams down last will have the file type associated with it.

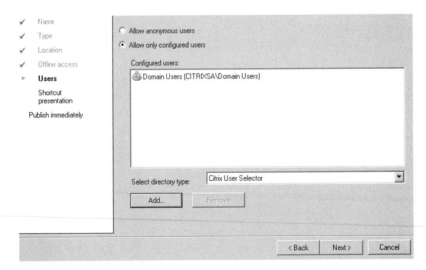

FIGURE 10.126

Users selection dialog box.

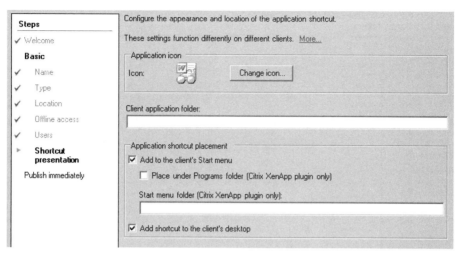

FIGURE 10.127

Shortcut presentation dialog box.

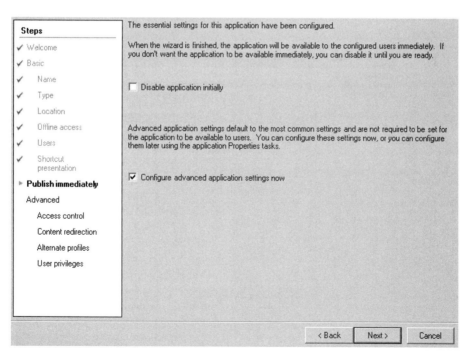

FIGURE 10.128

Publish immediately dialog box.

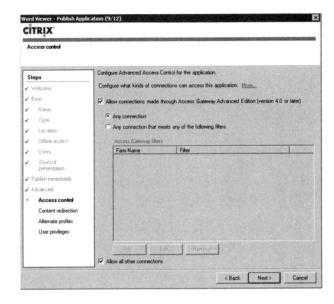

FIGURE 10.129

Advanced access control dialog box.

FIGURE 10.130

Content redirection – file types.

9. Click **Next** (see Figure 10.131).

Configure alternative application profile based on client IP range is a setting that enables you to define a location for the profile based on the client IP range. In the context of virtual desktops, this is useful if your virtual desktops exist in two separate datacenters, you can specify different application profile locations for the two datacenters.

10. Leave the **Run application as a least privileged user account** cleared, and click **Finish** (see Figure 10.132).

NOTE

Running the application with decreased privileges is a setting that is used for security purposes. If the user has administrative, or otherwise increased privileges, this setting would cause the application to execute with user-level privileges. This setting must be used with caution, as it could cause the application not to function correctly. When the XenApp streaming client authenticates the user, they will now be assigned the package based on their group memberships.

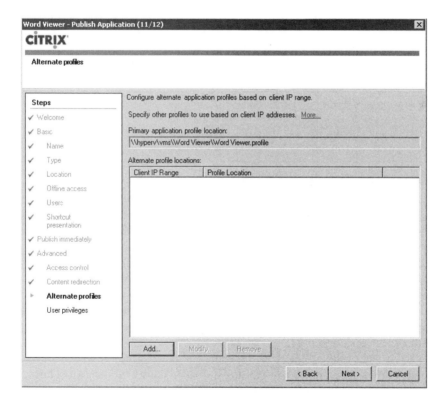

FIGURE 10.131

Alternative profiles locations.

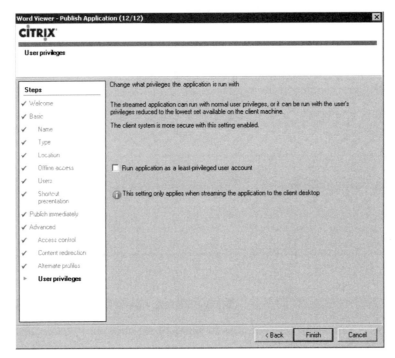

FIGURE 10.132

User privileges dialog box.

INSTALL VM-HOSTED APPLICATIONS

Conceptually, VM-hosted applications are similar to XenApp, with the exception that the applications are being hosted on a workstation operating system rather than a server operating system. Practically, the implementation of VM-hosted applications is actually just a variation of the standard Desktop Delivery Controller mechanism of XenDesktop.

The most common use case would be a requirement for an application that is Windows XP dependant, in an environment that is being standardized on Windows 7. There may be other use cases, where two applications required by the user require two different versions of Internet Explorer; however, in most cases, I would first consider XenApp before VM-hosted applications. VM-hosted applications, by their very nature, require a high level of server resources as one VM instance must exist for each user.

To install VM-hosted applications, you can choose to either install a second Desktop Delivery Controller and a separate farm, or you could use your existing XenDesktop farm, and create a separate Desktop Group that you are going to use to host the VM-hosted applications.

In this example, I will demonstrate how you would add a second farm to deploy VM-hosted applications.

Create the VM-hosted Application Virtual Machines – Step by Step

The recommended installation procedure is to load the XenApp FP2 CD first – XA50_FP2_WS03.iso.

1. Launch **Install XenApp** (see Figure 10.133).
2. Run the **Install VM-hosted Apps** (see Figure 10.134).

   This adds the registry key: [HKEY_LOCAL_MACHINE\SOFTWARE\Citrix\ManagementConsole]

   `"VMHostedAppsModeEnabled"=dword:00000001`

3. You are then prompted to mount the DDC_VDA.iso to your virtual machine (see Figure 10.135).

   The installation after this point follows exactly the same procedure as that of a standard XenDesktop installation. Refer to Chapter 2, "Installation of the Broker – Desktop Delivery Controller," for a step-by-step guide.

   In the previous sections, we have focused on Windows 7 as the guest operating system; in this section, the guest operating system used will be Windows XP as it is the most commonly used operating system for VM-hosted applications.

   Most of the tasks below are exactly the same as the procedure you would follow when using XenDesktop to provision virtual desktops.

1. Create a virtual desktop of the required operating system.
2. Install the required application.

FIGURE 10.133

Citrix XenApp installation welcome.

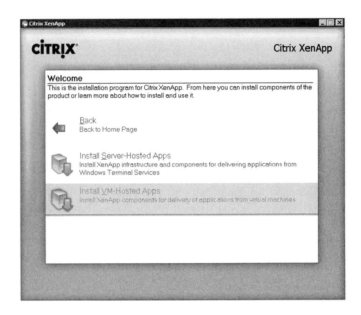

FIGURE 10.134

Citrix XenApp component selection.

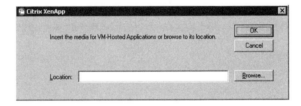

FIGURE 10.135

VM-hosted applications media location dialog box.

3. Install the Virtual Desktop Agent. Mount DDC_VDA.iso to the virtual desktop, and install the agent.

4. Browse to C:\Program Files\Citrix\ICAService\SeamlessInitialProgram. By default this is empty, and will provide the user full desktop, and you can add a shortcut to your application by right-clicking in the folder and selecting – **New | Shortcut**. Browse to your executable. Alternatively, you can simply drag and drop the shortcut into the folder. Change the security on the shortcut to allow your users access to the shortcut. Specifically a shortcut must be placed in the folder and not the executable (.exe) (see Figure 10.136).

5. Enter the path to the application or click the **Browse…** button to locate the executable. Click **Next** – Accept the Name, then **Finish** (see Figure 10.137).

In this example, I have browsed to Solitaire (sol.exe).

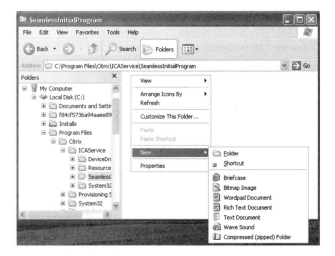

FIGURE 10.136

Seamless initial program folder.

FIGURE 10.137

Create shortcut wizard.

Important

Do not place more than one shortcut in the SeamlessInitialProgram folder.

6. Install the Provisioning Server Target Device software.
7. Copy the Target Device Hard Drive to a vDisk.
8. Change the vDisk mode to standard.

The following steps vary from how a similar task would be performed on XenDesktop.

9. Open the Delivery Services Console and expand your farm. Then right-click on **Desktop Groups**.
10. Select **Create desktop group** (see Figure 10.138).

Follow the wizard, as per normal.

11. When selecting the assignment type, select the check box **Use Desktop Group for VM Hosted Apps** (see Figure 10.139).

Important

This attribute cannot be changed after creation; the Desktop Group must be deleted and re-created. Failure to select this tick box results in the application not appearing correctly in a Seamless Window.

When specifying the Desktop Group name, bear in mind that this will be the display name of the application to the user, so assign a name that will be recognizable to the users (see Figure 10.140).

Changing the icon is useful in the context of an application. In terms of user experience, you are providing a familiar visual cue. Click **Change icon**…, and browse to the application folder (see Figure 10.141).

TIP

The application icon is sometimes stored in the application's folder, if there are no .ico files, select the application executable, the icon is most often embedded in the executable (see Figure 10.142).

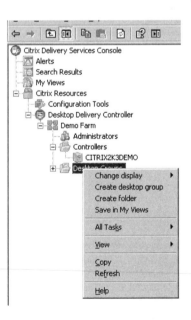

FIGURE 10.138

Create Desktop Group menu option.

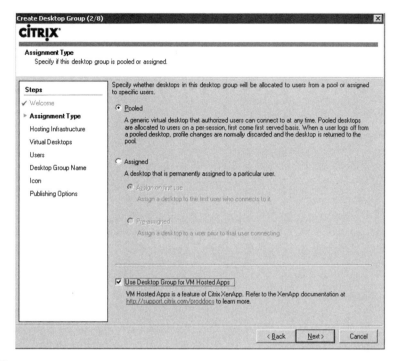

FIGURE 10.139

Assignment type dialog box.

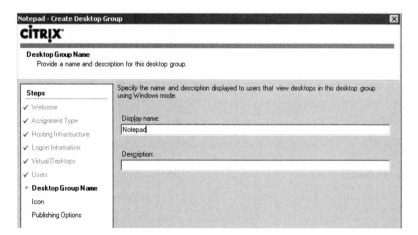

FIGURE 10.140

The Desktop Group name is the application display name.

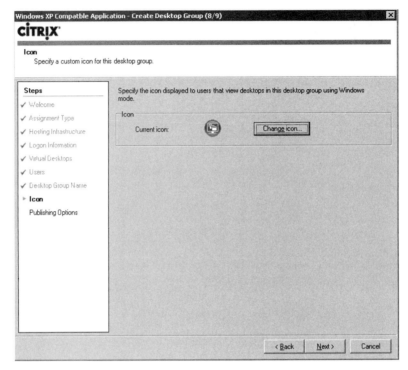

FIGURE 10.141

Changing the icon for a VM-hosted application.

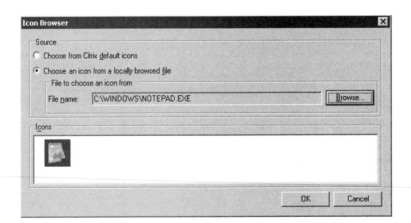

FIGURE 10.142

Selecting an application icon.

The simplest way to then configure VM-hosted applications is to use the XenDesktop Setup Wizard. The only difference between creating normal virtual desktops using the wizard and creating virtual desktops for application hosting is that the Desktop Group must be precreated. This is because the wizard does not have the facility to specify that the Desktop Group is intended for VM-hosted Apps.

Designating the Desktop Group as for "VM-hosted App" will automatically change how the application is presented to the users (see Figure 10.143).

When accessing the Web Interface site, an **Applications** tab is automatically created as shown in Figure 10.144. Resources are automatically filtered to be presented as either a desktop, or an application (see Figure 10.144).

Using farm aggregation, a Web Interface Services site can deploy both XenApp applications and VM-hosted applications into the virtual desktops. These will appear identically to the users.

In order to aggregate applications from multiple farms, Web Interface simply needs to be configured to communicate with both farms, and the applications from both farms will be displayed seamlessly to the user (see Figure 10.145).

FIGURE 10.143

Precreate a desktop group for XenDesktop Setup Wizard.

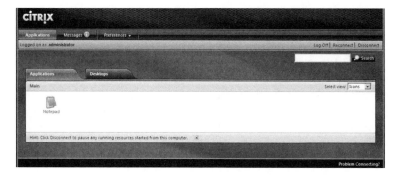

FIGURE 10.144

VM-hosted applications are added to the list of applications.

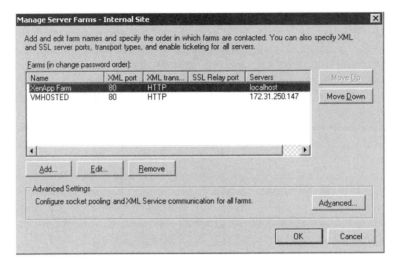

FIGURE 10.145

Farm aggregations in Web Interface.

MICROSOFT APP-V APPLICATIONS

Microsoft App-V is a standard application management infrastructure in many organizations. Microsoft App-V has functionality that overlaps with the XenApp streaming mechanism, but not with XenApp-hosted applications. It is advisable, from a standards perspective, to choose one mechanism to deploy your virtual applications. You could, for example, use both App-V to deploy virtual applications to your virtual desktops, and also use XenApp-hosted applications to present applications using HDX(ICA) into the virtual desktops.

Where we created streamed profiles using the Streaming Profiler, for App-V, we use the Microsoft Application Virtualization Sequencer. The sequencer is used to convert standard applications into Microsoft App-V sequences.

You can use traditional Microsoft methods to deploy App-V application to your virtual desktop.

Citrix has recently introduced a mechanism to deploy App-V packages using the Delivery Services Console.[A] You publish an App-V package in much the same way as you would a Citrix streamed application. When defining the application profile to be deployed, you specify the AppStreamingtoAppVConduit.profile. What this does is to call the App-V client on the virtual desktop to open a package sequenced with App-V.

In the above example, I have sequenced Word Viewer using App-V. I can then publish this to the user using the AppStreamingtoAppVConduit. This, as the name indicates, is a conduit for application streaming to App-V (see Figure 10.146).

This requires that the App-V 4.5 or 4.6 clients be installed on the virtual desktops.

[A]Please refer to the *Citrix White Paper – Application Streaming to App-V Conduit* for more details.

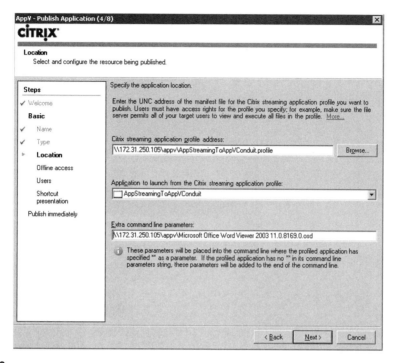

FIGURE 10.146

Publishing and App-V sequence.

The Citrix Receiver can now be used as the mechanism for App-V clients. There is an App-V plug-in for the Citrix Receiver. As with other base components, I recommend that the App-V client be installed as part of the base build, if you will be using App-V.

In the context of virtual desktops, the online plug-in authorizes the user to use an application, and calls

```
%PROGRAMFILES%\Microsoft Application Virtualization Client\sfttray.exe
```

(which is the App-V client) to execute the .OSD format (App-V) application.

SUMMARY

One of the keystones of the Citrix XenDesktop approach is that the components should be built out in a modular fashion. In this section, we addressed the provisioning of applications into our virtual desktops. We addressed the various different application virtualization mechanisms. We discussed very briefly the installation of XenApp servers, and then the configuration thereof. We focused on hosted applications, streamed to server-hosted applications, streamed to end point applications, and VM-hosted applications. This chapter dealt in depth with the installation, configuration, and publishing of these applications to the virtual desktop. Lastly, we discussed how Microsoft App-V applications can be integrated into a XenDesktop solution.

There have been many books written on the subject of Citrix XenApp, and this chapter doesn't attempt to cover all the details, but rather just to give you those details necessary to get you started in using XenApp within the context of XenDesktop.

Integrating Virtual Applications into the Virtual Desktop

INFORMATION IN THIS CHAPTER

- Configure the XenApp Client
- Precache XenApp-streamed Applications
- Precache App-V Applications

There are a number of different ways to deliver the applications to your users with the virtual desktop.

"Locally installed applications" into the base vDisk is a strategy commonly followed to perform a basic proof of concept. In many cases, the time frame makes this a good option. In production environments, streamed applications are generally a better choice.

"Streamed applications," whether using Citrix Application Streaming or Microsoft App-V are a better choice. Application virtualization makes the application environment far more manageable and flexible.

Streaming applications to the users "on demand" means that the applications are sent to the virtual desktop only when required. This causes delays when launching the application, and is not recommended. There are two ways in which the applications can retain the management functionality of application virtualization, while performing like locally installed applications.

1. Precache to the vDisk.
2. Precache to the write cache disk.

Precaching means that the files have been sent down to the virtual desktop, but the shortcuts have not been created. The application files are inaccessible to the user until they have authenticated through the XenApp (or App-V) client.

Precaching to the vDisk needs to be done while the vDisk is in Private image mode – as it is normally in read-only mode. Precaching to the write cache disk can be done at any time as it is inherently read/write.

> **NOTE**
> The strategy of using the write cache disk means that you would also need to reevaluate the write cache disk space requirements.

XenApp-hosted applications should not be discounted as an application delivery method. Presenting older Windows XP/2003 applications into a Windows 7 desktop is achieved simply by using XenApp. Additionally, applications that have complex requirements may not be well suited to streaming, and these should be placed on a XenApp server. An additional benefit would be that the application load is not incurred on the virtual desktops, but rather on the XenApp servers.

CONFIGURE THE XENAPP CLIENT

The Citrix XenApp client has now been renamed as the Citrix Receiver. The Citrix Receiver has been created to be a single point to update and control the various Citrix components. Download the Citrix Receiver from the www.citrix.com Web site (see Figure 11.1).

Download the Receiver for Windows, the online and the offline plug-in. The online plug-in is used for remote applications delivered to the user over the network using a Presentation Layer Protocol. The offline plug-in is used to deliver streamed applications that execute locally in an isolation environment.

Switch the base vDisk into Private image mode, such that the Citrix Receiver can be part of the base build.

Installing the Receiver and the Online Plug-in

The Receiver.msi is a silent installation, and the online plug-in is silent except for a success notification.

Installing the Offline Plug-in

The offline plug-in will be used for streamed applications. Execute the CitrixOfflinePlugin.exe executable that you have downloaded (see Figure 11.1).

1. Select the desired language, and click **OK** (see Figure 11.2).
2. Click **Next** (see Figure 11.3).
3. Toggle the radio button to accept the license agreement (see Figure 11.4).
4. Click **Install** (see Figure 11.5).
5. Click **Finish** (see Figure 11.6).
6. Click **Yes** (see Figure 11.7).

After a virtual desktop restart, the online plug-in will pop-up and request the location of the Web Interface server. This location will be used by both the online plug-in and the offline plug-in to retrieve assigned applications.

7. Enter the hostname of the Web Interface server, and click **Update** (see Figure 11.8).

> **TIP**
>
> Enter the FQDN of the Web Interface site – best practice would be to use a Citrix NetScaler to perform server high availability and load balancing. If you are not going to use these features, then a Citrix Access Gateway will also perform well. Remember that the Web Interface Web site must be configured as a XenApp Services site. The XenApp Services site must be configured as a "Dual mode Streaming" site to provision both hosted and streamed applications. Pass through authentication must be configured on the Web site to seamlessly pass the user's credentials through to the Web Interface server.

Receiver

Receiver for Windows 1.1	English	10/26/09	7.8 MB	.msi	Download ▶

Designed specifically for devices leveraging Microsoft Windows operating system platforms.

Plug-ins

Online plug-in	All Languages	9/29/09	13.8 MB	.exe	Download ▶
Offline plug-in	All Languages	9/29/09	12.9 MB	.exe	Download ▶
Dazzle	English	11/23/09	1.71 MB	.msi	Download ▶

FIGURE 11.1

The Citrix Receiver and plug-ins.

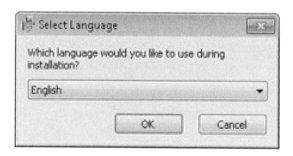

FIGURE 11.2

Select language.

FIGURE 11.3

Offline plug-in – welcome.

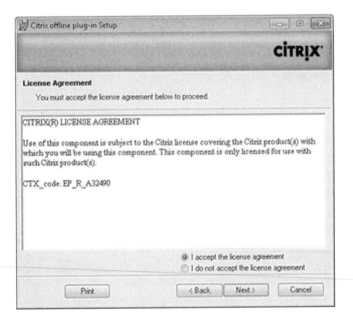

FIGURE 11.4

License agreement.

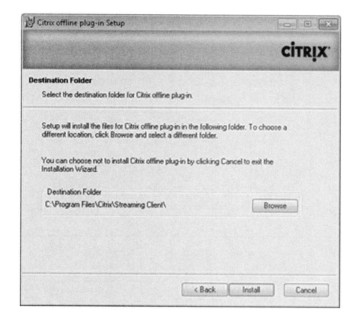

FIGURE 11.5

Destination folder.

FIGURE 11.6

Successfully installed dialog box.

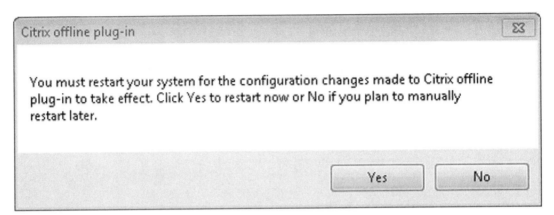

FIGURE 11.7

Restart.

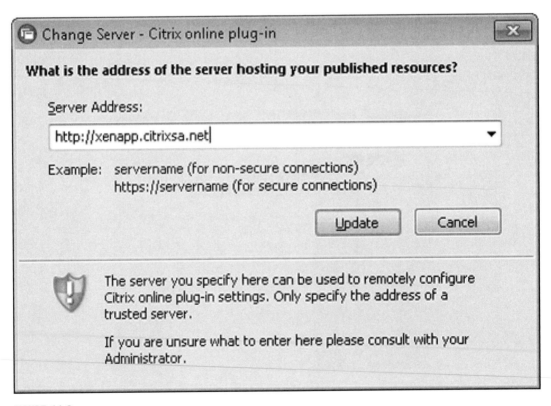

FIGURE 11.8

Online plug-in – server address.

PRECACHE XENAPP-STREAMED APPLICATIONS

When using a "Standard image" vDisk, the best practice for provisioning user applications to the user desktops is to have the packages actually built into the base build. This effectively deploys the applications in their entirety to the virtual desktops, but stops just short of actually granting them access. This prevents the applications from deploying over the network to the virtual desktops. It does, however, require that the base vDisk be preconfigured with the applications.

So, for example, if a user has five applications assigned to them, they would in a physical desktop scenario, download the applications on demand down to the local device. The virtual applications are cached to C:\Program Files\Citrix\RadeCache\<perappcache>, where the <perappcache> would be as per application folder designated by a randomized string – for example, *3055a6bb-bc81-4b41-8d2b-c0b56f4c163b_1*. The folder contains the entire application in its isolated environment. For the curious, if you look under that folder, you will find a "device" folder which contains the virtual "c" drive and all its contents. You would have five such folders, each containing one of the applications. In a virtual desktop environment, you may have many more folders, containing all the applications the user may need.

The question you may ask is why precache if it is a one-off task? And the answer is that the users vDisk is read only, and their "cache" folder will need to be refreshed after each reboot, which could potentially result in far more network traffic, as the creation of the files under Rade-Cache would occur as often as the device reboots. This is only true if you are using a "Standard image" vDisk – a "Private image" vDisk would persist and keep the files. The strategy is thus to create the RadeCache folder contents while the vDisk is in "Private image" mode – i.e., read/write.

Copy your existing production vDisk. Change the new vDisk into private mode, and mount it to a virtual machine. This process will be dealt with in detail in Chapter 12, "Implementing Virtual Profiles into the Virtual Desktop."

Open a command prompt. Type the following:

cd C:\Program Files\Citrix\Streaming Client

The radedeploy utility does not add itself to the path variables, so you will need to run it out of the folder. Radedeploy run without any switches returns usage information (see Figure 11.9). Use the following syntax to deploy the streamed application to the RadeCache folder (see Figure 11.9):

radedeploy /deploy \\<path to streamed packages>\<packagename>.profile

Repeat the process for each package you need to deploy.

It is important to note that this prepopulates the required files; however, it does not provide access to the application. The XenApp client authenticates the user and will push the shortcuts to the desktop or start menu (or both) depending on how you have published the application.

An application shortcut will point to the XenApp client (see Figure 11.10). For example, "C:\Program Files\Citrix\ICA Client\pnagent.exe" /CitrixShortcut: (1) /QLaunch "Word Viewer."

The application data is thus prepopulated, but access to the packages is managed by the XenApp Receiver.

The Citrix Receiver must have both the online plug-in and the offline plug-in, in order to use streamed applications. The offline plug-in provides the packages, and the online plug-in provides access by authenticating the user.

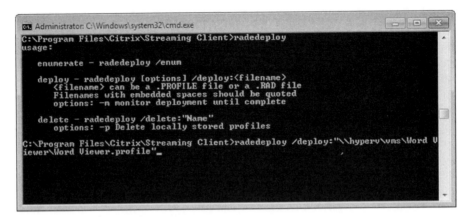

FIGURE 11.9

Using radedeploy to deploy packages.

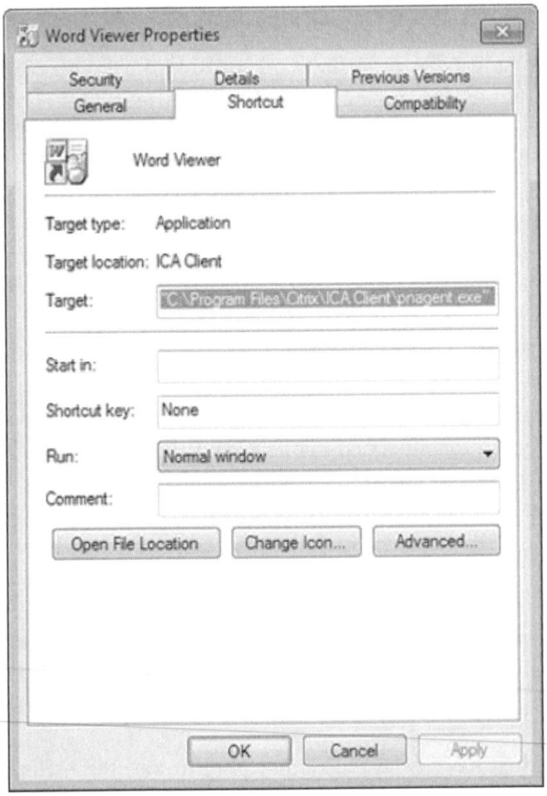

FIGURE 11.10

XenApp services application shortcuts.

PRECACHE APP-V APPLICATIONS

The logic behind precaching App-V applications is exactly the same as that behind precaching XenApp-streamed applications. Deploying virtual applications over the network is best avoided, particularly if it will need to be done repeatedly. Cached App-V applications are loaded into %AllUsersProfile%\Documents\App-V Client\OSD Cache, which is a common folder for all users using the virtual desktop. As the folder name "OSD Cache" indicates, this folder is used to store the OSD content.

Precaching the App-V files doesn't present the application to the user. The application access can be managed using the standard Microsoft mechanism, or as per Chapter 10, "Configure Citrix XenApp for Application Provisioning," the XenApp can be used to authorize the use of the application. Access to the applications are managed by the XenApp online plug-in the same as XenApp-streamed applications.

In order to load an App-V package into cache, the sfttray.exe executable can be used to manually populate the cache.

For example,

%PROGRAMFILES%\Microsoft Application Virtualization Client\ sfttray.exe /load \\172.31.250.105\appv\Microsoft Office Word Viewer 2003 11.0.8169.0.osd

This will load the application Word Viewer into cache. If the user is authorized to use the application, then the relevant icons are created automatically on the user desktop.

Checkpoint 5 Updating Packages in the Base Vdisk

This section leads you through a demonstration of updating a package on the base image. This would be best tailored to a technical audience who would then understand how the application packages and things like hotfixes can be updated in the virtual desktop environment.

The previous checkpoint was aimed at demonstrating the ease of implementation, and the functionality of XenDesktop. This checkpoint has the aim of demonstrating how XenDesktop can be managed from an operational perspective.

1. Open the Provisioning Server Console on the provisioning server, and indicate which vDisk is in use (see Figure 11.11).
2. Open the Delivery Services Console on the Desktop Delivery Controller; select **Modify desktop group properties** in the common tasks pane, select **Modify all properties** from the menu (see Figure 11.12).
3. Change the "Idle Desktop Count" to zero (see Figure 11.13).
4. Open the hypervisor console – XenCenter, SCVMM, or vCenter.
5. Shut down the virtual desktops through the relevant management console.
6. Returning to the provisioning server, show how the virtual desktops are marked as "Down" (see Figure 11.14).
7. Copy the vDisk and its .pvp (config) file and paste it into either another location, or rename the file in the same location (see Figure 11.15).
8. Open the Provisioning Server Console, right-click on the **Store** node, select **Add Existing vDisk...** (see Figure 11.16).
9. Click **Search** to discover the vDisk, click **Add** to add it to the store, and then click **Close** (see Figure 11.17). You now have multiple versions of the vDisk (see Figure 11.18).

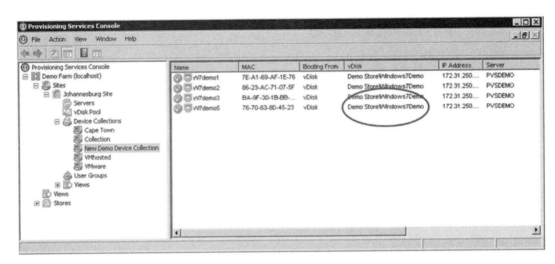

FIGURE 11.11

Provisioning Services Console – Device Collection vDisk.

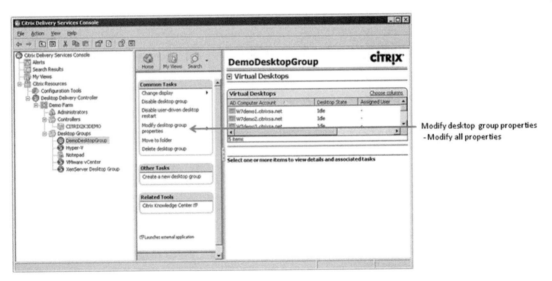

FIGURE 11.12

Delivery Services Console – Desktop Groups.

10. Right-click on **Device Collection**, select **Create Device Collection**. Assign the Device Collection a name – like Build or Development etc (see Figure 11.19).

11. Add a Target Device to the Build Device Collection using the procedure outlined in Chapter 7, "Fundamental Configuration of the Citrix Provisioning Server."

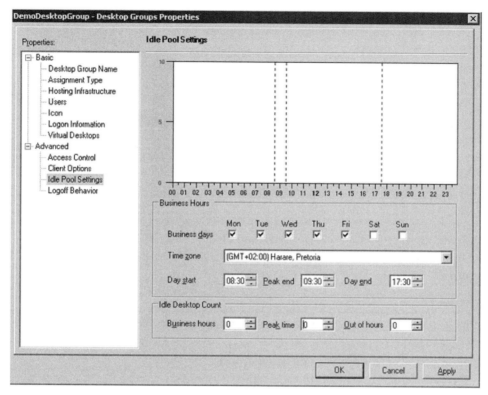

FIGURE 11.13

Desktop Group properties.

Name	MAC	Booting From	vDisk	IP Address
W7demo1	7E-A1-69-AF-1E-76	vDisk	Demo Store\Windows7Demo	Down
W7demo2	86-23-AC-71-07-5F	vDisk	Demo Store\Windows7Demo	Down
W7demo3	BA-9F-30-1B-BB-...	vDisk	Demo Store\Windows7Demo	Down
W7demo5	76-70-63-8D-45-23	vDisk	Demo Store\Windows7Demo	Down

FIGURE 11.14

Provisioning Services Console – Device Collection.

In order to keep things as simple as possible, I recommend that you create a build Target Device, and a build Device Collection. This is a good way to separate "build and test" from production workstations.

Important: The build Target Device should not be part of the production Desktop Group. This creates conflicts as the Desktop Delivery Controller will affect the power setting of the virtual desktop.

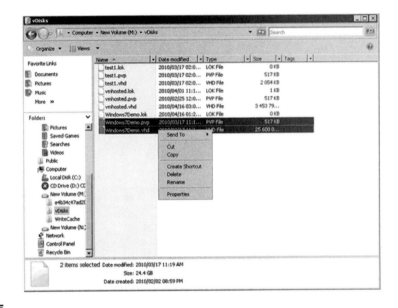

FIGURE 11.15

vDisk files.

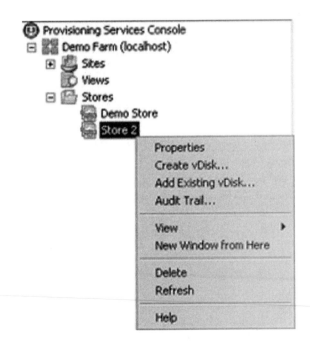

FIGURE 11.16

vDisk store options.

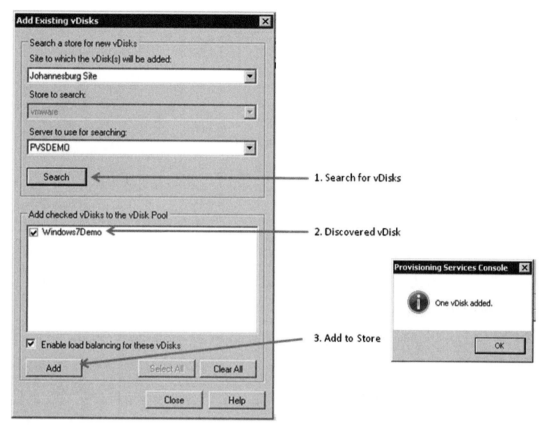

FIGURE 11.17

Add existing vDisks.

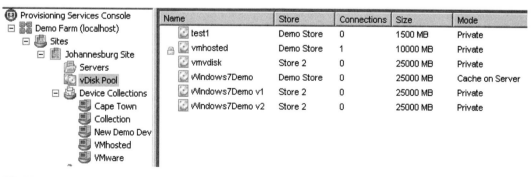

FIGURE 11.18

Multiple versions of a vDisk.

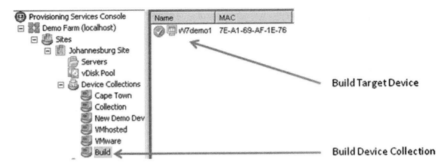

FIGURE 11.19

Provisioning Services Console – Device Collections.

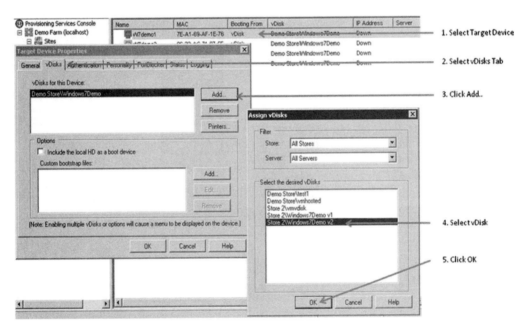

FIGURE 11.20

Assigning a vDisk to a Target Device.

12. Select the Target Device, right-click **Properties**, select **vDisk** tab, click **Add**..., select the vDisk you just copied, and click **OK** (see Figure 11.20).

You have now assigned your newly created vDisk to the Target Device.

13. Install something into your "build" vDisk, antivirus or antivirus update pattern files make a good demo (see Figure 11.21).

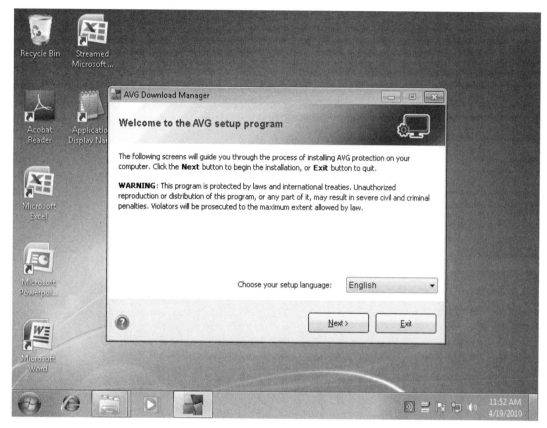

FIGURE 11.21

Virtual Windows 7 desktop.

14. Shut down the build Target Device – to release locks on the vDisk.

15. Change the vDisk from Private image to Standard image (see Figure 11.22).

16. "Drag and Drop" the new updated vDisk onto the **Device Collection**. Click **Yes** to accept the change to the vDisk assignments (see Figure 11.23).

NOTE

This will update all the virtual desktops in the Device Collection to the new build.

---

17. Amend the Idle pool on your desktop group to a nonzero number, to start the Desktop Group.

18. Log into one of the virtual desktops and indicate the updated content.

19. Demonstrate how the "Drag and Drop" of the "version 1" vDisk back onto the Device Collection can be used to simply "roll back" to an older version of the vDisk (see Figure 11.24).

FIGURE 11.22

vDisk – access mode.

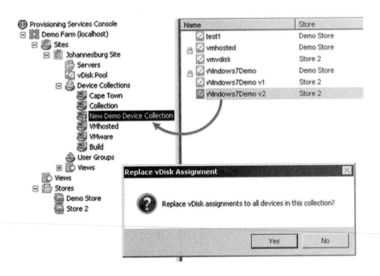

FIGURE 11.23

Replace vDisk assignment.

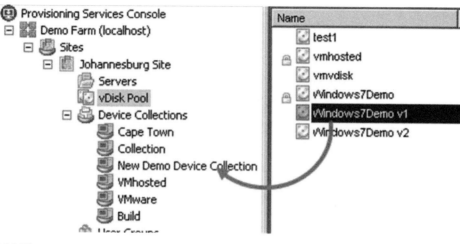

FIGURE 11.24

Roll back vDisk assignment.

Discussion Point

This is a good point at which to raise the question as to which components should be part of the base build, and which components should be streamed in. Antivirus, for example, would be part of the base build, but applications should normally be streamed in.

SUMMARY

This chapter covered application provisioning from the perspective of the virtual desktops. The previous chapter covered how the application provisioning is configured from the server side, and this chapter dealt with how the Citrix Receiver should be configured to present the applications to the user. We also covered how to prepopulate the application cache for best performance.

The checkpoint in this chapter is a demonstration of how the vDisks can be manipulated to operationally manage updates in the context of virtual desktops.

Implementing Virtual Profiles into the Virtual Desktop

INFORMATION IN THIS CHAPTER

- What Is a Profile?

In a traditional desktop environment, user settings are stored on the local device. In a virtual desktop environment, the user receives a standard build operating system, without any user settings. It is particularly important in a virtual desktop environment to have a mechanism to maintain user personalization. Hosted applications delivered to the virtual desktop also require individual user settings. Microsoft desktop operating systems use a mechanism called a user profile to store user-specific settings.

WHAT IS A PROFILE?

A user profile comprises the registry keys and files where the user's settings are saved. The user profile is located at C:\Documents and Setting\%username% in Windows XP and at C:\Users\%username% in Windows 7 as shown in Figure 12.1.

The user's HKEY_CURRENT_USER registry hive is loaded from NTUSER.DAT at logon, and saved at logoff. Likewise, application-specific files – for example, the user's Microsoft Word template is saved in the profile. Local profiles save the user settings to the local machine.

Roaming profiles are for users using multiple environments. Roaming profiles entail saving the user settings to a network location, the user settings are downloaded at logon, and saved at logoff as shown in Figure 12.2.

Most applications save user-specific settings to the user locations; however, some applications save settings into HKEY_LOCAL_MACHINE and to the application installation folder, rather than to the profile. In these cases, roaming profiles do not save the user's settings.

Roaming profiles have a further issue; they tend to "bloat." Over time, more and more files get added to the profile; some of these are temporary application files, or things like temporary Internet files. The profile must be downloaded at logon to receive the user settings, and as the profile grows in size, the logon time increases.

Virtual Profiles are an enhancement of the roaming profile concept. Virtual Profiles extend the roaming profile concept by allowing the administrator to include files and registry keys held outside of the standard locations. We could specify that "HKEY_LOCAL_MACHINE\Software\StrangeApplicaton\Settings" be saved to the Virtual Profile, and be injected at logon like the standard settings. This extends the user personalization to nonstandard applications.

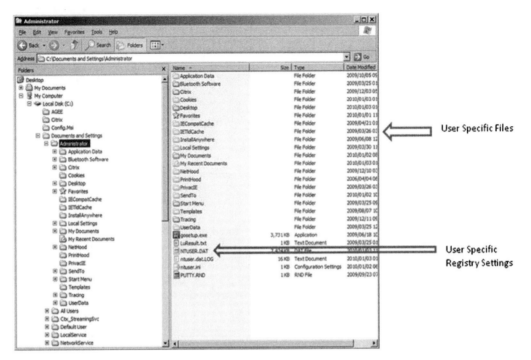

FIGURE 12.1

User profile stored on the workstation.

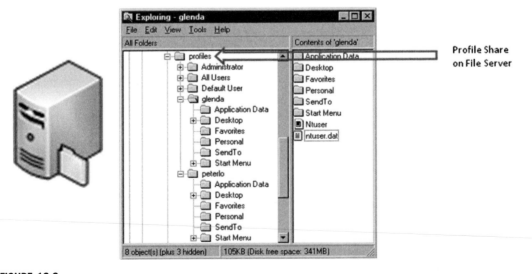

FIGURE 12.2

Roaming profiles are stored on a file server.

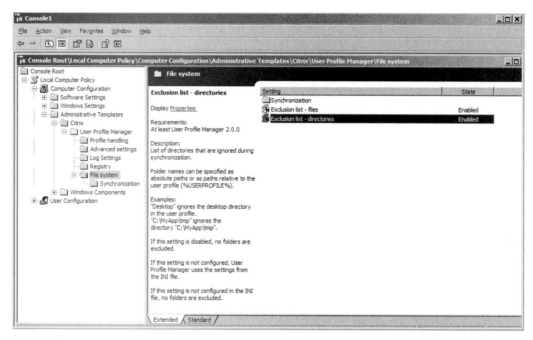

FIGURE 12.3

Creating a Virtual Profile exclusion list.

Using Virtual Profiles, the administrator could also specify that some files or registry settings held in the profile be excluded from being saved, as shown in Figure 12.3. This enables the administrator to control what is saved in the user settings at a far more granular level. The size of the Virtual Profile can be managed and slow logon times eliminated.

Additionally, Virtual Profiles add an enhanced mechanism for merging profile settings – hosted application settings with streamed application settings – providing a more consistent, robust profile.

> **TIP**
>
> For Windows XP, virtual desktops use UPHCLEAN from Microsoft in conjunction with Profile Management. It is not necessary with Windows 7 as UPHCLEAN is integrated into the operating system.

Installation of Virtual Profiles

Citrix Profile Manager can be downloaded from the Citrix Web site. It is part of the XenDesktop downloads under the Components section. Extract the contents of the download; you should have something as shown in Figure 12.4.

The .msi (Microsoft Installer) packages are for installation into the target virtual desktop. The .adm file is to be loaded into a Group Policy Management Console to control the Profile Manager settings.

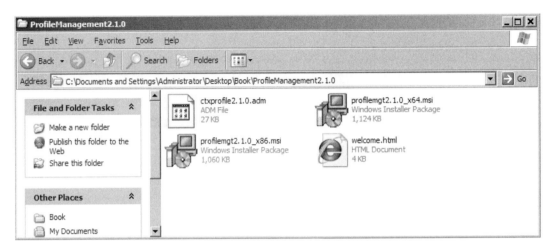

FIGURE 12.4

Profile Manager installer packages.

There are two versions of the .msi: the 64-bit version and the 32-bit version. Execute the version relevant to your desktop operating system. If you are using provisioning server, you should mount the build vDisk in Private mode to add the Profile Manager to the base build.

Install Profile Manager – Step by Step

1. Double-click the profilemgt2.1.0_x86.msi (profilemgt2.1.0_x64.msi if your Windows XP/ Windows 7 is 64 bit).
2. Click **Next** as shown in Figure 12.5.
3. Accept the license and click **Next** as shown in Figure 12.6.
4. Select the default path as shown in Figure 12.7. Click the **Change…** button to install the files in a different location. Click **Next** when finished.
5. Click **Install** as shown in Figure 12.8.
6. Click **Finish** as shown in Figure 12.9.
7. Click **Yes** as shown in Figure 12.10 to reboot the system or **No** to reboot later.

Once the virtual desktop has restarted, you will see that the Profile Manager has installed as a service on the virtual desktop as shown in Figure 12.11.

Configuration of Virtual Profiles

Citrix Profile Manager is configured by using a Group Policy. The ctxprofile2.1.0.adm file is included with Profile Manager. The .adm file extends the standard Group Policy to include the Citrix Profile Manager settings. Profile Manager also has a legacy .ini file mechanism that can also be used. The simplest way to configure the settings is by using a Group Policy.

Group Policies are preferable as you can dynamically manage the settings and the settings can be set differently for different groups of machines or users.

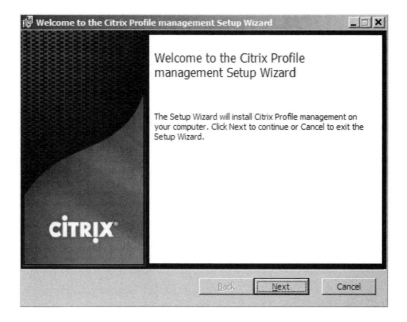

FIGURE 12.5

Profile Management Setup Wizard.

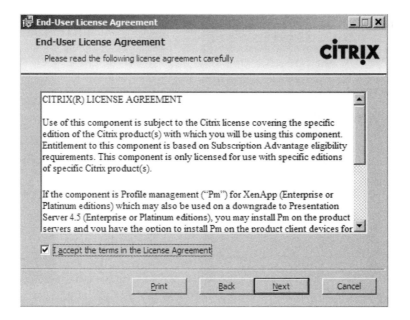

FIGURE 12.6

Citrix license agreement.

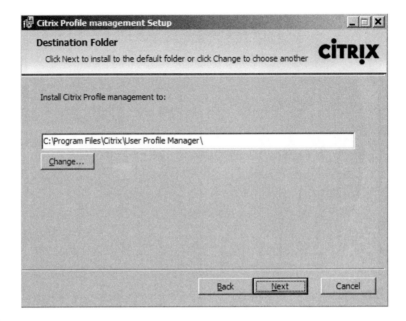

FIGURE 12.7

Destination folder dialog box.

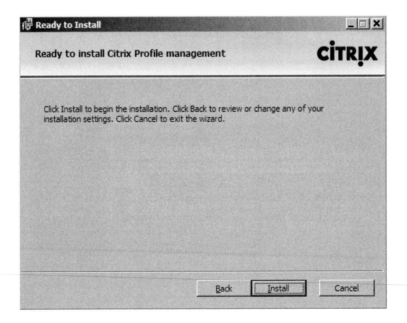

FIGURE 12.8

Ready to install dialog box.

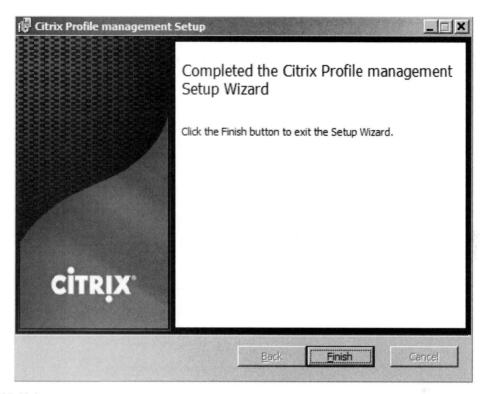

FIGURE 12.9

Successful completion dialog box.

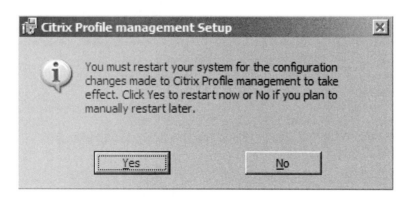

FIGURE 12.10

Restart system dialog box.

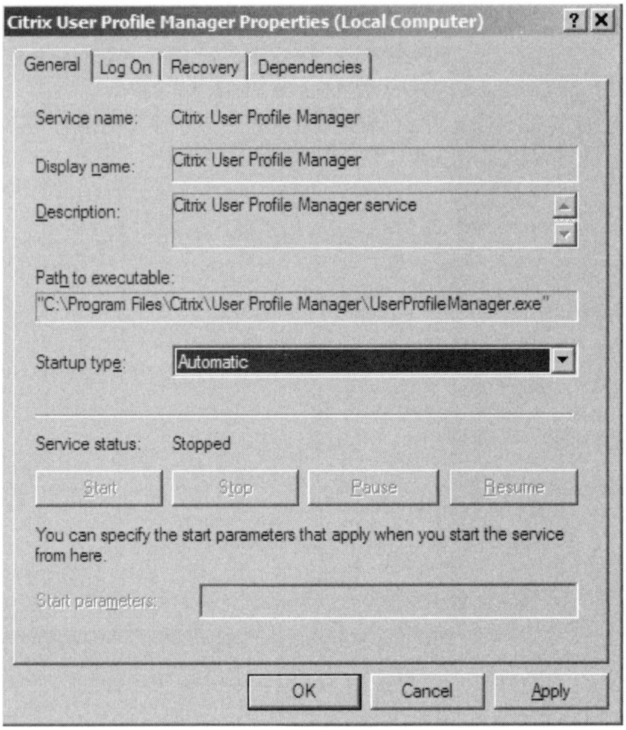

FIGURE 12.11

The Citrix User Profile Manager service.

In some instances, you may not have permissions to edit the Group Policies. If you are conducting a proof of concept, consider implementing the setting by just using a Local Machine Policy. Local Machine Policies are less flexible, and bear in mind that the vDisk of your virtual desktop will need to be in private mode when making changes.

Configure Virtual Profiles – Step by Step

1. From the *Run* command, execute gpedit.msc.
2. Under **Computer Configuration**, right-click on **Administrative Templates** – select **Add/Remove Templates**... as shown in Figure 12.12.
3. Click **Add**... and browse to Profile Management Folder as shown in Figure 12.13.
4. Select **ctxprofile2.1.0.adm** – open as shown in Figure 12.14.
5. Select **Enable Profile management** – Set to Enabled as shown in Figure 12.15.
6. Select **Path to user store**.
7. Set the path and click **OK** as shown in Figure 12.16.

The default location is in the user's home directory, under the Windows subdirectory. For a proof of concept or pilot, you may want to isolate the virtual desktop environment from the current environment. In this case, use the following syntax: \\fileserver\sharename\%username%.

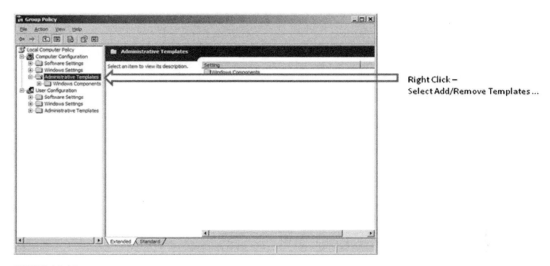

Right Click –
Select Add/Remove Templates...

FIGURE 12.12

Microsoft Group Policy editor.

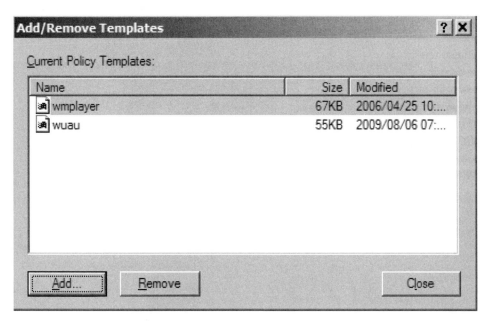

FIGURE 12.13

Add/Remove templates dialog box.

FIGURE 12.14

Browse to ctxprofile2.1.0.adm file.

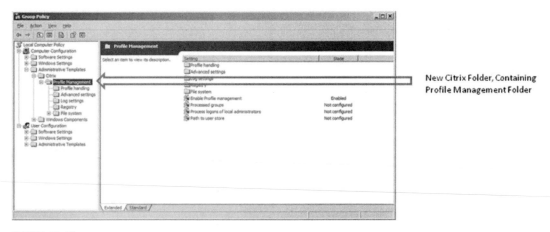

FIGURE 12.15

Citrix folder in Group Policy Management Console.

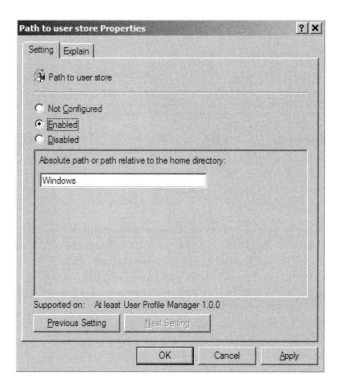

FIGURE 12.16

Path to user store properties.

%username% is an environment variable that resolves to the user's logon name. The security settings for the "sharename" folder needs to include "Full Control" for "Creator Owner."

Profile Manager uses the user's logon credentials to Read/Write to the share, and one of the most common issues with Profile Manager is simple file/folder permissions.

By default, all of the standard profile settings are now saved to the specified location.

Additional Profile Manager Settings

If required extra files/folders or registry settings can be added to the Virtual Profile. Some applications, like terminal emulators, don't save their settings to the standard profile location. Filemon from Microsoft can be particularly useful to find where an application is saving its settings.

You may also choose to exclude some files/folders to prevent your profile growing unnecessarily large. Registry keys that you don't want saved can also be excluded as shown in Figure 12.17.

If required, logging can be enabled. The logs are granular, and they record each step of the process during the logon and logoff as shown in Figure 12.18.

Virtual Profiles are configured through a Microsoft Group Policy, and we believe more and more settings will be moved into Group Policies as it is adopted as a standard control mechanism.

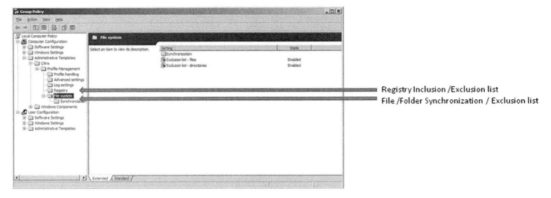

FIGURE 12.17

Inclusion/exclusion lists for Virtual Profiles.

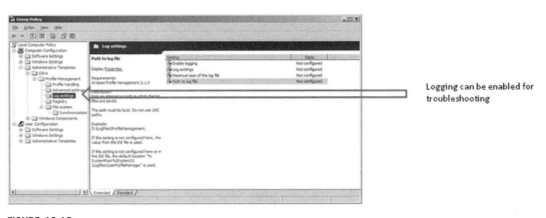

FIGURE 12.18

Enable logging for troubleshooting.

Citrix Streamed User Profiles

The "Profile Streaming" feature is currently out in "Tech Preview" as part of Profile Management 3.0, which means it is available for testing, but not yet for production. By the time this goes to print, it may well be out for general availability (GA), which means it has been regression tested for production.

Profile Streaming is a mechanism that allows the profile to be pulled down "on demand." Using normal "roaming profiles," or the existing Profile Management 2.1, the entire user profile must be fully downloaded before the user's session is initiated. This mechanism allows you to partially download the profile, only downloading the required components, and thus dramatically improving the logon time – by as much as five times faster.

SUMMARY

In this chapter, we considered how user personalization settings should be handled in a virtual desktop environment. We discussed how standard roaming profiles work, and then looked at how Virtual Profiles can extend on that principle. We then discussed the step-by-step procedures for installing, and then configuring Virtual Profiles. Lastly, we briefly discussed how "streamed" profiles will be used in the future.

Advanced XenDesktop Client Settings – Audio and Video and Peripherals

INFORMATION IN THIS CHAPTER

* Citrix Client-side Configuration

The user experience afforded by Citrix XenDesktop aims to be the equivalent or better than a physical desktop system. Configuring a desktop that fulfils the business and security requirements is not enough, the usability of the virtual desktop directly influences your users' productivity. The Citrix user-side technologies have been grouped under a broad umbrella called HDX – High Definition User Experience.

Different organizations will have varying requirements for these technologies. This chapter has been included last, not because it is an afterthought, but rather because this is where we have passed the stage of functional testing, and we now need to "tweak" the settings for the best user experience.

> This chapter discusses primarily the client-side configuration. Bear in mind that these settings may be overridden by Citrix Policy Settings. Your configuration of graphics, USB devices, audio and files access for example, will all need to also be configured using the Citrix Policies discussed in Chapter 5, "Desktop Delivery Controller – Advanced Configuration Settings."

CITRIX CLIENT-SIDE CONFIGURATION

The latest Citrix clients are optimized for XenDesktop. Using existing older Citrix clients won't give you the options presented here.

The Microsoft RDS client has always had a connection bar, which would autohide at the top of the screen. The Citrix Receiver places the connection bar in the same location, and it similarly autohides when not selected.

TIP

If the Desktop Viewer Toolbar is not present, it is most likely due to the changes on the Web interface or how it was installed. The XenDesktop setup program enables the setting:

```
ShowDesktopViewer=On
```

In the file: WebInterface.conf – the default path is C:\Inetpub\wwwroot\Citrix*DesktopWeb*\conf\ the drive letter and the DesktopWeb folder may vary depending on your installation.
If the Desktop Toolbar is missing, find the following line:

```
#ShowDesktopViewer=Off
```

To enable the Desktop Toolbar, remove the hash that comments out the line, and change the setting to **On**, as per the pervious example.

The XenDesktop Connection Bar shown in Figure 13.1 allows the user to configure his or her session settings. On the far left-hand side, you can select the desktop of the physical host. The virtual desktop connections are tiled in the center of the bar – if you have more than one virtual desktop open, you can use this to switch between desktops – the icon shows the screen background of the physical or virtual desktop, which make this intuitive to the users. The **Ctrl + Alt + Del** key combination sends the key sequence to the virtual desktop – which would otherwise be intercepted locally. The **Preferences** button presents a dialog box to configure the session settings. The **USB** button presents a drop down of all the USB devices connected to the physical device, giving the user the option to connect or disconnect devices from the virtual desktop.

The display settings include the following (see Figure 13.2):

1. **Scale to Fit** – keeps the geometry and simply resizes (this can cause a blurry display).
2. **Actual Size** – keeps the screen size and resolution – display it in a Window if smaller, or with scroll bars if bigger than the host display.
3. **Change Resolution** – the default, automatically resizes, and alters the resolution accordingly.

The **USB** tab (see Figure 13.3) have the following options:
When the desktop starts, you can choose to automatically connect all the USB devices, display the list to the end user, or do nothing.

When a USB device is inserted while using the desktop – we have the same options – you can choose to automatically connect all the USB devices, display the list to the end user, or do nothing.

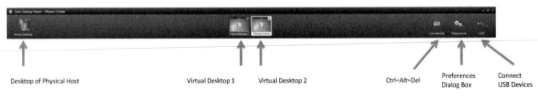

Desktop of Physical Host   Virtual Desktop 1   Virtual Desktop 2   Ctrl–Alt–Del   Preferences   Connect
                                                                                                    Dialog Box   USB Devices

FIGURE 13.1

The Desktop Viewer Connection Bar.

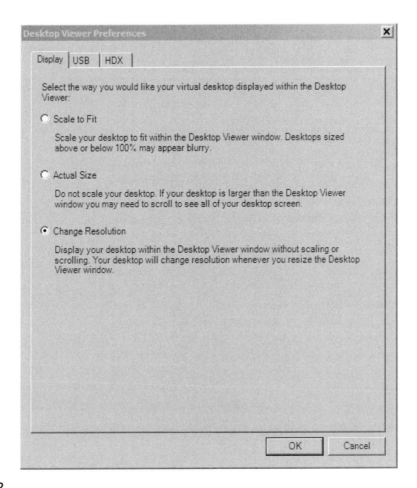

FIGURE 13.2

The Desktop Viewer Preferences dialog box.

NOTE

Bear in mind that Citrix Policy Settings can override USB settings. Security policies sometimes requires USB ports be disabled.

The **HDX** tab (see Figure 13.4) have the following options:
Flash Acceleration can be set to **Disabled**, **Enabled**, or **Prompt**.

NOTE

Flash Acceleration requires configuration in two places: at the farm level and at the client.

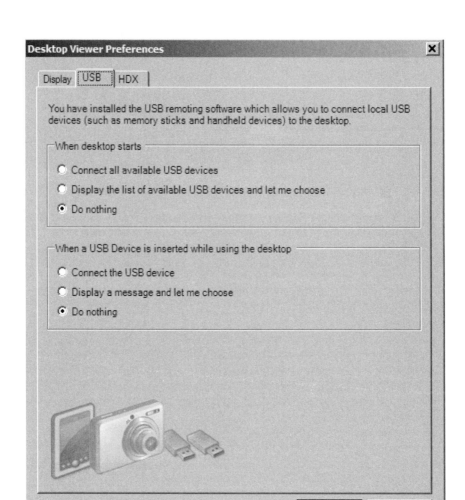

FIGURE 13.3

The Desktop Viewer – USB settings.

File Access determines the level of file access the virtual desktop has to the physical device. This can be set to **Disabled, Read Only, Read Write**, or **Prompt**.

Microphone, allows the use of a microphone at the physical end point. This can be set to **Enabled, Disabled** or **Prompt**.

NOTE

Both the File Access and Microphone settings can be overridden at a Citrix Policy level.
Selecting the **Remember my selection** checkbox will retain the setting for subsequent sessions.

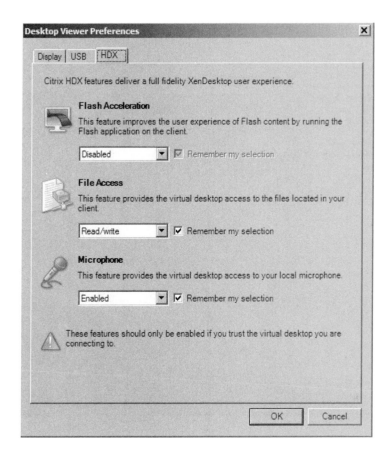

FIGURE 13.4

The Desktop Viewer – HDX Settings.

HDX Media Stream – Streaming Content

Flash streaming is a relatively new technology, which enables Adobe Flash content to be streamed directly to the physical end point, rather than rendering the content to the virtual desktop, and then displaying the content through the ICA stream.

DESIGN DECISIONS

The streamed media will consume significantly more bandwidth than the standard Independent Computing Architecture (ICA), so much so that you could actually degrade performance. This does perform very well over LAN (and LAN-like) networks, and should certainly be enabled if you are not bandwidth constrained.

To enable Adobe Flash Player, open the Delivery Services Console, right-click on the **Farm** and select **Properties** (see Figure 13.5).

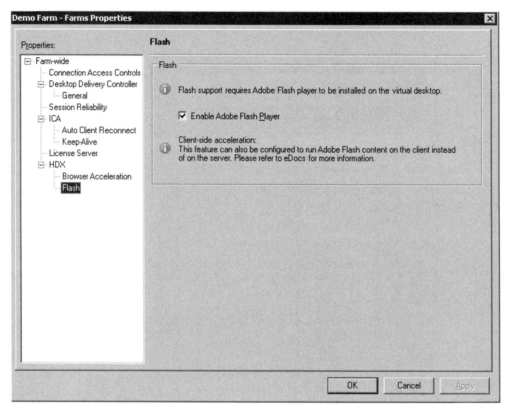

FIGURE 13.5

Enable Adobe Flash Player.

Select **HDX | Flash**, and check **Enable Adobe Flash Player**.

Adobe Flash Player will also need to be installed on the virtual desktop, and should be included in the base build.

The streaming capabilities are not limited to Adobe Flash. Windows Media and RealPlayer streaming are also featured. The Windows Media Player in the virtual desktop will be automatically enabled for use with XenDesktop.

TIP

In some rare cases, HDX Multimedia streaming can cause issues, see the article CTX122963. This article contains an explanation of how to manually disable multimedia streaming.

Select **HDX | Browser Acceleration** (see Figure 13.6).

Unlike Flash Acceleration which is a client-side technology, Browser Acceleration is a server-side technology, which alters how Web-based content is rendered over the wire to the user. Images

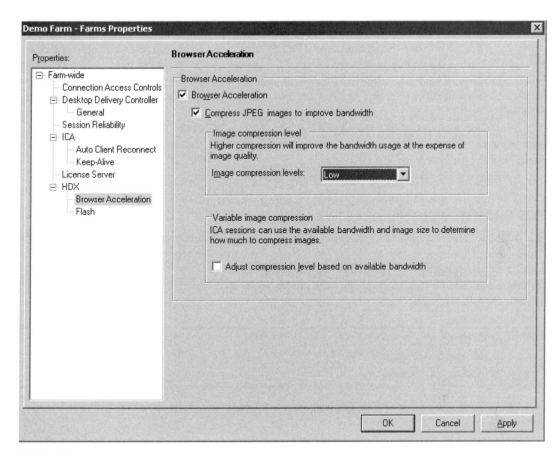

FIGURE 13.6

Enable Browser Acceleration.

embedded in Web pages can be compressed to high, medium, or low compression. The user experience is affected, the graphics embedded in the Web pages will display with degraded resolution.

There is an additional option to enable "Variable image compression," which leverages the adaptive capabilities within ICA to adjust the image compression based on the available bandwidth.

DESIGN DECISIONS

Browser Acceleration should be enabled for slow WAN links, but is unnecessary for LAN-based connections.

Related topics – Image Acceleration. Image Acceleration is a "Speedscreen" technology, which is enabled by default. Please refer to Chapter 5, "Desktop Delivery Controller – Advanced Configuration Settings," for the policies relating to Speedscreen Image Acceleration.

HDX Plug and Play – USB Redirection

There have been a number of important technical developments to make the user experience in the area of USB redirection. The process has changed from being a form of emulation to doing native USB redirection. This vastly improves the compatibility of USB devices. The Citrix client now introduces client-side USB drivers; in fact, the USB redirection will not work without a reboot after installation.

USB devices can now be introduced plug and play. That is, they can be introduced during a session without requiring a session restart. The redirection results in the virtual desktop detecting USB devices in the same way as a physical PC.

USB devices can now include isochronous devices like webcams.

HDX Real-time Bidirectional Audio and Video

The advances in the audio and video capabilities make it possible to use bidirectional audio and video devices within a virtual desktop. Video conferencing using webcams is feasible and there has been in-depth testing of VoIP solutions.

Cisco and Avaya soft phones have been tested on XenDesktop. The audio codecs available give the user high (CD) quality audio.

DESIGN DECISIONS

Enabling high-quality audio will increase the bandwidth requirements of each session utilizing audio. These requirements should be measured and accounted for as part of your design.

Microsoft OCS

Microsoft Office Communications Server (OCS) USB phones can be integrated directly into your virtual desktop. I have personally tested this and I must confess that I am impressed by the USB plug and play of the device and the audio quality.

TIP

Attach the OCS phone to the build virtual desktop, while the vDisk is in Private image mode. The OCS installation files will be loaded in the base image, and won't need to be copied up when attaching an OCS phone.

HDX 3D

HDX 3D opens the possibility of using graphically rich applications on a virtual desktop. Applications like OpenGL and DirectX applications perform well. Virtual desktops running graphical applications can even be run over WAN links.

These technologies can even be used in conjunction with Picture Archiving and Communication Systems (PACS).

Graphical settings can be configured through Citrix Policies.

DESIGN DECISIONS

Lossy compression will give the best performance but may not be appropriate in some environments – like medical images.

HDX Broadcast and HDX Intellicache

HDX Broadcast refers to some of the built in optimizations of the ICA protocol. Being adaptive, it varies according to available bandwidth. The protocol is self tuning. HDX Intellicache refers to the added compression you can achieve by utilizing Citrix branch repeaters. Branch Repeaters are compression/caching devices, which will further compress the ICA protocol datagrams, and even cache graphic requests for reuse. Branch Repeater compression appliances are highly recommended for WAN links.

Installing the HDX Experience Monitor

The HDX monitor shown in Figure 13.7 is a useful tool that you can use to analyze how the HDX technologies are being utilized by the virtual desktop. This can also be a useful troubleshooting tool, as it will show you each installed component, and how they are configured.

FIGURE 13.7

The HDX monitor.

Download and install the hdx-monitor-x86.msi (or hdx-monitor-x64.msi for 64 bit) on the virtual desktop. The installation can be downloaded from http://hdx.citrix.com/hdx-monitor.

This monitor interrogates the ICA virtual channels, allowing you to monitor bandwidth usage of the components. The Smart Card and Printing ICA channels are also available to be monitored.

SUMMARY

In this chapter, we discussed the Citrix HDX technologies. We specifically looked at how these settings can be configured on the client device side. We discussed configuring media streaming on the XenDesktop farm. We then looked at the details of the settings covered in the first part of this chapter:

- HDX Plug and Play
- HDX Real-time
- HDX Media Stream
- HDX 3D
- HDX Broadcast and HDX Intellicache

Lastly, we briefly discussed using the HDX experience monitor to look at details of an individual user's session. This chapter was intended to assist you in fine tuning the client device.

Appendix

POC PREREQUISITE CHECKLIST

Hardware, network, and a hypervisor of choice need to be in place before proceeding.

I have provided numbers wherever possible; however, each Proof of Concept (POC) will have a different number of required workstations for testing purposes. "Xx Workstations" below refers to the number of workstations for your POC.

Components

Broker – to manage virtual desktops. Provides access to users.	Citrix XenDesktop
Virtual Disk Server – mounts a virtual disk to the virtual desktops. One vDisk can boot multiple virtual desktops.	Citrix Provisioning Server (PVS)
Virtual Application Server – XenApp can provision applications to users into the virtual desktops. User applications are based on AD user or group memberships.	Citrix XenApp
Virtual Workstations	Windows XP, Vista or 7

The prerequisites are listed with two options: preferred or required. This is because there is either the simple way, or the more time-consuming way. Try for push for the simpler preferred option wherever possible.

Networking

Required – IP addresses

- 1x build workstation IP address
- 1x provisioning server IP address
- 1x XenApp server IP address
- 1x DDC server IP address
- Xx workstation IP addresses; each virtual desktop will need an IP address

All IP addresses should be in the same range as the server. Workstation addresses should also be in the server range.

> We are putting workstations in the datacenter – we will need access over ICA TCP 2598 to all the workstations *inside* the datacenter.

Preferred

A separate VLAN for the XenDesktop servers and workstations.

> On your switches, disable Spanning Tree or enable PortFast (STP Fast Link).
> A DHCP scope in the server range with DHCP enabled.

Scope options for PXE enabled
066 IP address of the provisioning server
067 boot file name **ARDBP32.BIN**

If this is not possible, then use the PVS to create an individual boot.ISO file for each workstation and mount the .ISO to each workstation. If you can get DHCP but not the scope options, then you can use one boot.ISO for all the workstations – which is still considerably less effort.

Active Directory Requirements

1. Active Directory accounts for the following:
   a. 1x build workstation
   b. 1x provisioning server
   c. 1x XenApp server
   d. 1x DDC server
   e. Xx workstations
2. Dedicated organizational unit (OU)
3. Account operator privileges for PVS – create computer accounts or at least manage them.
4. Once off full control to create group objects and permissions in the OU – this one is that could be done using a RUNAS when launching the AD Configuration Wizard.
5. User account for managing the PVS/DDC/XenApp servers, with administrator privileges on those servers.
6. In a Multiple Server Provisioning Server environment, an Active Directory Service Account for the Provisioning Server Stream and Simple Object Access Protocol (SOAP) service.
7. Basic user account for user testing.

If the security precludes getting a dedicated OU, then use http://support.citrix.com/article/ctx118976 to configure the workstations to a static DDC address.

Hardware

- 1 GB for the Desktop Delivery Controller and Citrix XenApp Server, and 2 GB for the provisioning server
- 1 GB per physical host (hypervisor)
- 1 GB per workstation – XP or
- 2 GB per workstation – Vista/Windows 7

More is better. This could be blades or tower servers.

So a single server POC would start with 5 GB or more of memory per workstation.

Software
Required
- Windows 2003 media and licenses – required for DDC (2003 R2 – 32 or 64 bit, if integrating with SCVMM)
- Windows 2003 or Windows 2008 media and licenses – required for PVS (2008 preferred)
- XenDesktop 4 software – either the .ISO or the media
- Desktop operating system media – Windows 7/Windows XP

Preferred
- Microsoft SQL 2000 or 2005
  Or
- Oracle 11 g Release 1

Hypervisor

XenServer 5/5.5, or VMware (any version from 3 to vSphere) preferably with vCenter and the SDK, Hyper-V, and preferably SCVMM.

The SDK (for VMware) or SCVMM are required for integration purposes, i.e., the XenDesktop Setup Wizard and for the DDC to power on or off VMs as required.

Permissions
- XenServer – full control
- SCVMM – full control of the SCVMM
- vCenter – full control of the resource group assigned to the project

Storage

If fiber channel/iSCSI storage is used:

- 1x provisioning server – 150 GB
- 1x XenApp server – 20 GB
- 1x DDC server – 20 GB
- 1x build workstation – 20 GB

I tend to "oversize" the PVS in case it needs to be used as a software repository/profile server/ XenApp package repository.

You can comfortably request 500 GB LUN. It needs to be presented to all the physical boxes.

Fiber channel will give better performance than iSCSI, but iSCSI performance has improved and may be sufficient for your needs. Enterprise Storage is recommended for production systems, local storage can be used for pilots or very small environments.

XenApp 6 FOR WINDOWS 2008 R2

The XenApp content in this book is based on the XenApp 5 Feature Pack 2 version of the product. At the time of writing XenApp 6 for Windows 2008 R2 has been released in the Tech Preview form. Broadly speaking, the settings that need to be configured haven't changed significantly, but rather the management consoles have been simplified.

VMware SDK INTEGRATION

The interaction between the Citrix components (the Desktop Delivery Controller and the XenDesktop Setup Wizard) and the VMware hypervisor stack is done through the VMware SDK.

The VMware SDK is normally only accessible through HTTPS. The SDK security settings can, however, be changed to allow this communication to occur over HTTP. This is the first choice of many IT engineers – who hear the word "Certificates" and break out into a cold sweat! Humor aside, security policies don't always allow you to change the settings to HTTP. I would recommend HTTP for a proof of concept environment, but for a production environment, it would be advisable to use secured communications.

The XenDesktop Setup Wizard requires the changes be made on the provisioning server.

Changing the SDK Requirements to HTTP

In order to change the SDK to allow HTTP access, one has to edit the proxy.xml file on the Virtual Center/vCenter Server. The proxy.xml file is in the "All Users" profile, which is C:\Documents and Settings\Application Data\VMware\VMware VirtualCenter\proxy.xml under Windows 2003, and C:\Users\Application Data\VMware\VMware VirtualCenter\proxy.xml on Windows 2008.

```
Open the proxy.xml
<e id="5">
        <_type>vim.ProxyService.LocalServiceSpec</_type>
        <accessMode>HTTPSWithRedirect</accessMode>
        <port>8085</port>
        <serverNamespace>/sdk</serverNamespace>
</e>
Change the section "HTTPSWithRedirect" to "HTTPAndHTTPS"
<e id="5">
        <_type>vim.ProxyService.LocalServiceSpec</_type>
        <accessMode>HTTPAndHTTPS</accessMode>
        <port>8085</port>
        <serverNamespace>/sdk</serverNamespace>
</e>
```

Connecting Using HTTPS

This was fairly easy to manage in versions 3 and 3.5, unfortunately changes to how the certificates are created for vCenter (version 4) has made this trickier for the latest version of VMware's software.

Versions 3 and 3.5

1. Locate RUI.CRT on the Virtual Center Server under C:\Documents and Settings\All Users\ Application Data\VMware\VMware VirtualCenter\SSL on Windows 2003, or C:\Users\All Users\Application Data\VMware\VMware VirtualCenter\SSL on Windows 2008.
2. Copy the certificate to the Desktop Delivery Controller (or provisioning server).
3. Double-click on the certificate.
4. Click **Install Certificate**... (see Figure A.1).
5. Click **Next** to step forward through the wizard.
6. Change the selection to **Place all certificates in the following store** and click **Browse**... (see Figure A.2).
7. Tick the **Show physical stores** – select **Trusted Root Certification Authorities** and the subcontainer **Local Computer**, and click **OK** and then **Next**.
8. Click **Finish**.

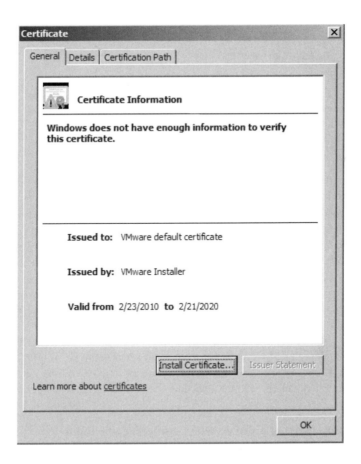

FIGURE A.1

Certificate details.

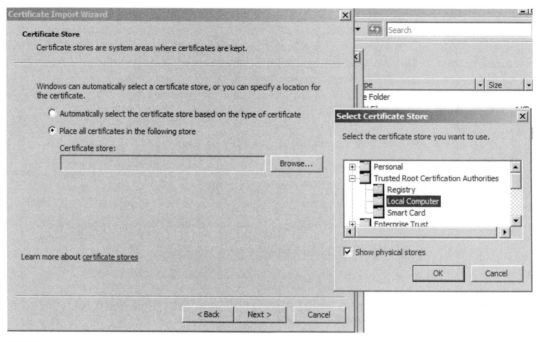

FIGURE A.2

Certificate Import Wizard.

This adds a certificate for "vmware" to the Desktop Delivery Controller.

Also on the Desktop Delivery Controller, open the file C:\Windows\System32\drivers\etc\hosts with a text editor like notepad. Under the line:

```
"127.0.0.1             localhost"
Add the line:
"xxx.xxx.xxx.xxx     vmware"
```

Where xxx.xxx.xxx.xxx is the IP address of your Virtual Center Server. Remember to use a <tab> between the IP address and the name.

Basically what we are doing is using the self-signed certificate built into Virtual Center to secure communications. The default certificate assigned to the Virtual Center is to the hostname "vmware," and using the host's entry, we are "tricking" the Desktop Delivery Controller into thinking that it is communicating with a host called vmware, and thus the certificate matches the hostname.

Version 4/vSphere

VMware recommends the use of a Commercial Certificate Authority to replace the default vCenter certificates. This involves obtaining a certificate from one of the trusted CAs like VeriSign, Thawte, Baltimore, or Entrust. You need to obtain a certificate of the "Web Server" type. You can also alternatively create a self-signed certificate using OpenSSL. Documentation for changing the vCenter certificate can be found at www.vmware.com/files/pdf/vsp_4_vcserver_certificates.pdf.

This will give you the steps to create a new root certificate – RUI.CRT. Once you have replaced the root certificate, follow the same steps as with the earlier versions to import the certificate into the Desktop Delivery Controller (or provisioning server).

CITRIX XenServer

Citrix XenServer is the free hypervisor available for use with XenDesktop. Citrix Essentials for XenServer ships as part of the XenDesktop Enterprise and Platinum license. The hypervisor is free to use provided it is running "Citrix" loads – the XenDesktop management servers, XenApp and the workstations, may all be run without charge.

Even in scenarios where there is an existing hypervisor environment, it may be simpler to run XenServer in parallel with the existing environment. The first proof of concept system should always be installed in a development/test environment. Avoid installing the proof of concept system on live/production servers.

Installing your own environment frees you from being constrained in someone else's hypervisor environment. You are free to add/remove storage, change network settings (like VLANs), and so on, without having to wait for a change window.

DOWNLOADING CITRIX SOFTWARE
Your Organization Has Bought the Software

The software required for your Citrix XenDesktop implementation can be downloaded from www.mycitrix.com.

When you buy Citrix software, Citrix will send you an e-mail containing your username and password. If you have not received the e-mail, contact your Citrix reseller to find out who was registered as the contact person in your organization.

If some of the download files have a closed padlock icon next to them, this is due to the version of XenDesktop you have purchased.

XenDesktop Editions:

1. VDI Edition
2. Enterprise
3. Platinum

For a full feature list, see the Citrix Web site, the most significant differences in my view are:

- VDI Edition gives you the XenDesktop broker, but no XenApp or provisioning server.
- Enterprise Edition adds XenApp and provisioning server.
- Platinum Edition adds to Enterprise, Password Manager, EdgeSight Monitoring, the Branch Repeater (WanScaler) software client, and the Access Gateway SSL VPN.

You Are Evaluating the Software

The software required for your Citrix XenDesktop implementation can be downloaded from www.mycitrix.com.

If you are a new user, you will need to register to create a new Login for yourself. Login to the portal. Select **Downloads | XenDesktop 4 Evaluation**. From here, you can download the Evaluation software and an Evaluation License File.

Obtaining the License File

1. Log on to www.mycitrix.com.
2. Select **Product Previews/Beta Releases – License Retrieval** – (see Figure A.3) if you have already received a license serial number through e-mail, select **Activation System/Manage Assets** – jump to Step 5.
3. Click **Retrieve License** (see Figure A.4).
4. Click on one of the license serial numbers (see Figure A.5).
5. Click **Continue** (see Figure A.6).
6. Select your country, and search for your reseller (I have chosen cannot find my reseller as I am doing this for demonstration purposes) – click **Continue** (see Figure A.7).
7. Click **Submit** to confirm your contact details (see Figure A.8).
8. Confirm company details – click **Submit** (see Figure A.9).

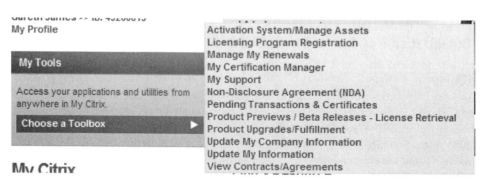

FIGURE A.3

The MyCitrix toolbox.

FIGURE A.4

License retrieval.

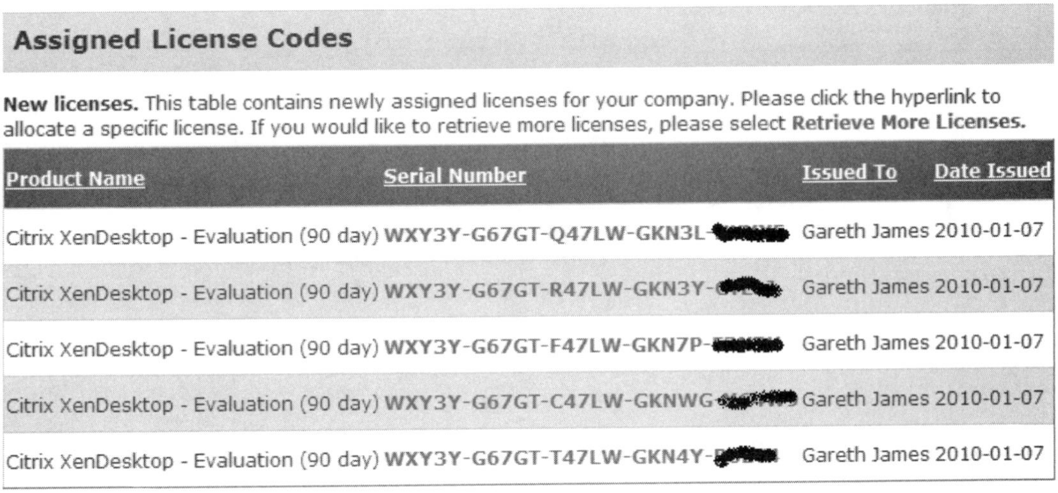

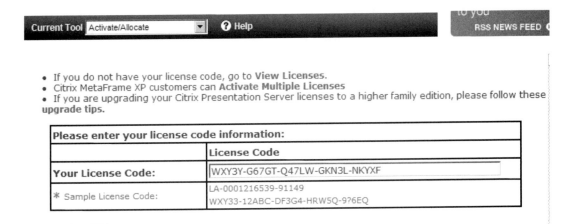

FIGURE A.5

Select serial number.

FIGURE A.6

Activate/allocate the license code.

9. This is the area where most people experience problems. If the license file doesn't *exactly* match your hostname, then it will not work. The most reliable way to obtain your hostname is from the command line. Click **Continue** (see Figure A.10).

10. Before you proceed to the next step, log on to the license server, and open a command prompt – **Start | Run | CMD**.

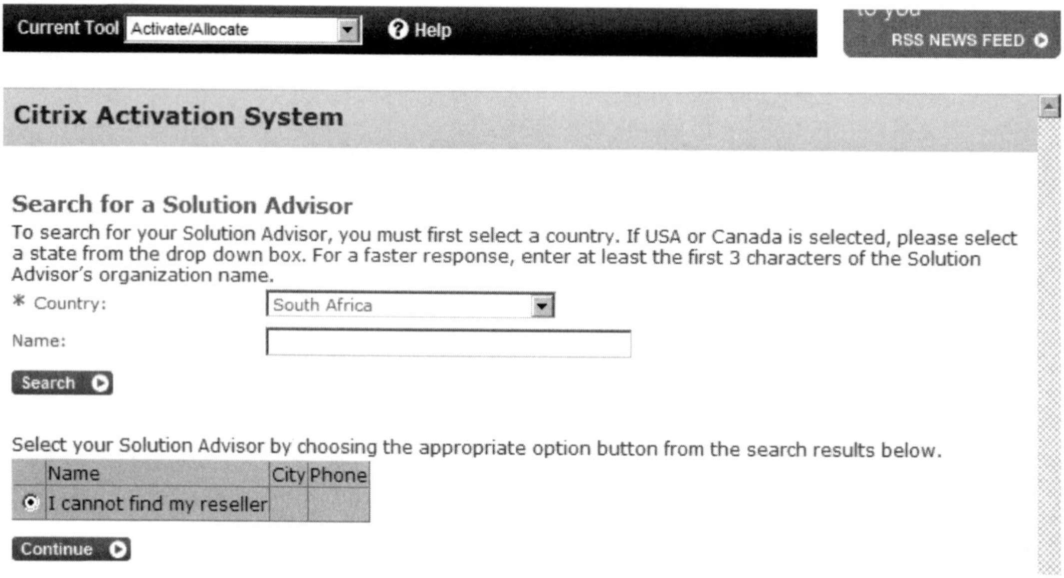

FIGURE A.7

Search for a reseller.

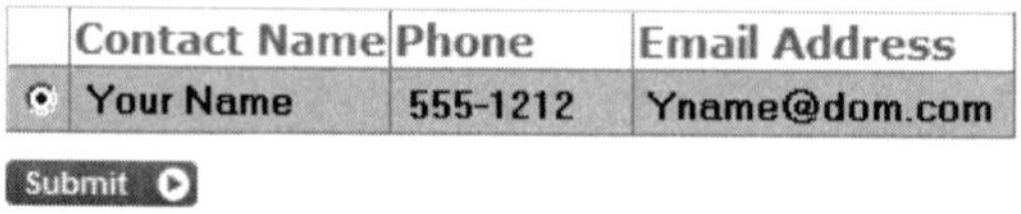

FIGURE A.8

Contact details.

11. Type hostname.

This is the name you need to use, be careful to take note of upper and lower case letters (see Figure A.11).

12. Enter the hostname and click **Allocate**. Remember upper and lower case matters (see Figure A.12).

13. Click **Confirm** (see Figure A.13).

14. Click **Download License File** (see Figure A.14).

Save the license file to a suitable location, and then copy to your license server (see Figure A.15).

Adding the license file to the license server is discussed in Chapter 3, "Configuring the Desktop Delivery Controller."

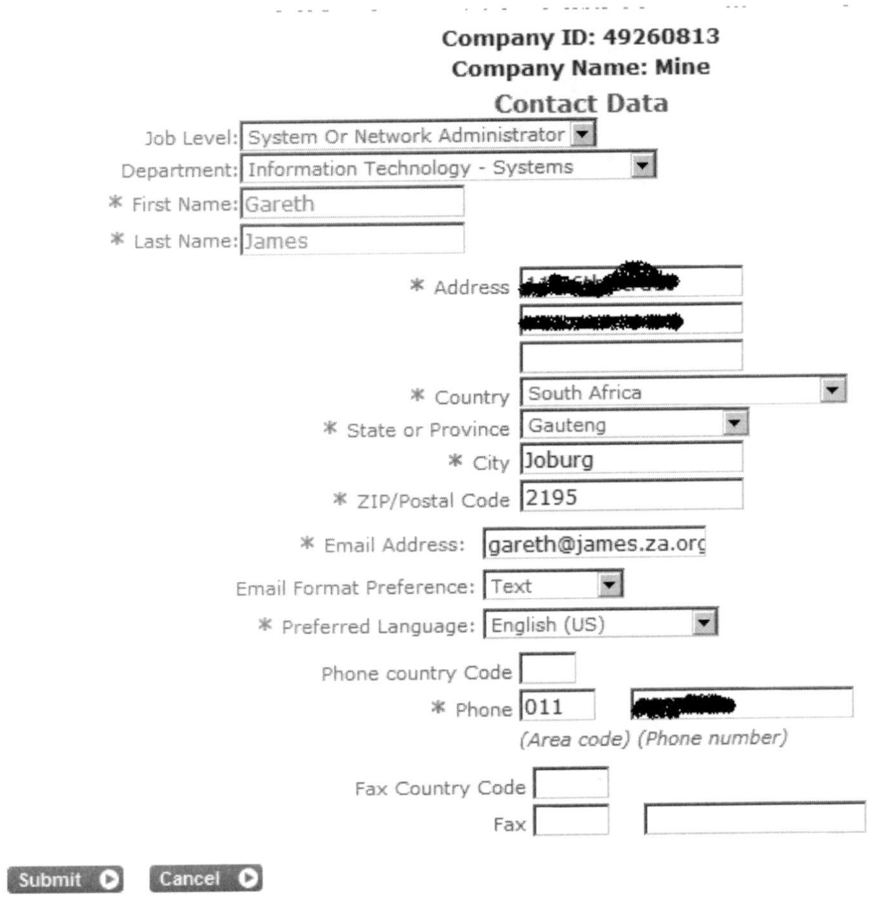

Company ID: 49260813
Company Name: Mine
Contact Data

Job Level: System Or Network Administrator
Department: Information Technology - Systems
* First Name: Gareth
* Last Name: James

* Address [REDACTED]
[REDACTED]

* Country South Africa
* State or Province Gauteng
* City Joburg
* ZIP/Postal Code 2195
* Email Address: gareth@james.za.org
Email Format Preference: Text
* Preferred Language: English (US)
Phone country Code
* Phone 011 [REDACTED]
(Area code) (Phone number)
Fax Country Code
Fax

Submit ⊙   Cancel ⊙

FIGURE A.9

Company details.

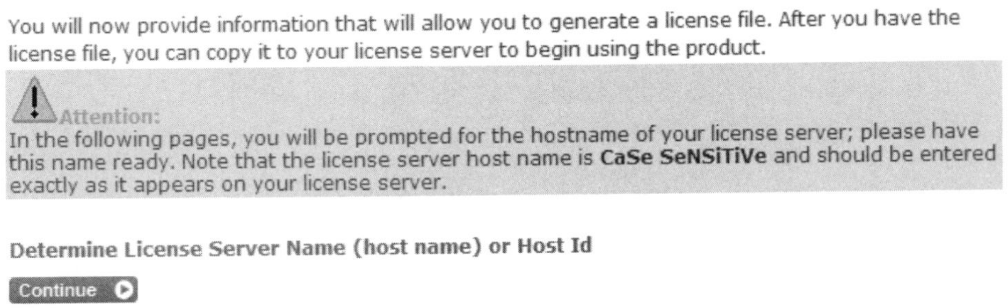

You will now provide information that will allow you to generate a license file. After you have the license file, you can copy it to your license server to begin using the product.

⚠ Attention:
In the following pages, you will be prompted for the hostname of your license server; please have this name ready. Note that the license server host name is **CaSe SeNSiTiVe** and should be entered exactly as it appears on your license server.

Determine License Server Name (host name) or Host Id

Continue ⊙

FIGURE A.10

Hostname warning.

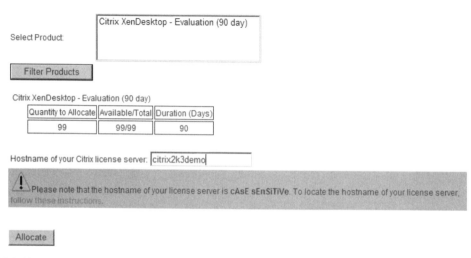

```
Command Prompt

Microsoft Windows [Version 5.2.3790]
(C) Copyright 1985-2003 Microsoft Corp.

C:\Documents and Settings\Administrator.CITRIXSA>hostname
citrix2k3demo

C:\Documents and Settings\Administrator.CITRIXSA>_
```

FIGURE A.11

Hostname determination from the command prompt.

Select Product:
> Citrix XenDesktop - Evaluation (90 day)

[Filter Products]

Citrix XenDesktop - Evaluation (90 day)

Quantity to Allocate	Available/Total	Duration (Days)
99	99/99	90

Hostname of your Citrix license server: citrix2k3demo

⚠ Please note that the hostname of your license server is cAsE sEnSiTiVe. To locate the hostname of your license server, follow these instructions.

[Allocate]

FIGURE A.12

Hostname entry.

Confirm your Selection

Citrix XenDesktop - Evaluation (90 day)

Quantity to Allocate	Available/Total	Duration (Days)
99	99/99	90

Hostname of your Citrix license server: citrix2k3demo

⚠ Please note that the hostname of your license ser
follow these instructions.

[Confirm] [Cancel]

FIGURE A.13

Confirmation.

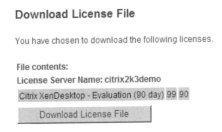

Download License File

You have chosen to download the following licenses.

File contents:
License Server Name: citrix2k3demo

Citrix XenDesktop - Evaluation (90 day) 99 90

Download License File

FIGURE A.14

Download license file prompt.

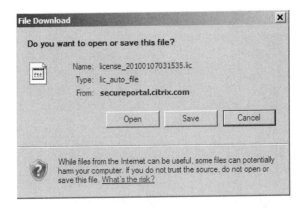

FIGURE A.15

File download dialog box.

INSTALLING MICROSOFT SYSTEM CENTER VIRTUAL MACHINE MANAGER – SCVMM – STEP BY STEP

In order to integrate properly with Microsoft Hyper-V, it is necessary to install the SCVMM Administrator Console on both the Desktop Delivery Controller and on the Citrix Provisioning Server.

Note: Windows 2003 R2 or above is required for SCVMM.

1. VMM Administrator Console setup (see Figure A.16).
2. Select **I accept the terms of the agreement** and click **Next** (see Figure A.17).
3. Select to enable Microsoft Update, and click **Next** (see Figure A.18).
4. Click **Next** (see Figure A.19).
5. The Prerequisite Check will return any tasks that need to be performed before installation. Click **Next** (see Figure A.20).
6. Choose the path to install SCVMM. Click **Next** (see Figure A.21).
7. Leave the SCVMM port at the default (see Figure A.22).
8. Click **Install** (see Figure A.23).
9. A successful installation will return a positive result. Click **Close** (see Figure A.24).

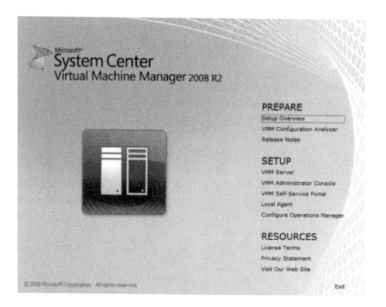

FIGURE A.16

System Center Virtual Machine Manager setup.

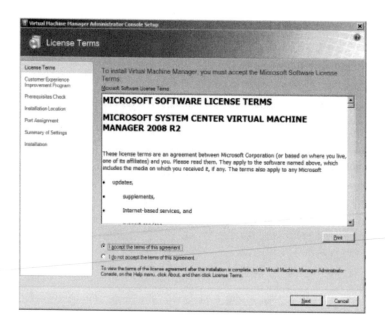

FIGURE A.17

License terms agreement.

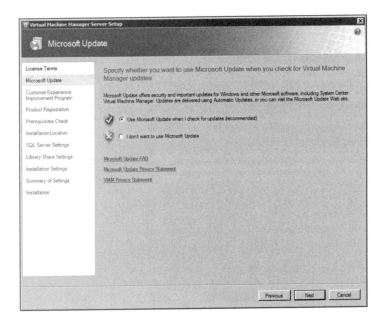

FIGURE A.18

Microsoft updates option.

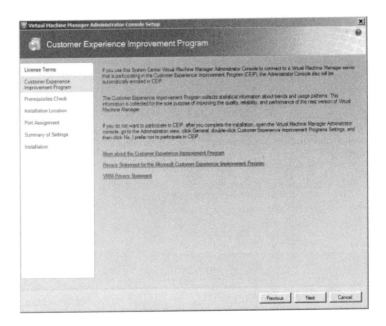

FIGURE A.19

Customer Experience Improvement notification.

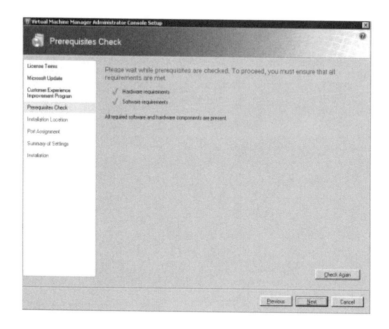

FIGURE A.20

Prerequisite check.

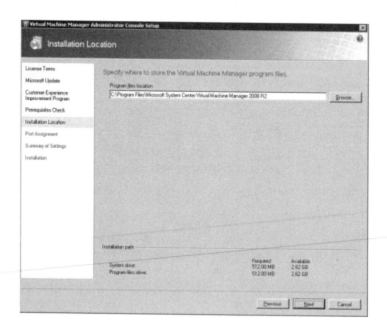

FIGURE A.21

Installation location.

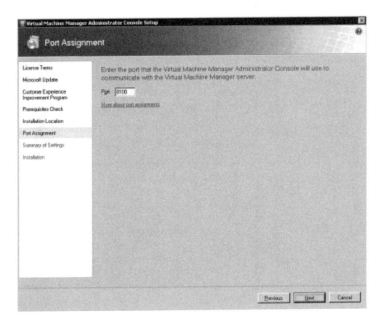

FIGURE A.22

Port assignment.

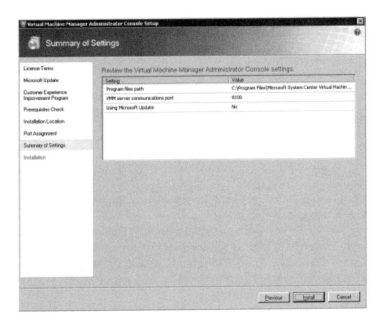

FIGURE A.23

Summary of settings.

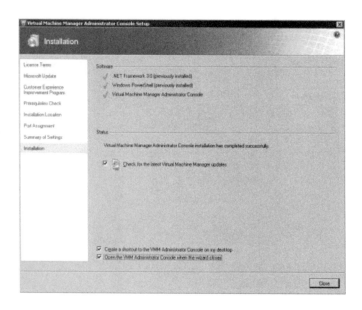

FIGURE A.24

Successful installation notification.

MICROSOFT LICENSING

If you want to use Microsoft desktop operating systems, you will inevitably need to pay Microsoft at some stage. This cost is something that should be considered up front as part of the project cost. Each of your virtual desktops will require a license.

Virtual Servers

Those components of the infrastructure that you have chosen to virtualize can take advantage of Microsoft's licensing options for virtualized servers. The best choice of licensing will depend on the number of virtual servers that you can run on a physical host.

Windows Server Standard Edition licenses are a simple 1:1 ratio. Each virtual edition needs a Standard Edition license.

Windows Server Enterprise Edition has a 4:1 ratio. Each Enterprise license entitles you to run four virtual instances of the Enterprise Edition.

Windows Server Datacenter Edition has an "all you can eat" kind of license. The Datacenter Edition is licensed per processor, but you can run as many virtual instances as you want on the physical host.

Use Microsoft's "Windows Server Virtualization Calculators" to calculate which option would be the most cost effective for your company.

Virtual Desktops

Microsoft has launched its VECD license specifically for virtual desktops. VECD, which stands for Virtual Enterprise Centralized Desktop, covers a connecting device to access up to four virtual machines running a Windows desktop operating system per device. This is obviously important for scenarios where the user may require access to legacy applications on Windows XP and additionally to run a Windows 7 desktop.

From a XenDesktop perspective, this could also include VM-hosted applications.

There are two versions:

1. With software assurance
2. Without software assurance

The pricing will vary depending on your Microsoft agreements. The key point to note is that buying VECD is significantly cheaper with software assurance.

VDI Suites

Microsoft has released two VDI suites. These suites are aimed at providing all the building blocks you would use to build out a Microsoft VDI environment. Microsoft Virtual Desktop Infrastructure Standard Suite includes licensing for Hyper-V Server, System Center Virtual Machine Manager, System Center Configuration Manager, System Center Operations Manager, Remote Desktop Services (CAL), and Microsoft Desktop Optimization Pack (MDOP).

Remote Desktop Services (RDS) was previously referred to as Terminal Services (TSCALs). The Standard Suite includes the Remote Desktop Services rights to virtual desktops only – not to Windows Server RDS. It is important to note that MDOP includes desktop licensing for App-V.

The Premium VDI Suite includes RDS CALs to connect to Windows Server RDS. Additionally it also includes App-V for RDS, this is so that you can use App-V on the Windows Server RDS based desktops too.

From a XenDesktop perspective, if you are going to use XenApp to provision hosted applications to the virtual desktops, then the Premium VDI Suite will, in many instances, be more cost effective than buying the RDS CALs separately.

USING SNAPSHOTS

Snapshots are an ideal way to take backups at significant points in the installation process. I recommend taking a snapshot before making any significant changes to any component of your environment. If an installation fails or is not error free, it is most often better to revert to the preinstall state, and begin the installation again rather than trying to "fix" the buggy installation.

NOTE

Use of snapshots in a production environment should be managed. Remember a snapshot is a "point in time" image of a state, the further the virtual machine moves from that state, the larger the snapshot. I have seen instances of snapshots left "running" for months, which are actually larger than the original virtual machine. In other words, delete old snapshots and don't use them as a long-term backup mechanism.

Take a snapshot of your virtual machine at this stage.

XenServer

Click **Take Snapshot** from the **Snapshots** tab (see Figure A.25).

SCVMM

Right-click on your virtual machine, and select **New checkpoint** (see Figure A.26).

FIGURE A.25

Using XenServer snapshots.

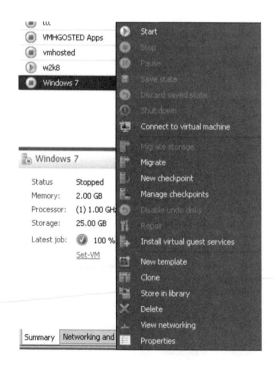

FIGURE A.26

Using SCVMM to create a checkpoint.

VMware

Right-click on the virtual machine, select **Snapshot** and click **Take Snapshot**… (see Figure A.27).

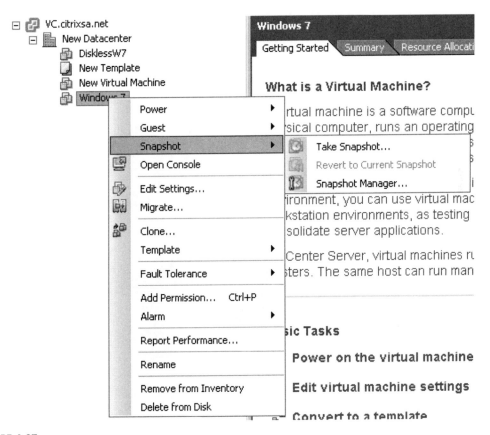

FIGURE A.27

Taking a snapshot using vCenter.

Index

Page numbers in *italics* indicate figures and tables.